Hayden's PowerBook

Power Book

Ross Scott Rubin

Dedication

This book is dedicated to the memory of my uncle Herbie, whose joyful embrace of life will always inspire me.

Hayden's PowerBook Power Book

Copyright © 1992 by Hayden.

A Division of Prentice Hall Computer Publishing.

All rights reserved. Printed in the United States of America. No part of this book may be used or reproduced in any form or by any means, or stored in a database or retrieval system, without prior written permission of the publisher except in the case of brief quotations embodied in critical articles and reviews. Making copies of any part of this book for any purpose other than your own personal use is a violation of United States copyright laws. For information, address Hayden, 11711 N. College Ave., Carmel, IN 46032.

Library of Congress Catalog No.: 92-70548

ISBN: 0-672-48520-6

This book is sold *as is,* without warranty of any kind, either express or implied. While every precaution has been taken in the preparation of this book, the publisher and author assume no responsibility for errors or omissions. Neither is any liability assumed for damages resulting from the use of the information or instructions contained herein. It is further stated that the publisher and author are not responsible for any damage or loss to your data or your equipment that results directly or indirectly from your use of this book.

94   93   92   4   3   2   1

Interpretation of the printing code: the rightmost double-digit number is the year of the book's printing; the rightmost single-digit number the number of the book's printing. For example, a printing code of 92-1 shows that the first printing of the book occurred in 1992.

Hayden's PowerBook Power Book is based on Apple Computer's family of notebook computers.

Publisher	Mike Britton
Associate Publisher	Karen A. Bluestein
Managing Editor	Neweleen Trebnik
Editors	Cheri Clark
	Erik Dafforn
	Jodi Jensen
Technical Editor	Christian "Xtian" Jacobsen
Editorial Production Coordinator	Karen Whitehouse
Cover Designer	Katherine Hanley
Designer	Michele Laseau
Production Team	Jeff Baker, Paula Carroll, Brad Chinn, Jeanne Clark, Keith Davenport, Mark Enochs, Audra Hershman, Phil Kitchel, Bob LaRoche, Linda Seifert, Louise Shinault, Suzanne Tully, Lisa Wilson, Phil Worthington, Johnna VanHoose

Composed in ITC Garamond, Avant Garde, and MCPdigital by Hayden

Trademark Acknowledgments

There are too many trademark acknowledgments to list on one page. To acknowledge every product and every company would require that we double the size of this book. However, because we are environmentalists, and because paper is a valuable (and therefore costly) commodity, we are limiting our trademark acknowledgments to the following statement:

All products mentioned in this book are either trademarks of the companies listed in the product directory in the back of this book, registered trademarks of the companies listed in the product directory in the back of this book, or neither. We strongly advise that you investigate a particular product's name thoroughly before you use the name as your own.

About the Author

Ross Scott Rubin

Ross Scott Rubin, a New Yorker, has been working with computers since childhood and with Macs since 1985. A technology advisor for McKinsey & Company, Inc., he has written articles on enhancing productivity for MacUser magazine, cover story features for *inCider/A+* and *PC Today* magazines, and the manual for Icom Simulations' On Cue II. He received his Bachelor of Science degree from Cornell University in 1989.

Photo Acknowledgments

We gratefully acknowledge the following people and companies for supplying photographs for inclusion in this book:

Chapter One photographs courtesy of Apple Computers (photographer John Greenleigh), Kensignton Microware Ltd., Dayna Communications, Inc., Radius (courtesy of A&R Partners), Microtech International-Europe, Ltd., Outbound Systems, and Liberty Systems.

Back cover photograph of Mr. Rubin courtesy of Susannah Levy.

Acknowledgments

Special thanks...

To Mom and Dad, whom I am happy to have made proud, and to my brother Jared, whose radiant sense of humor shows an understanding and perspective beyond his years.

To Mike Britton and Karen Bluestein of Hayden Books, for believing in and pushing this project, and Karen Whitehouse, who was the consummate liaison, coach, coordinator, juggler, and magician, pulling a PowerBook out of thin air. Thanks also to Steve Poland of Prentice Hall Computer Publishing, who made me feel welcome.

To Gene Zelazny, Arvind Saxena, Michael Alliston, Olina Sulak, and all of Computing and Analytic Services at the New York office of McKinsey & Company, Inc., whose generous consideration enabled me to write.

To Michele, whose encouragement made the book possible and whose friendship I will always treasure.

To Eileen, whose understanding kept me going through the final crazy days, and who gave sleepless nights creating the vendor directory.

To Susie, who braved the fierce New York winter for a photo shoot near the scenic East River.

To the majority of vendors, who eagerly offered honest appraisals of their products.

To The Commitments, Marc Cohn, Dire Straits, Squeeze, and Joe Jackson, who provided the soundtrack.

We Want to Hear from You

What our readers think of Hayden is crucial to our sense of well-being. If you have any comments, no matter how great or how small, we'd appreciate your taking the time to send us a note, fax us a fax, rhyme us a rhyme, etc.

We can be reached at the following address:

Mike Britton/Karen Bluestein
Hayden: The Cool Mac Publisher
11711 N. College Ave. (a boring address, but we assure you we're anything but boring)
Carmel, IN (yes, Indiana—not California...) 46032
(317) 573-2500 voice
(317) 573-2583 fax

If this book has changed your life, please write and describe the euphoria you've experienced. Do you have a cool book idea? Please contact us at the above address.

Overview

Introduction 1

PART I: UP AND RUNNING
  1 **Portable Power** 5
  2 **A Diminutive Desktop** 27

PART II: CREATING AND COMMUNICATING
  3 **Application Software** 49
  4 **Yakety Mac** 67

PART III: THE UTILITARIAN APPROACH
  5 **Managing Time and Contacts** 95
  6 **Productivity Enhancers** 123

PART IV: ROAD HAZARDS
  7 **Safe Computing** 147
  8 **Diffusing the Bomb** 165

    Product Directory 187
    Index 201

Table of Contents

Introduction 1

PART I: UP AND RUNNING

1 Portable Power 5
   In the Chips 5
   Field of Dreams 7
   Family Ties 8
      Keyboard 8
      Trackball 9
      Other Pointing Devices 10
      Screen 10
      Serial Ports 10
      SCSI Port 11
      Sound Out 12
      Hard Disk Space 12
      Internal Slots 13
      Power Saving Features 14
   Differences Among the Models 15
      The PowerBook 100 15
      The PowerBook 140 17
      The PowerBook 170 17
   More Than You Bargained For 18
      The Bleak Outlook 18
      The Fast Lane 21
      The Power Play 21
      The Numbers Game 22
      Mo' Better Modems 23
      Stop the Presses 23
      RAM Tough 24
      'Book Bags 25
   To Seventh Heaven 26

2 A Diminutive Desktop 27
   First Impressions 28
   Directory Listing 29
   Finding Yourself 30
   Keys to Success 31

Hayden's PowerBook Power Book

A Bolder Folder 33
The Font Issue 34
Desktop and Debris 36
Virtual Reality 37
Preferred Shares 39
Special Editions 40
RAM Cram 42
Seven Can Wait? 43
7.0.1 for the Road 43
    Caps Lock 44
    RAM Disk 44
    Sleep Command 45
    The Battery DA 46
    Portable Control Panel 47
Off and Running 48

PART II: CREATING AND COMMUNICATING

3 Application Software 49
Integrated vs. Lean Applications 50
Integrated Software 52
    Microsoft Works 52
    GreatWorks 53
    ClarisWorks 55
    BeagleWorks 56
    HandiWorks 57
Lean Applications 57
    Word Processing 58
    Spreadsheets 61
    Databases 62
    Graphics 63
    Communications 64
Outliners 65
Conclusions 66
Reaching Out 66

4 Yakety Mac 67
The PowerBook's Portals 67
Stock Exchanges 69
    Flipping Floppies 69
    Ready, Willing, and Cable 69
    Remote Controls 71
    Building Bridges 74

Contents

Sharing Alike	74
File Groupies	76
Conversation PCs	77
Se Habla "DOS"	78
Easy DOS It	79
XTNDing Yourself	80
ASCII Jumps	82
Graphic Contents	82
Sending a Cable	83
C> Shells	83
Big Blue in a Box	84
Look Who's Talking Too	86
Net Worth	87
Wired to the World	88
America Online	88
CompuServe	89
CONNECT	91
GEnie and Delphi	91
Prodigy	91
All the Fax	92
Reaching Out	94

PART III: THE UTILITARIAN APPROACH

5 Managing Time and Contacts 95

Forget-Me-Nots	95
Smart Alarms and Appointment Diary	96
Alarming Events	97
Easy Alarms	98
First Things First	99
Right on Schedule	101
DayMaker	101
In Control	103
AgentDA	104
Up-to-Date	106
The Far Side Calendar	108
Jot Lag	109
QuickDEX II	110
INTouch	111
Playing the Fields	113
Dynodex and Address Book Plus	114
TouchBASE	116

Hayden's PowerBook Power Book

    Making Connections 118
    Selling the Dream 120
    On the Horizon 120
    Conclusions 121

6 Productivity Enhancers 123
    Power Launch 124
    Nailing Files 127
    The Squeeze Play 129
        Champs of the Clamps 130
        Your Main Squeeze 131
    Hitting Cruise Control 134
        QuicKeys 2 134
        Frontier 136
        KiwiPowerWindows 136
        Magic Typist 137
    Swiss Army Utility Knives 138
        Now Utilities 138
        QuickTools 141
    Other Aids 143
        Intertie 143
        Read My Lips 143
    Safe at Any Speed 145

PART IV: ROAD HAZARDS

7 Safe Computing 147
    Security Software 147
    The Basics and Beyond 148
    Shareware Showcase 151
    FolderBolt 151
    Access Management Programs 153
    Security Summary 155
    The Terrible Trio 156
        How Serious Is the Threat? 156
        DOS Viruses 162
        The Bottom Line 162
    The Bomb Squad 163

8 Diffusing the Bomb 165
    The Hard Facts 166
        Disk-o-Tech 166
        Beating the System 168

The Soft Touch 170
    What's Wrong, Doc? 171
    Interrupting This Program 171
    Weighing Your Options 172
    INIT-Wits 174
    Extension Headaches 175
    The Norton Anthology 179
    Last Resort 181
    What Knowledge Lurks 182
    Hanging on a Heartbeat 184
    Crashing the Party 185

Product Directory **187**

Index **201**

Introduction

It was love at first sight when I saw it shining in the window of the dealership. The sleek, efficient, dark-gray design would be mine for just a few thousand dollars. It was so small, yet so powerful. I knew I could take this little road warrior anywhere I wanted to go. And, of course, the best part about it was the famous five-letter name of the company that created this masterpiece: Honda.

I drove the car down to the local Apple dealership, where the people were still buying Macintosh Classics and Portables to meet their needs for a Mac they could take with them on the road. The trade magazines had been abuzz with talk of a new breed of portable Macs that Apple was working on, but unresolved questions abounded. Would Apple again stumble with size and weight? How powerful would the new Macs be? How do they get those ships into those bottles, anyway?

My fears proved unwarranted. Several months later, Apple unleashed the tiny trio of PowerBooks into the world. In many respects, there is little revolutionary about the new machines; they simply take the advanced Macintosh computing environment and reduce it to a size slightly larger than a student notebook. In other ways, though, the PowerBooks signify a new opportunity for two groups of people.

One group needs a small, powerful portable computer. Typically novices, this group dreads the arcane interfaces of IBM PC-compatibles. These portables reduce the size, but not the complexity, of their desktop cousins.

Hayden's PowerBook Power Book

Then, there are the Macintosh faithful who have long wanted a second, portable machine. These veterans know the ins and outs of the Mac, but some are reluctant to use new advances in the Mac platform such as System 7.0 because the system they're currently using seems comfortable.

This book caters to the second group because I wanted to create a concise solutions guide that you could stuff into a PowerBook carrying case. I do not see the point in writing a book that weighs more than the computer it discusses. Therefore, this book complements Apple's PowerBook documentation, to help answer the question, "Where do I go from here?"

As a result, this book lacks the room to answer most concerns of absolute beginners. Many outstanding references, however, can help get them up to speed, from the Getting Started and User's Guide manuals and the Macintosh Basics overview that come with the PowerBook, to the scores of books, videotapes, and classes geared toward beginning users.

I hope those familiar with the standard Macintosh environment—those who understand fonts and desk accessories and RAM and memory partitions—will find this book to be a valuable resource for solutions to their PowerBook needs.

Four parts comprise the book's eight chapters. Part I, "Up and Running," introduces the characteristics that bind and separate the three PowerBook models. In addition, the section points out some third-party accessories providing capabilities Apple does not include. A chapter about System 7.0 explains the new features of the operating system for old hands experiencing it for the first time on the PowerBooks. This chapter also discusses the system software features included just for PowerBook owners' benefit.

Part II, "Creating and Communicating," discusses applications suitable for use with the PowerBooks, including relevant integrated software. Of course, creating something is of limited value if you can't share it, so I've included a comprehensive chapter on communications, including networking options and MS-DOS compatibility.

Part III, "The Utilitarian Approach," explains how you can use popular time management and contact management software. With these applications, you can keep in touch with other users on the road and maximize the time you spend using your PowerBook.

Introduction

Part IV, "Road Hazards," tells how to protect your computer from human and software enemies, and outlines a holistic approach to troubleshooting that can help you diffuse pesky system bombs.

To sum up, this unique source book caters to people who understand the basics. If time and space were less pressing, I would include more, but, like most PowerBook users, I have to get going.

RSR
New York City
February, 1992

Portable Power

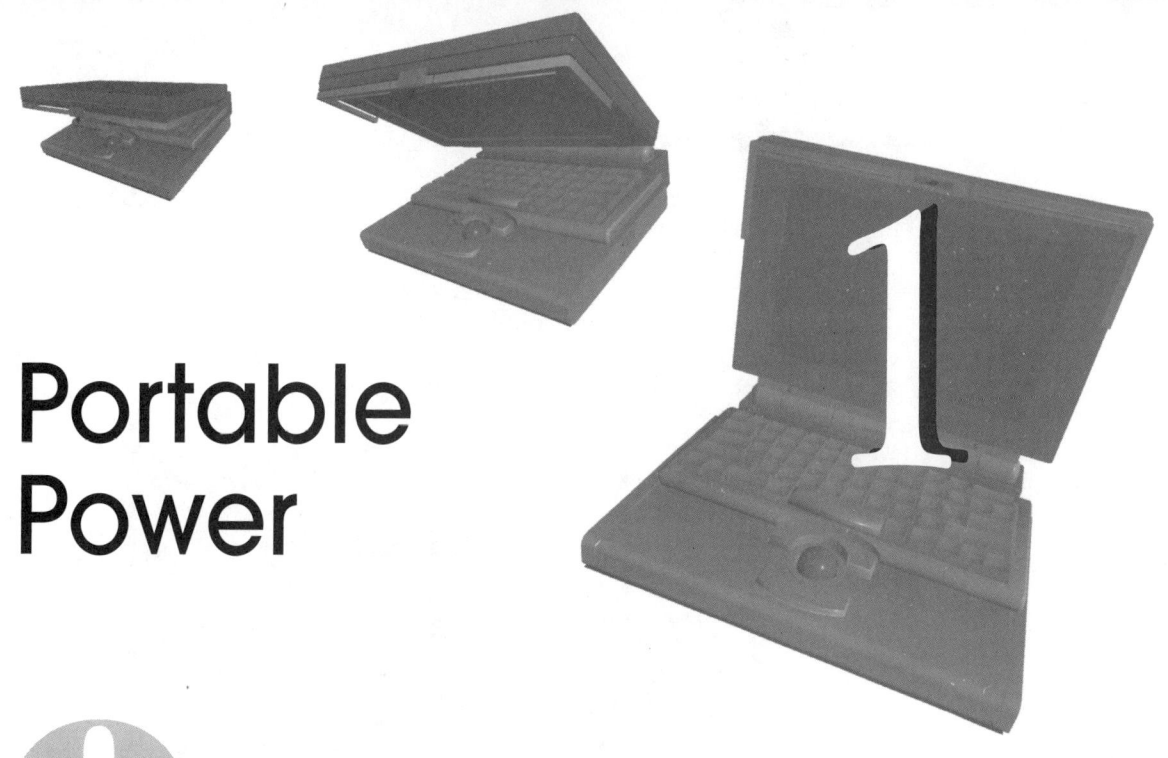

On October 21, 1991, Apple Computer delivered three times on what had been one of the most elusive promises in its 14 years: a truly portable Macintosh. Amidst an ocean of IBM-compatibles at the industry trade show COMDEX, Apple showed off its three new arrivals: the PowerBooks 100, 140, and 170 (see figure 1.1). The names have no significance except that they describe the relative power of the different models. The higher numbers are progressively more powerful, with the 140 being closer to the 170 than the 100. The PowerBooks answer the critics who questioned whether Apple could create a small and lightweight—yet powerful—notebook computer. Getting Mac users to recognize the allure of the PowerBooks weighs heavily in Apple's ambitious plan to capture 20 percent of the portable computer market.

In the Chips

All Macs are based on a series of CPUs (central processing units) from a company called Motorola. (Yes, Motorola has come a long way since car radios.) The first Macintosh used the Motorola 68000 (pronounced "sixty-eight thousand"). Since that time, the chip maker produced more capable models: the 68020, 68030, and 68040. Although each chip has gotten faster, each (more or less) can accept the same

1 Hayden's PowerBook Power Book

instructions. Consequently, software written for the relatively slow 68000 used in the Macintosh Classic can run on the blazing 68040 used in the Macintosh Quadra line. Occasionally, compatibility problems arise when software companies don't follow Apple programming guidelines. For the most part, however, software that runs on one Mac runs on all of them, including the PowerBooks.

Fig. 1.1. The small and lightweight, yet powerful, Macintosh PowerBooks.

As a general rule, the higher the chip number, the faster the Macintosh. Chips are further differentiated by clock speed, measured in megahertz (abbreviated MHz). The PowerBook 100 has a 16-MHz 68000 chip, the same chip as in the original Macintosh Portable which weighed three times as much as the 100. It is roughly twice the speed of a Mac Classic, Apple's least expensive Macintosh that has an 8-MHz 68000 chip. The 140 has a 16-MHz 68030 chip, making it about three times as fast as a Mac Classic, and the 170 has a roaring 25-MHz 68030 chip paired with a special math chip, making the 170 up to five times faster than a Mac Classic.

You don't own a Mac Classic, you say? To further compare with Apple's popular desktop Macs, the three PowerBooks break new ground in size and weight, but their computing power lands them in the mainstream of the Macintosh product line. The PowerBook 100 is comparable to a Macintosh LC, Apple's least-expensive color Mac. The 140 is a twin with the Macintosh Classic II, and is about 30 percent faster than the Macintosh LC. The 170 has the same main processor and math processor as the venerable Mac IIci, and performs similarly. Often, though, the PowerBooks seem a little slower than these other models because the notebooks' screens are not as responsive as desktop monitors.

Note that these speed ratings are relevant only for tasks that require heavy use of the CPU, such as calculating, sorting, and finding. Tasks such as copying disks require about the same amount of time on all PowerBooks. These tasks depend mostly on hard disk speed, which is virtually identical in all PowerBooks. Similarly, the speed at which you transfer a file electronically depends on the speed of the modem or network you use, not the speed of your computer.

Field of Dreams

In terms of the competition, companies such as Colby and Dynamac produce more portable cases for the boards of Macintosh logic boards (the "brains" of the computer). The only other company that produces notebook Macs, though, is Colorado-based Outbound Systems, which sells the Outbound Notebook System (see figure 1.2). The upgradable Outbound Notebook System's design more closely resembles that of traditional laptops, but the Outbound Notebook can run almost all Mac software. The Outbound computers can run Macintosh system software and applications because Outbound Systems has agreed with Apple to use Apple ROM (read-only memory, which contains patented information) on Outbound Systems' own logic boards. Since the Outbound computers use older versions of Apple ROM, however, there is a potential for minor incompatibilities.

Fig. 1.2. The Outbound Systems Notebook resembles a traditional laptop.

1 Hayden's PowerBook Power Book

The best feature of Outbound is that it offers a wide range of configurations, including a model faster than the PowerBook 170. Upgrading an Outbound Notebook is easy: you simply remove the hard disk, CPU, and RAM. Currently, there is no way to upgrade from one PowerBook to another, although upgrading from a 140 to a 170 might be a future option because both systems use the same case. Although some of the models are not directly comparable to the PowerBooks, pricing is competitive.

Outbound Systems also has thrown in some nice software features. For example, the Outbound Notebook can display DOS disks on the desktop (PowerBooks require separate software). On the other hand, the Outbound Notebook does not include AppleTalk Remote Access (ARA), although you can purchase ARA separately and use it with the Notebook. The Outbounds Notebooks also are less finicky about which system software you use, so, if you feel you can live without System 7.0 (see Chapter 2, "A Diminutive Desktop"), you can use System 6.0 and save some RAM for applications.

A common complaint about the Outbound Notebook is its pointing device, called a trackbar. The trackbar is a small metal rod that you roll forward or backward to move the cursor up and down, and slide left or right to move the cursor horizontally. People comfortable with the trackbar swear that you can use it effectively after a few hours of practice, but the trackbar certainly has a learning curve. In any case, the Outbound Notebook definitely deserves serious attention if you're still in the market for a notebook Mac. While this book does not refer to Mac clones explicitly, many topics in this book are still relevant should you make the decision to buy an imitation Mac.

Family Ties

All PowerBooks share a number of standard options. Some of these options are traits most computers share, while others make Apple's notebooks unique.

Keyboard

Apple claims that the PowerBook has a full-size keyboard, although the PowerBook's keys appear slightly narrower than their desktop counterparts. The PowerBook keyboard feels mushier than most Apple keyboards and is relatively quiet for taking notes at meetings. At times,

Portable Power 1

you may feel your hands are a little cramped for room, especially when you hit certain command-key combinations, such as Command-S for Save. Overall, though, typing is very comfortable, even for long periods of time.

The Esc and Enter keys flank the Spacebar. This placement seems a bit odd, but since these keys are rarely important in daily Mac use, the layout doesn't matter much unless you accidentally strike one of these keys.

Trackball

The PowerBook's pointing device is a trackball, which operates like a big mouse turned upside-down. Because you move the ball directly, you don't need as much desk space available as you need with a mouse. Trackballs first became popular in the Atari arcade game Missile Command. In that game, you marked where your missiles would detonate with an on-screen cursor controlled by a trackball that was so large and heavy you had to use your whole palm to operate it. Not to worry—the trackball on the PowerBook 140 and 170 measures 25 mm across, considerably smaller than trackballs for desktop systems such as the Kensington Turbo Mouse.

The trackball is centered below the keyboard, enabling the trackball to accomodate both right- and left-handed people. Its placement makes the PowerBooks the first Macs to allow control of the cursor with both hands on the keyboard. You easily can control the trackball with either thumb, which touch typists normally find lurking around the Spacebar anyway.

Two buttons that perform the same action lie both above and below the trackball. You may find the top button more convenient for a quick click when you're controlling both trackball and mouse button with the same hand. The lower button may be better suited for mouse-intensive operations.

Partly because of the placement of the trackball, there is extra space below the keyboard. This space around the trackball acts as a built-in wrist rest providing more comfort when typing—especially in cramped quarters. All PowerBooks also have two knobs in the rear corners that snap to provide stilts or feet that lift the rear or the machine, enabling you to type on an inclined keyboard. There's not a single electronic component in either the wrist rest or feet, but they are among the machine's most innovative hallmarks.

Other Pointing Devices

If you've traditionally disliked trackballs because they tend to be imprecise, the PowerBook's trackball might turn you around because it can be used effectively even by people who are literally "all thumbs." In any case, it is much less awkward than clip-on trackballs made for IBM PC-compatibles.

Still, the PowerBook's ADB (Apple Desktop Bus) port can accommodate standard Macintosh input devices such as mice and other keyboards. If you attach one of these devices, it fights the built-in controls of the PowerBooks if you try to use both at once. For example, if you attach a Macintosh keyboard to your PowerBook, you and an equally bored friend can see whether you can type faster than she or he can delete. (Hey, not all computer time can be productive.)

Where better to play Microsoft Flight Simulator than on an airplane? Be advised, however, that if you decide to add an ADB device (such as a joystick) to your PowerBook, that such devices draw power from your battery. Ideally, you should use low-power ADB devices. To determine the power requirements of an input device, contact the device's manufacturer.

Screen

The PowerBook has an integrated, black-and-white display with an adjustable viewing angle. The screen tilts so far back that you can type standing up with the PowerBook on a table for limited periods. The PowerBook screen measures roughly nine inches diagonally (like the Macintosh Classic and SE/30 screens), but displays a larger number of pixels (dots on the screen). Actually, the display is slightly shorter than that of the Apple 13-inch RGB display, the one most commonly paired with Macintosh II computers. Like the Apple 13-inch display, the PowerBook can display the full width of a page and nearly half the length of one.

Backlighting makes working in dim light easy. If you can work in bright light, though, you can turn off backlighting and reduce a significant drain on the battery. Incidentally, the screen gets brighter when the PowerBook is plugged in.

Serial Ports

All PowerBooks have at least one serial port, a standard port that can be used to connect the types of printers you're most likely to use with the machines. If you don't mind the confusing terminology, you also

can attach an external modem to the printer port, although most people prefer to use an internal modem.

Macs have always had the capability of easily sharing peripherals such as printers, and with the advent of System 7.0 (see Chapter 2), Macs can share files as well. You can network a PowerBook by attaching a PhoneNET-type connector to its printer port. For more information on networking, see Chapter 4, "Yakety Mac."

SCSI Port

Like all Macs since 1986, the PowerBooks have a high-speed SCSI (Small Computer System Interface, pronounced "scuzzy") port. This port enables you to attach a wide variety of devices to your PowerBook, such as portable hard disks by Liberty (see figure 1.3) and portable CD-ROM drives by Chinon. In addition, you can attach transportable Bernoulli removable drives from Iomega (these drives can hold 90 megabytes on thin disks) and hand-held scanners such as the LightningScan by Thunderware, Inc. Of course, you can also attach larger devices such as a desktop scanner, but you aren't as likely to travel with them.

Fig. 1.3. A Liberty Systems' external SCSI hard drive can back up or supplement a PowerBook's internal hard drive.

To conserve space on the back of the PowerBooks, Apple used a smaller SCSI port than that found on desktop Macs. Typically, the SCSI port is a wide trapezoid, but on the PowerBooks, the port is a small square. Because the port is a unique shape, you must purchase Apple's HDI-30 SCSI System Cable if you want to attach a normal SCSI device (such as the devices described in the preceding paragraph) to the PowerBook. This cable should not be confused with the HDI-30 SCSI Disk Adapter, which is used to "dock" a PowerBook 100 to a desktop Mac (see Chapter 4, "Yakety Mac").

1 Hayden's PowerBook Power Book

Sound Out

All PowerBooks have a built-in speaker adequate for projecting system beeps, voice, and other monaural sound. PowerBooks also have a sound-out jack in the back of the system that accepts headphones or miniature speakers, in case you want to listen to a series of voice annotations privately.

Hard Disk Space

All PowerBooks contain thin, low-power hard disks that must conform to Apple's specifications. As a result, PowerBook hard disks are available only in small capacities, especially when compared to modern desktop alternatives. Although the scarcity of hard drives with larger capacities will probably continue for some time, Microtech is shipping the RoadRunner 80M internal hard disk (see figure 1.4) and 100M models might not be far off.

Fig. 1.4. Microtech's miniscule RoadRunner 80 is a faster and larger alternative to Apple's internal PowerBook hard disk.

Conserving hard disk space is a constant battle for PowerBook users. If you know you can live without something, do so. Many programs do not need translators or help files that consume significant chunks of hard disk space. On the other hand, be wary of randomly trashing supplemental files with purposes you don't understand; some programs do not launch unless they can find certain files.

Avoid redundant files. If you use several programs that deal with text, a quick search of your hard disk for the term "dictionary" may reveal several applications' dictionaries. Such files may use several thousand bytes apiece. Dictionary (and thesaurus) files can quickly add up to consume several megabytes of disk space. You may want spell-checking abilities in several programs that use different dictionaries,

Portable Power 1

and even in some programs that don't offer spell-checking out of the box. If this sounds appealing, check out Thunder 7 from Baseline Publishing, an extension that uses one set of dictionaries to check spelling in a variety of different programs.

To save hard disk space, use an automatic compression program such as AutoDoubler. These extraordinary utilities can enable you to keep more of what you need close at hand, especially if you're not as concerned about power consumption. To find out more about these utilities, see Chapter 6, "Productivity Enhancers."

Internal Slots

PowerBooks have two tiny internal expansion slots, one for extra RAM and one for a modem. The slots are filled differently, depending upon which configuration you buy. All PowerBooks can accommodate up to 8M of RAM by adding or replacing a RAM card. Table 1.1 illustrates the memory expansion options for PowerBooks. With RAM upgrade options for the PowerBooks, you can run more programs at once and open larger files.

Table 1.1 RAM upgrade options.

If Your PowerBook Came With	To Get 4M RAM	To Get 6M RAM	To Get 8M RAM
2M RAM	Add 2M card	Add 4M card	Add 6M card
4M RAM	N/A	Remove 2M card Add 4M card	Remove 2M card Add 6M card

Note: Some third parties sell memory kits that "piggy back" onto existing cards so that you don't have to remove the 2M card in a 4M PowerBook to have 8M in your PowerBook.

RAM tends to follow the MTV credo, "Too much is never enough." The more RAM you have, the more applications you can run at once. Allocating more RAM to applications enables the applications to work with more and larger documents. With extra RAM, you also can customize your system with some of the productivity enhancers discussed in Chapter 6. You also can set aside RAM for an extra-fast RAM disk that speeds your work (see Chapter 2, "A Diminutive Desktop").

The PowerBooks use "pseudo-static" RAM, which preserves the contents of memory using very little power. As you might guess, the RAM chips themselves are much smaller than normal RAM chips. The chips also contain special circuitry designed to keep their power requirements low.

All Apple notebooks have a modem slot. This slot already is occupied in the PowerBook 170 by the Macintosh PowerBook Fax/Data Modem, a 2400-baud modem that can also send faxes at 9600 baud. An authorized Apple dealer can install that modem, or third-party alternatives such as PSI's PowerModem, in the other PowerBooks.

> *Tip:* Internal modems draw power as long as they are on, even if the modems are not transmitting data. To conserve power, quit your communications program as soon as you finish using it.

Power Saving Features

In addition to being on or off, the PowerBook can be in sleep mode (although a better analogy might be coma mode). Sleep turns off—among other circuits—two of the machine's biggest consumers of battery power: the screen and hard disk. The PowerBook uses only enough power to preserve the contents of the system memory (RAM), so you don't lose changes you have made to your work. You can put the PowerBook to rest manually or have it sleep automatically after a specified period of time.

The blank screen and quiet hard disk prevent you from determining whether a PowerBook is off or sleeping. There is, however, a simple method for finding out whether the PowerBook is in sleep mode. Touching any key except Caps Lock wakes a sleeping PowerBook. If that doesn't work, try pressing the power button.

In addition to sleeping, all PowerBooks take advantage of system rest. This feature keeps the machine working but slows down the main processor. There is nothing to configure for system rest; you probably won't know whether it's active unless you continually monitor the performances of your applications.

The PowerBook warns you twice when the battery power is getting low, and then forces itself to sleep. To wake up the PowerBook at that point, you should plug the system in or put in a fresh battery.

Portable Power 1

Differences Among the Models

The PowerBooks are more alike than dissimilar, but there are significant differences among the trio in addition to their computing speed.

The PowerBook 100

The PowerBook 100 looks different from the other two PowerBooks. The 100 incorporates the curved front that Apple started using with the Macintosh LC and IIsi. The lightest, smallest, and cheapest PowerBook, the 100 is a true notebook computer, with a width and depth of 8 1/2" by 11", a height of 1.8", and a weight of just over five pounds.

In building the 100 following Apple specifications, Sony traded bulk for inconvenience. One reason the 100 is so light is that it lacks an internal floppy disk drive. Floppy disk access, therefore, is limited to an external floppy disk drive. Like the SCSI port on all PowerBooks, the external floppy port exclusive to the 100 is narrower than the ports on desktop Macs. So, you must purchase an external floppy disk drive that can plug into the port. As you might guess, Apple makes just such a beast: the HDI-20 External 1.4 Megabyte Floppy-Disk Drive (see figure 1.5).

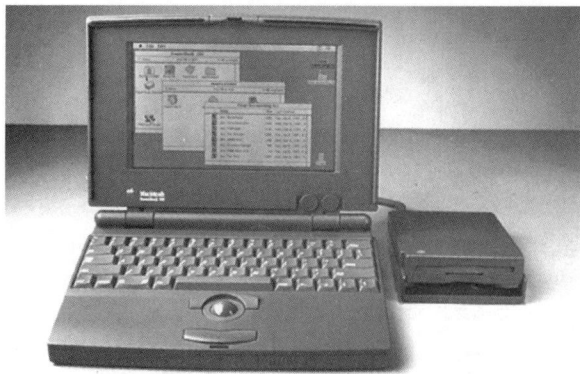

Fig. 1.5. Apple offers an external 1.4M floppy drive to complement the PowerBook 100.

Apple also offers the PowerBook 100 without the floppy disk drive. Although you occasionally may want to forego the external bulk of the already thin drive, you risk limiting the convenience with which you

1 Hayden's PowerBook Power Book

can transfer information. Using the correct cables and software, the 100 can still communicate with other Macs and PC-compatibles, but swapping floppies is much easier. For more information on transferring data, see Chapter 4, "Yakety Mac."

The 100 does not have an on/off button like its more powerful siblings. Instead, you turn it on by touching any key except Caps Lock. It also has a storage switch that you should use when you're not using the machine for a long period of time.

Because the 100 is the only Mac with only one serial port, you must use a switchbox to connect both an external modem and a printer. Of course, using an internal modem frees the port for whatever use you want.

Although the 100 lacks a microphone, you can use the printer port to accommodate a small microphone such as Premier Technology's MacMike or Macromind-Paracomp's MacRecorder Voice Digitizer. These microphones, paired with the MacRecorder Driver software (available from online services and user groups) give you practically all the benefits of the Apple microphone.

> ***Tip:*** If you experience problems connecting serial devices to the printer port, AppleTalk might be on. To turn off AppleTalk, select Chooser from the Apple menu. Then, select the Off button next to the AppleTalk option in the Chooser dialog box.

Because the 100 uses a different battery technology than the other PowerBooks, you must specify that you want extra PowerBook 100 batteries if you plan to be without an electrical outlet for more than four hours. Unlike the lead-acid batteries that slip into the side of the machine (used in the 140 and 170), the 100's NiCad battery slides into the front of the computer.

Apple also sells a PowerBook 100 battery recharger separate from the one used to recharge 140 or 170 batteries so you can recharge as you work. Compared to the batteries for the 140 and 170, the 100 battery takes approximately a half-hour less to charge to 80 percent capacity, but takes up to an additional hour to fully recharge.

The 100 has brightness and contrast knobs at the base of the screen, whereas the 140 uses slide controls. The 100's restart and interrupt buttons are in a more traditional location: on the left side toward the rear. The restart and interrupt buttons appear at that location on most

Portable Power

compact desktop models such as the SE and SE/30. When pushed simultaneously, these two buttons restart the system if there is a system error.

Because the central processor of the 100 does not support a function called paged memory management, PowerBook 100 users cannot use virtual memory. This system software trick treats unused hard disk space as a slower form of RAM. Although virtual memory has its benefits, it depletes the battery faster than real RAM because it greatly increases the amount of work the hard disk has to do. When the PowerBook is plugged in, though, virtual memory is a nice option to have.

The PowerBook 140

The PowerBook 140 is similar to a laptop version of Apple's Macintosh Classic II, but shares the body design of the more powerful 170. The 140's 68030 chip runs at 16 MHz, which means the 140 can take full advantage of System 7.0. The middle child in the PowerBook family, the 140 shares the same physical design of its more powerful sibling, the 170—but like the 100—the 140 has a lower-quality supertwist screen. For control of brightness and contrast, the 140 uses slide controls instead of the dials used on the 100. Although the screen is quite readable, you might notice that the cursor fades when you drag the mouse quickly.

The PowerBook 170

Sharp display and speed are the hallmarks of the PowerBook 170, which packs the computing muscle of a Macintosh IIci in a computer weighing under seven pounds (see figure 1.6). The 170's 25-MHz 68030 chip places the machine in the upper echelon of mainstream Macs. Its alluring screen incorporates the controversial active-matrix technology. Although the debate continues about trade barriers imposed on importing the displays, no one disputes their quality. The 170's crisp, responsive display outshines others when it comes to speed and clarity.

The 170 is the only PowerBook with a math coprocessor, the same 68882 chip found in the Mac IIci. This coprocessor makes a big difference if you're performing math-intensive tasks such as working with large spreadsheets or manipulating complex CAD drawings. For most users, though, the math coprocessor doesn't significantly affect daily computer use.

1 Hayden's PowerBook Power Book

Fig. 1.6.
Sharp display and speed are the hallmarks of the PowerBook 170.

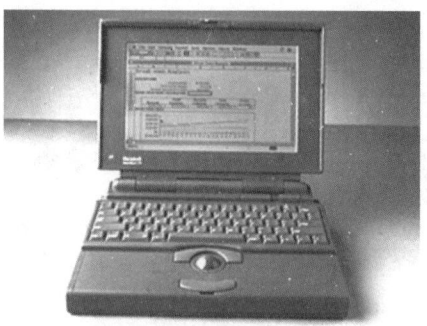

Although all PowerBooks have power management features (see Chapter 2, "A Diminutive Desktop"), the 170 has a unique Power Saver feature that slows down the speed of the CPU to 16 MHz whenever no activity is detected. This feature buys some extra battery time (about a half hour) while still providing satisfactory performance.

As noted previously, the 170 comes standard with the internal Apple send-only fax/data modem available for all PowerBooks.

More Than You Bargained For

In Apple's promotional brochure, the company claims that when designing the PowerBooks, "We couldn't bring ourselves to leave out anything." On the contrary, although the PowerBooks feature standard options considered extra on competing laptops, third parties are racing to fulfill a rich add-ons market.

The Bleak Outlook

The biggest gripe most people have with PowerBooks is that there is no standard way to project a screen image onto another monitor because PowerBooks lack the "video out" ports available on many laptops. A number of vendors have come up with solutions for this. A popular approach is to pass the video signal through the SCSI port. This approach frees you from having to open the PowerBook case yourself (and thus void the warranty) or having to pay an authorized—and willing—Apple dealer to open it for you.

Among the mainstream Mac video specialists, Radius has created a relatively inexpensive and easy-to-install (if cumbersome) solution with the Radius PowerView (see figure 1.7). The PowerView is an SCSI

Portable Power 1

device that enables you to attach a wide variety of monitors including Radius' popular Pivot display and the Apple 13-inch RGB display. However, the PowerView's response time lags behind those of internal cards. The PowerView currently works only with the PowerBook 140 and 170, although Radius is working on a software upgrade to enable it to work with the 100.

The PowerView mimics a Radius video card and even allows the use of Radius' useful RadiusWare software. This software features such enhancements as an enlarged font menu and a built-in screen saver (a nice touch because you might not be toting one with your PowerBook). Unfortunately, the lightweight PowerView itself is rather bulky and requires a sizable power supply, an extra power cord and the special Apple PowerBook SCSI cable Radius includes.

After you set your preferences via the controls in the PowerView and Monitors control panels, you will find that the PowerView can imitate what is on your Mac screen—but very slowly. The PowerView can keep up with you as you type, but presentations—especially visual effects such as sweep left and dissolve—crawl along. In the acid test, we ran a Macromind Director animation file on a PowerView-equipped 140. Without the PowerView attached, the animation was in sync with the musical accompaniment. When we attached the PowerView, the music finished far ahead of the blocky animation.

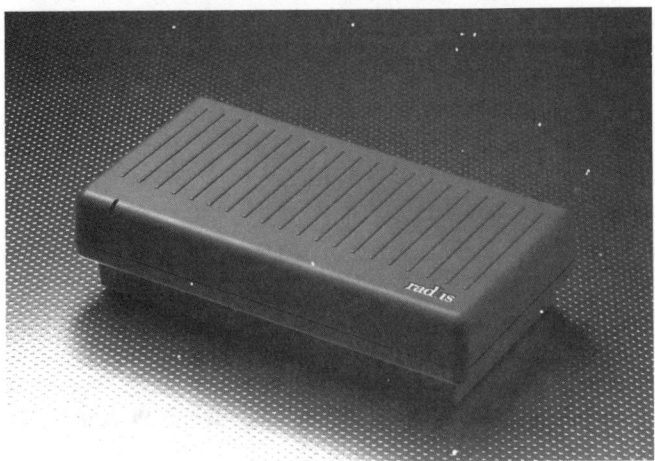

Fig. 1.7. The Radius PowerView enables you to use different monitors with your PowerBook.

With an entire external box with which to work, Radius could have gained a competitive advantage by putting video RAM in the PowerView, but it didn't. Like the internal adapters, the PowerView

1 Hayden's PowerBook Power Book

relies on the RAM in your PowerBook to create the video signal. Consequently, be prepared to beef up your RAM if you want to carry along color presentations for use on an Apple 13-inch display.

Radius' archrival RasterOps provides a less versatile but arguably more convenient solution in its upcoming ClearVue/SD21 two-page grayscale monitor. This monitor can accept video signals directly from the SCSI port; the case contains all the required video circuitry.

Envisio and Computer Care took the road less traveled: the internal one. Their internal display adapters lack the considerable bulk of external SCSI boxes like those from Radius. Both Envisio and Computer Care recommend installation by a certified Apple dealer to keep the PowerBook warranty intact, but they claim that anyone who's not afraid of a screwdriver and can follow directions can install their products.

Envisio offers six different Notebook Display Adapters that can piggy-back onto a RAM card already occupying the PowerBook's RAM slot. Three adapters are for the PowerBook 100, and the other three can be used in either the 140 or the 170. The 100's video ports emerge through the backup battery door and can display only black and white because of the computer's limitations; on the 140 and 170, the ports emerge at the base of the screen and can produce 256 colors on certain displays.

Envisio bundles nearly all of its video cards with RAM so that you can upgrade your PowerBook's RAM and video-out ability simultaneously. The PowerBook also can sense when a video cable is attached and spare the required battery power when not in use. In addition to the more expensive cards with RAM such as those that Envisio sells, Computer Care offers a model called the BookView. The BookView outputs the standard image of the PowerBook screen to another monitor, regardless of how much bigger the other monitor is.

Tip: If you're planning to use a projector with your PowerBook to display presentations, most projectors are compatible with any video boards that support the Apple 13-inch RGB Display. These projectors should work in conjuction with the PowerView or the internal cards.

Portable Power 1

The Fast Lane

The problem of how to get a Mac lacking a suitable expansion slot onto a high-speed Ethernet network is not a new one. Companies such as Asanté and Nuvotech offer external SCSI devices that enable such computers as the Macintosh Plus and Classic (not equipped with internal slots) to get onto any kind of Ethernet cabling scheme, whether thick, thin or twisted-pair wiring.

Dayna Communications continues that tradition with the DaynaPORT SCSI/Link (see figure 1.8), an external SCSI device that boasts a smaller form factor than traditional external SCSI devices. Dayna's SCSI/Link can accommodate different Ethernet connections so that your PowerBook can transfer data over an Ethernet LAN at speeds higher than those possible with LocalTalk.

Fig. 1.8. With Dayna's SCSI/Link, you can transfer data at speeds faster than with LocalTalk.

Tip: SCSI/Link won't speed up network connections over a modem made with AppleTalk Remote Access. For that, you'll need a faster modem.

The Power Play

Apple's original Macintosh Portable was larger and heavier than any of the PowerBooks, but it had a much longer battery life. In addition to

PowerBook battery rechargers, Lind Electronic Design offers an external battery pack that the company claims quadruples your available battery computing time, and an adapter that delivers juice from your car's cigarette lighter.

The Numbers Game

In at least one respect, the PowerBooks mark a throwback to the days of the Mac 512K, they keyboard of which lacked a numeric keypad. At that time, Apple sold a keypad that matched the style of the 512K keyboard; this time, two third-party developers beat Apple to the punch. Kensington, one of the largest Macintosh accessories producers, and the ADB wizards at Sophisticated Circuits, created numeric keypads for all the spreadsheet jockeys to match the design of the PowerBook itself. The Kensington model also has function keys for use with terminal emulation and macro software (see figure 1.9). Kensington's Notebook Keypad is a boon for number-crunching travelers who have fallen victim to the horizontal placement of the PowerBook's number keys.

Fig. 1.9. Kensington's Notebook Keypad is great for number-crunching travelers.

Tip: You can compensate somewhat for the lack of a numeric keypad by using a free keyboard definition file called Num Lock by Masaaki Takahashi. Num Lock lets you use nine of the keys on your keyboard to simulate a numeric keypad, greatly facilitating numerical data entry.

Portable Power 1

Mo' Better Modems

If you purchased a PowerBook 170, you received Apple's send-only fax modem free of charge. But if you've got a 140 or 170, you may be able to get more baud for the buck than you can with Apple's offering. PSI offers the PowerModem, which can receive faxes as well as send them.

For the ultimate telecommunications tool, Global Village Communications may even be able to persuade owners of the 170 to remove their Apple modems in favor of the PowerPort/v.32, a 9600-baud internal modem. This modem, although a bit pricey, competes with other premium modems offering such high speeds. A 9600-baud modem can transfer information approximately four times as fast as a 2400-baud modem. This speed results in briefer long-distance calls and less on-line time at expensive services that support high-speed access, such as CompuServe. Better yet, Global Village offers excellent fax-sending and receiving software (just hold down the Option key as you choose Print to fax instead) included with the PowerPort/v.32.

In addition, several small, portable, external modems work with the PowerBooks. One worth mentioning is the QBlazer from Telebit Corporation, a small, fast, external modem that runs for three hours on batteries.

Stop the Presses

Apple's StyleWriter is the closest the company can come to offering a portable printer, and it's not that bad of an attempt. An inkjet printer capable of packing 360 dots per inch, the lightweight, compact, and economical StyleWriter complements the PowerBooks. The printer does, however, require a power supply and a great deal of patience because of its speed.

A smaller inkjet of lower, but acceptable, print quality is GCC Technologies' WriteMove printer (see figure 1.10). The WriteMove printer was available long before the PowerBooks, but it makes a perfect match for Mac notebook users who need a small, battery-powered, near-laser-quality printer. The tiny 3-pound printer uses the same hardware as the popular Diconix 150M Plus printer by Kodak, and GCC, one of the oldest makers of Mac peripherals, includes a Chooser selectable printer driver and a spooler. The WriteMove also accepts cut-sheet or tractor-fed paper. For power needs, the WriteMove comes with an AC adapter for wall outlets and can accept five NiCad rechargeable C-size batteries that actually sit inside the printer roller to save space. You can recharge the batteries while they are still installed in the printer.

1 Hayden's PowerBook Power Book

Fig. 1.10. The GCC WriteMove Printer makes a perfect match for PowerBook users.

RAM Tough

How much RAM is enough? The answer depends upon how much memory you want to work with and the type and level of work you want to do. Chapter 3, "Application Software," discusses how integrated and lean applications minimize the amount of RAM you need for a project.

A 2M PowerBook is a purchase you should carefully consider, although you will find plenty of tips for the RAM-poor in later chapters. Even with a pared-down System Folder without sounds, fonts, and extensions (see Chapter 6, "Productivity Enhancers"), System 7.0 takes up more than 1M of RAM. This leaves you with—at best—approximately 800K to 900K of RAM with which to work. This is enough RAM to squeeze in a single application, or perhaps two "lean" applications described in Chapter 3, but such tight RAM constraints limit much of the PowerBook's multitasking potential.

Each PowerBook can accommodate up to 8M of RAM. Using Apple or third-party memory expansion cards, you can upgrade a PowerBook to 4, 6, or 8M of RAM. If you want to make the jump from 2M to 8M, for now you must rely on third parties such as Newer Technologies, one of the few companies offering 6M PowerBook upgrade cards. Keep in mind that, as with all products that involve exposing the PowerBook's innards, you risk voiding your warranty if you damage the PowerBook while installing RAM. If you're thinking about installing additional RAM, either combine an accurate set of instructions on PowerBook RAM installation with technical confidence, or find an Apple dealer willing to install the RAM for you.

Portable Power 1

'Book Bags

To protect your PowerBook (and to stow the cables, disks, and possibly the printer you want with you), a slew of third parties offer carrying cases expressly for Apple's little darlings. Kensington Microware has two carrying cases: one for just the PowerBook and another that lets you hold other goodies as well. Magenta7 offers MagentaCase cases in a variety of colors (if you order more than five cases). With a MagentaCase, you can use your PowerBook while it's still in its case. The company also maintains a registering service in case your PowerBook is lost (although the Surgeon General warns against holding your breath waiting for a missing PowerBook to return).

T/Maker, publisher of the acclaimed WriteNow word processor and ClipArt graphic images, offers the PowerBundle: a carrying case for the PowerBook stuffed with five software programs (see figure 1.11). T/Maker's PowerBundle carrying case packs a collection of useful software, most notably its speedy WriteNow and Power Up!'s versatile Address Book Plus. Also included in the bundle are ClipArt for faxes, if:X Expense Reports, and America Online. The access software for America Online is available free from America Online. In addition, WriteNow and Address Book Plus are among the leaders in their classes, and the other two programs add further value. If your needs match those of the typical new user, the PowerBundle may contain the right stuffing.

Fig. 1.11. T/Maker's PowerBundle carrying case packs a collection of useful software.

With many carrying cases selling for well over $100, you may wish that some of the manufacturers would get a grip. Actually, that's what Premier Technology has in mind. For a mere $29.95, its add-on handle replaces the PowerBook feet. The handle offers no protection for the PowerBook, but it does make toting your machine more convenient.

1 Hayden's PowerBook Power Book

To Seventh Heaven

The PowerBook is probably not your first exposure to the Macintosh environment, but you may notice some changes if you are using older versions of system software. Chapter 2, "A Diminutive Desktop," explains what's new in System 7.0 for old Mac hands and discusses some important system features that cater to users of the new machines.

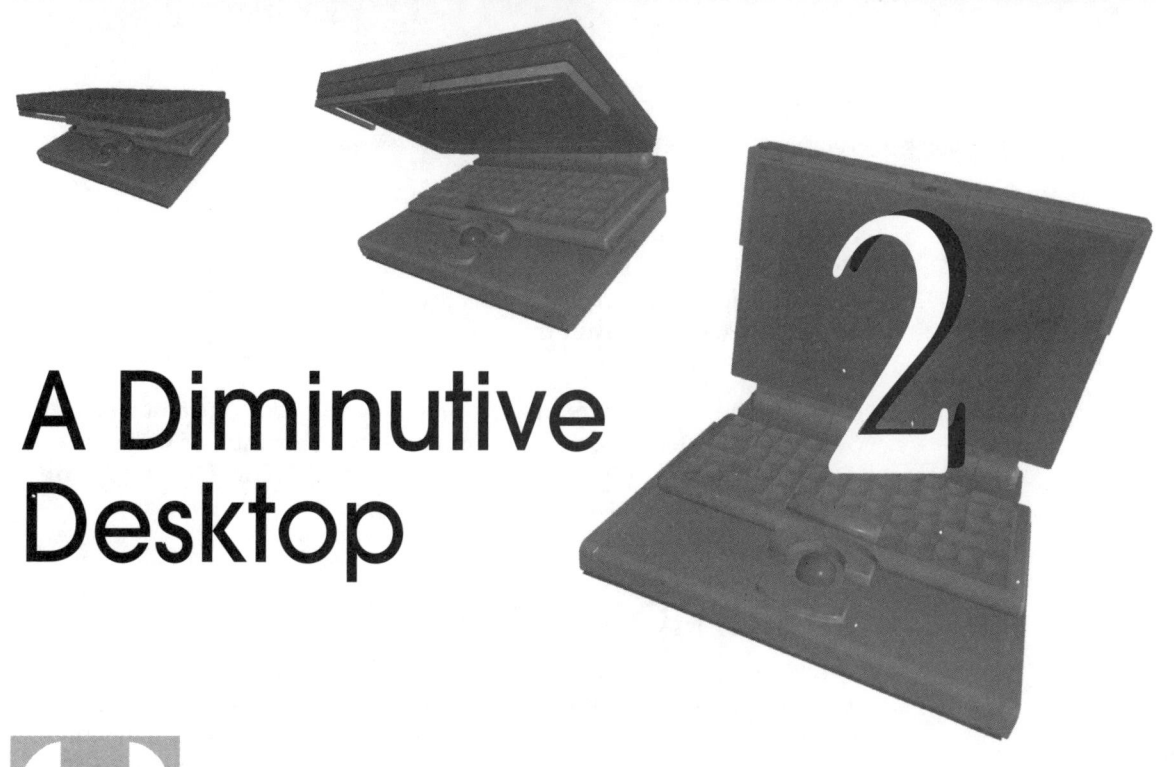

A Diminutive Desktop

The CEO of an influential Mac software developer once remarked that Apple should get out of the hardware business and just write software. He may have had second thoughts after seeing the PowerBooks, but his comments captured a sentiment often heard in the Macintosh community: for a hardware company, Apple writes great software.

Nowhere has Apple's software shined as brightly as it has on the Macintosh computer. Eight years after its introduction, the Mac continues to advance standards for elegance and ease of use in the microcomputer industry while others scramble to become more "Mac-like." Indeed, popular MS-DOS portables have features the PowerBooks lack, such as color screens, faster processors, video ports, and function keys. But the MS-DOS portables all lack System 7.0—the soul of the Macintosh interface that ties everything together.

System 7.0.1 (a minor update to System 7.0 that the PowerBooks require) marks the ongoing improvements to the operating system that pioneered the graphical interface in an affordable computer. Release 7.0 had a daunting charter: to make an already powerful, friendly computer more powerful and more friendly. And 7.0 had to accomplish that without changing the Macintosh interface so radically that people had to relearn how to do things. With few exceptions, System 7.0 succeeded, proving stable enough to entice experienced users and invite new ones.

If you are a new user, take the time to review "Macintosh Basics," a HyperCard tutorial stack that comes with all PowerBooks. You may be surprised at how much the stack covers and how well it conveys information. Also consult the "Getting Started" and "Learning" sections of Apple's *Users' Guide*.

If you are an experienced user, you may have been reluctant to adopt System 7.0 for fear of change, compatibility, reliability, or memory requirements. If you've invested in a PowerBook, much of the apprehension will disappear once you understand the new features.

First Impressions

The Finder holds the most dramatic changes to the system software. After the familiar "Welcome to Macintosh" message, you notice that the Finder has a new menu, Label (discussed later), and two small icons on the right of the menu bar. The far-right icon may resemble the old MultiFinder icon you used to switch among open programs. Using MultiFinder, however, is no longer an option with System 7.0; it is now a standard feature. Fortunately, Apple enhanced switching from program to program. An application menu from which you can select any open application (see figure 2.1) replaces the MultiFinder icon at the right of the menu bar.

Fig. 2.1. The application menu replaces the old MultiFinder icon.

Instead of having to click repeatedly to new applications, you select them, optionally hiding the windows of other applications. The application menu also can deal with the window clutter associated with running multiple applications. You can hide all of an application's

A Diminutive Desktop 2

windows by choosing "Hide <the program name>" from the application window or to hide all windows belonging to other programs by choosing "Hide Others." Because System 7.0 treats desk accessories (DAs) as applications, open DAs also appear in this menu.

> *Tip:* To hide all other windows as you switch to an application, hold down the Option key as you choose the application's name from the application menu.

The comics-style balloon to the left of the application icon is the Balloon Help menu, used to turn Balloon Help on and off. Balloon Help provides explanations for virtually everything on the screen by "talking" through a comics-style balloon. To find out what the Trash does, you can point to the trash can. If you need a menu item to be explained, pull down the desired menu and drag the pointer to select a particular item.

Balloon Help can explain new features or new applications quickly. It cannot, however, substitute for the more detailed explanations found in Microsoft Word, Aldus PageMaker, and other applications that contain their own online help. Many applications do not yet take advantage of Balloon Help, but more applications are being added to the list each month.

> *Tip:* When Balloon Help is on, the balloons may distract experienced users. Fortunately, a shareware program called Helium, as well as popular commercial programs such as QuicKeys 2, let you turn balloon help on or off with a keystroke.

Directory Listing

Viewing files by name, size, date, or label produces a list view of your files. You can change the sorting order of the directory listing by clicking on column titles. Clicking the top of the File Name column alphabetizes the files by file name; clicking the top of the Size column sorts files and folders by size. To sort folders by size, however, you must select "Calculate folder sizes" in the Views control panel.

The new list view features small triangles to the left of folders (see figure 2.2). Clicking a triangle that points to the right (or pressing Command-right arrow) displays a folder's contents without opening the folder. Clicking the triangle again (or pressing command-left arrow) hides the contents. You also can drag across files to select them in the list view and see the total used and free disk space without switching back to icon view.

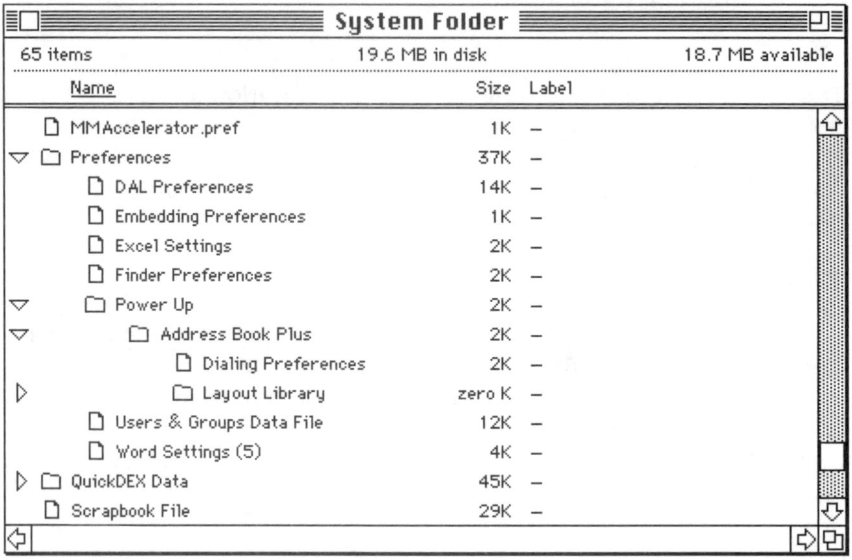

Fig. 2.2. Triangles appear to the left of folders.

Name	Size	Label
MMAccelerator.pref	1K	—
▽ Preferences	37K	—
DAL Preferences	14K	—
Embedding Preferences	1K	—
Excel Settings	2K	—
Finder Preferences	2K	—
▽ Power Up	2K	—
▽ Address Book Plus	2K	—
Dialing Preferences	2K	—
▷ Layout Library	zero K	—
Users & Groups Data File	12K	—
Word Settings (5)	4K	—
▷ QuickDEX Data	45K	—
Scrapbook File	29K	—

System Folder — 65 items — 19.6 MB in disk — 18.7 MB available

You can replace icons by copying an icon from one Get Info window and pasting the icon into another Get Info window. Icon names can appear in any font and can range in size from 6 to 36 points. You also can choose to keep your icons organized in either of two grids.

Finding Yourself

Finder 7.0 received more muscle in addition to its facelift. For starters, 7.0 is the first version of the Finder that actually can perform searches. By selecting the Find command from the File menu, you can search any available disk for all files based on any part of the file's name, its size, its type, or the date the file was last changed (see figure 2.3). The Find command replaces the less powerful Find File desk accessory of older systems.

A Diminutive Desktop 2

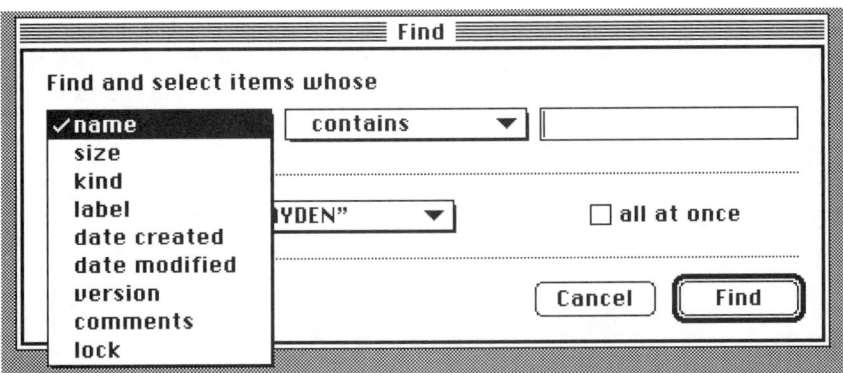

Fig. 2.3.
The Find command.

The Finder automatically opens the proper window and selects the file you want, or it simultaneously can select all files that match your criteria. This capability makes it easy, for example, to move all MacWrite files from a disk to a folder called "Word Processing Files."

> *Tip:* If you've selected many files at once, you can narrow your selection by choosing Find Again in "More Choices." This approach lets you search for files from among those files already selected.

You also can search on the basis of labels. The Label menu replaces the old Color menu. Assigning one of eight customizable labels to any icon lets you designate a file as "Important," "Personal," "In Progress," and so on. To apply a label, select the icon or icons you want to label and choose the appropriate label from the Label menu.

Keys to Success

The Find command and Label menu are two of the many ways in which Finder 7.0 makes your files more accessible. If you are an experienced Mac user, you've probably wished for a way to control the Finder from the keyboard. Even if you are a new PowerBook user, you will appreciate System 7.0's methods of keyboard control.

Typing the first few letters of an icon's name in a window selects that icon. You can select other icons in the window by using the arrow keys or select the next icon in alphabetical order by pressing Tab. You can select the previous icon by pressing Shift-Tab. When editing icon

names, a small rectangle surrounds the text to let you know you are in renaming mode. When not renaming icons, pressing keys selects files. You can rename a selected icon by pressing Return, typing the new name, and pressing Return again (see figure 2.4).

Fig. 2.4.
Renaming a folder.

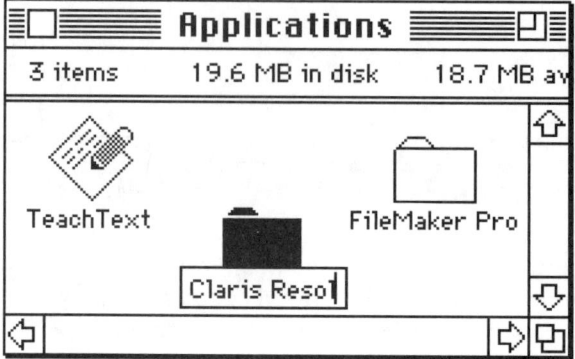

Mimicking the standard Open and Save dialog boxes, Command-up arrow opens the folder containing the file you're viewing, and Command-down arrow opens the file you've selected. You can close all Finder windows by pressing Command-Option-W. You also can remove disks from the desktop by selecting them and pressing Command-Y. (You don't need to remember any of these key combinations because they are documented in the Finder Shortcuts menu item in the Balloon Help menu.) Of course, the mouse still works the same way it always has.

System 7.0 also eases organization by using aliases. Aliases are copies of a disk, folder, or file icon that do nothing more than point to the original icon. Alias names appear in italics. With aliases, you can have files act as though they are in two places at once. For example, if you use MacDraw Pro often, you may want to keep the application icon on your desktop, but you also may want an alias of the MacDraw Pro icon in your "Graphics Applications" folder.

With System 7.0, you can keep just the alias of the program's icon on the desktop. Aliases are simple to create; you merely select any icon and choose Make Alias from the File menu. An underrated part of System 7.0, aliases provide freedom from programs that require files to be in certain places. Using aliases, you can keep applications in their appropriate folders and still access the applications from the Apple menu (a process discussed in the next section).

A Diminutive Desktop 2

The sophistication of aliases also can make communicating easier for PowerBook owners who use AppleTalk Remote Access. This software enables you to access data on your desktop Mac from remote locations. For more about AppleTalk Remote Access, see Chapter 4, "Communications."

A Bolder Folder

The System Folder remains crowded in System 7.0, but five special folders greatly ease System Folder organization (see figure 2.5). Special folders exist for Extensions (formerly called "INITs"), Control Panels (formerly called "cdevs"), and Preferences files. But don't worry about remembering which files go where. When you drag control panels and extensions to the System Folder as you always have, the Mac tells you where each item should go. If you like, the Mac even puts the files in the proper folders for you. Applications create Preferences files, and as more programs become "System-7.0 savvy," you'll find fewer Preference files cluttering your System Folder.

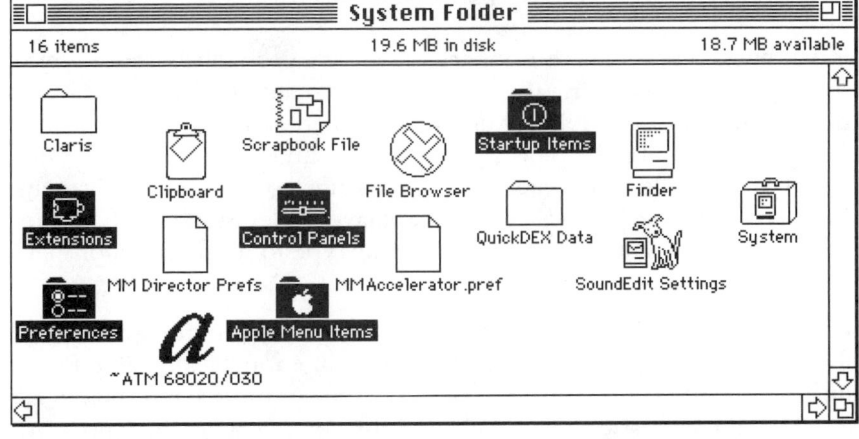

Fig. 2.5.
The five special folders in the System Folder.

The Apple Menu Items folder provides instant access to often-used files. Originally, you could access only 15 desk accessories (DAs) from the Apple menu, and the only way to get the DAs onto the Apple menu was to use a hideous utility called the Font/DA Mover. Mac veterans are pleased to discover that System 7.0 makes the Font/DA Mover obsolete.

Dragging a file's icon or its alias into the Apple Menu Items folder makes the file instantly appear under the Apple menu. From the Apple menu, you can open more than 50 items ranging from the Calculator to PageMaker. You also can open control panels and desk accessories by double-clicking their icons.

The Startup Items folder in the System Folder replaces the old Set Startup command in the Special menu. Dragging applications or documents (or their aliases) into the Startup Items folder causes the item to open automatically when your machine starts. You even can drop a System 7.0 sound file into the Startup Items folder for your Mac to play upon startup.

The Font Issue

System 7.0 incorporates a new font format called TrueType. Introduced with Apple's Personal LaserWriter LS and StyleWriter, TrueType produces good-looking text at large sizes both on-screen and on printers that do not support PostScript. (PostScript is Adobe's page description language that produces high-quality images on many different printers.)

If that doesn't sound revolutionary to you, it's probably because you've seen it done before using the Adobe Type Manager (ATM) control panel. The control panel delivers similar functionality using Type 1 PostScript fonts. TrueType is slightly faster than ATM, but the TrueType font files are larger. TrueType fonts have a distinct advantage over Type 1 fonts: they are easier to manage under System 7.0. All the information the Mac needs to draw a TrueType font on-screen or in a printer exists in a single file (see figure 2.6).

PostScript fonts have two components: a bitmapped font responsible for displaying output on-screen, and an outline font responsible for imaging the font in the printer. The functions of these components get a little confusing when using ATM, because that program also uses the outline font to display attractive large type.

Apple has apparently either had a change of heart or received a lot of hate mail regarding Type 1's second-class citizen status. The computer maker now promises that a future version of System 7.0 will treat Type 1 and TrueType fonts more similarly. Perhaps to show its sincerity,

A Diminutive Desktop 2

Apple already has plans to incorporate Adobe Type Manager into System 7.0. For now, however, the two font formats seem to coexist (as long as you don't install both versions of the same font).

Fig. 2.6.
The "Get Info" window of a TrueType font reveals the font's versatility.

Tip: In System 7.0, installing PostScript fonts is counter-intuitive. You drag bit-mapped (screen) fonts into the System file or the System Folder (which places them in the System file for you). Oddly enough, you drag outline fonts into the Extensions folder. Sure enough, the Get Info window of a TrueType font indicates that it's a "font," although PostScript fonts are labeled "extensions." You can use a utility like Fifth Generation System's Suitcase II to place a font in a more intuitive folder (one named "Fonts," for example), but this seems like a marginal reason to keep a utility.

Desktop and Debris

System 6.0 dealt with the Trash and the Desktop inconsistently. For example, when you were in the Finder, certain icons appeared to be on the Desktop. However, when you viewed the icons from within an application, however, the icons appeared to be on the top layer of the hard disk.

Similarly, under System 7.0, the Trash doesn't empty until you choose Empty Trash from the Special menu. Under System 6.0, however, restarting the Mac took the contents of the Trash away automatically (sort of like a built-in sanitation department).

Although you can skip warning messages by deselecting "Warn before emptying" in the Trash's Get Info dialog, Finder 7.0 is safer than Finder 6.0 because the new finder never erases files in the Trash until you select Empty Trash from the File menu—even if you turn off your Mac.

> *Tip:* If you want even more control over your Trash, you may want to look into the trashiest utility ever created: HandOff Corporation's TrashMaster. TrashMaster lets you selectively delete items thrown in the Trash and permanently erase the files so that file recovery software can't recover confidential files.

The Clean Up command in the Special menu performs different tasks depending on which modifier key you hold down when you select Clean Up (see figure 2.7). Zoom boxes also are more useful in System 7.0, opening up just large enough to display a window's contents. Command-clicking a window's title reveals a pop-up menu from which you can select the folder that contains that window. Windows also scroll automatically when you drag within them.

Other amenities abound. Open and Save dialog boxes have been augmented with better keyboard access. A Desktop layer allows for fast switching among available drives. You can even copy and paste sounds into the Scrapbook.

The Mac has always been versatile when it comes to customizing your environment. System 7.0 incorporates parts of customization utilities such as Norton Utilities' Layout program. Dedicated customization programs such as Dubl-Click Software's fun ClickChange control panel and Thought I Could Software's well-received Wallpaper work on the

A Diminutive Desktop 2

PowerBooks (Wallpaper requires a PowerBook 140 or 170), but the programs do take up hard disk space and RAM. If you're using either of these programs, you probably can leave behind many of their color-optimized patterns.

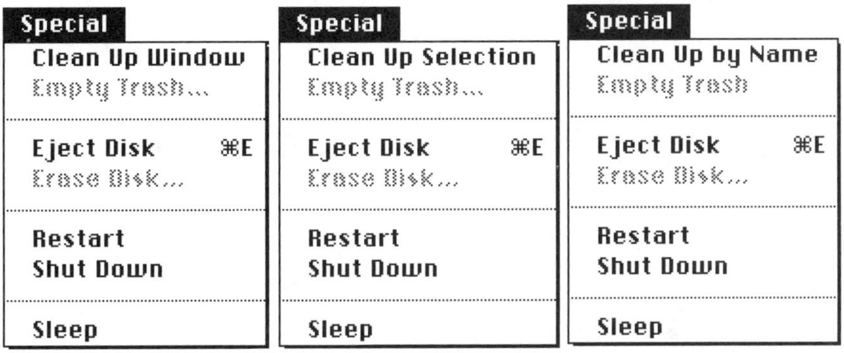

Fig. 2.7.
The Clean Up command when no keys, the Shift key, and the Option key (respectively) are held down.

Tip: You can use ClickChange to replace the normal I-beam cursor (used when editing text) with a cursor that's easier to see.

Virtual Reality

The Memory control panel provides two methods for expanding available system memory in System 7.0, but the usefulness of both methods is severely limited on a PowerBook (see figure 2.8).

The disk cache sets aside a certain amount of RAM to store recently used information. The popularity of System 6.0's disk cache—like the popularity of MultiFinder—convinced Apple to incorporate the feature into System 7.0. The disk cache option also moved from the General control panel to the Memory control panel, where it probably feels more at home.

A larger cache reduces the number of disk accesses the PowerBook must perform. This translates into more computing time per battery charge. Unfortunately, with a larger cache, less memory is available for running applications. If you have only 2M of RAM in your PowerBook, you may have to set the cache as low as possible to run anything at all.

2 Hayden's PowerBook Power Book

Fig. 2.8.
The Memory control panel.

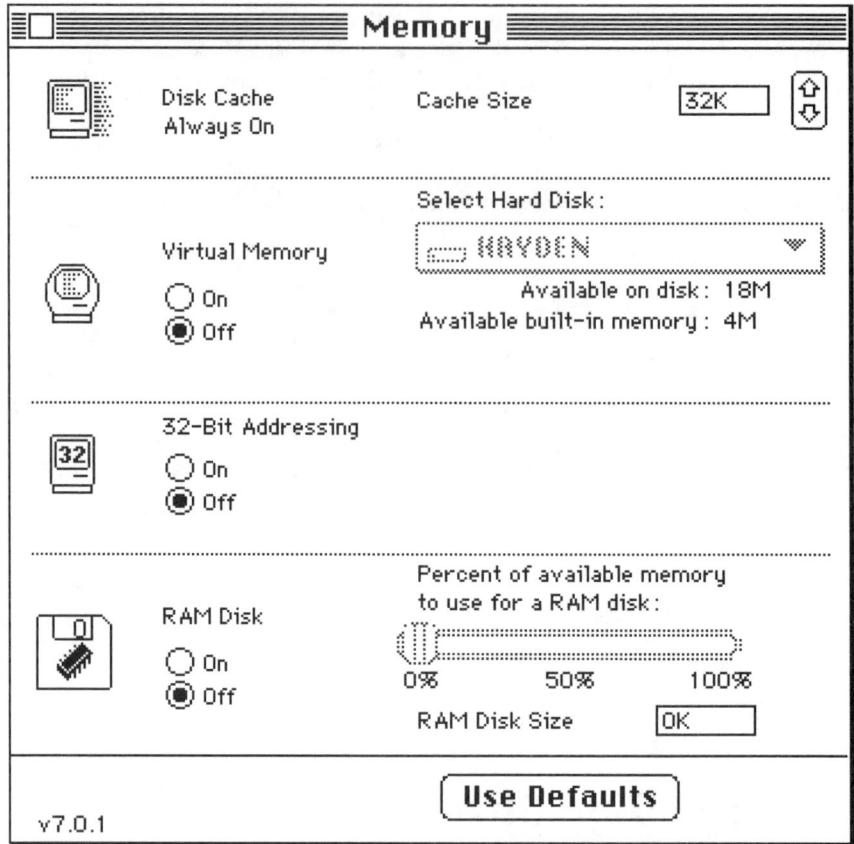

Virtual memory tricks the Mac into using hard disk space for RAM. This feature is unavailable on the PowerBook 100 because that machine lacks a memory-management chip called a PMMU (paged memory management unit). On the PowerBook 140 and 170, the PMMU is built into the 68030 processor chip.

By turning on virtual memory, you can allocate at least 13M of your hard disk space (if it's available to behave like RAM). This allocation may lead you to believe that you can run as many programs as you like on your PowerBook. In reality, however, the constant swapping of data between hard disk and RAM drains the battery like a leech. On a PowerBook, simply turning on virtual memory yields a dialog box warning you of reduced battery life.

Therefore, when you're working without a power outlet, heed the warning and forget about using virtual memory. On the other hand, when your PowerBook is plugged in, virtual memory can be helpful

A Diminutive Desktop 2

when you need to use more RAM. Remember, though, that using virtual memory slows down your PowerBook, because even a fast hard disk is slower than real RAM. Virtual memory also does not work well with sound and animation programs.

On the PowerBook 140 and 170 models, the Memory control panel also has an option for 32-bit addressing, which normally enables a Mac to access more than 8M of RAM. Although PowerBooks cannot accommodate more than 8M of RAM, turning on 32-bit addressing also enables you to use more than 13M of your hard disk for virtual memory.

If you turn on 32-bit addressing, you must make sure that all the software you use is "32-bit clean." This means that the software does not interfere with how the Mac uses additional memory addresses. Software that is System 7.0-compatible should also be 32-bit clean. Contact the software vendor if you have any doubts.

Preferred Shares

System 7.0 capitalizes on the Mac's built-in networking by enabling you to share files across a network. Selecting the Sharing command from the Finder's File menu when a folder is selected enables you to designate who can view the folder's contents and make changes to that folder. By double-clicking on the Users and Groups control panel, you can specify users and groups (such as Marketing and Management) and define privileges. You can share any disk or folder and determine network users' access through access privileges (see figure 2.9).

To create a shared folder, you must turn on file sharing in the Sharing Setup control panel and wait a few seconds for file sharing to begin. Then select the folder you want to share and select the Sharing command from the File menu. Indicate which users and groups can access the folder and choose from nine security levels. You can share up to ten folders on your hard disk, but those folders each can contain an unlimited number of folders. This flexible file-sharing option enables offices with small networks to save money by avoiding the purchase of a file server.

You access a shared disk or folder exactly as you access an AppleShare file server. From the Chooser, select the AppleShare icon. You will see a list of available shared folders and file servers. Select the disk or folder you want to use and enter your name and password. In a moment, the server icon appears on the desktop. This icon acts like any other disk on your desktop.

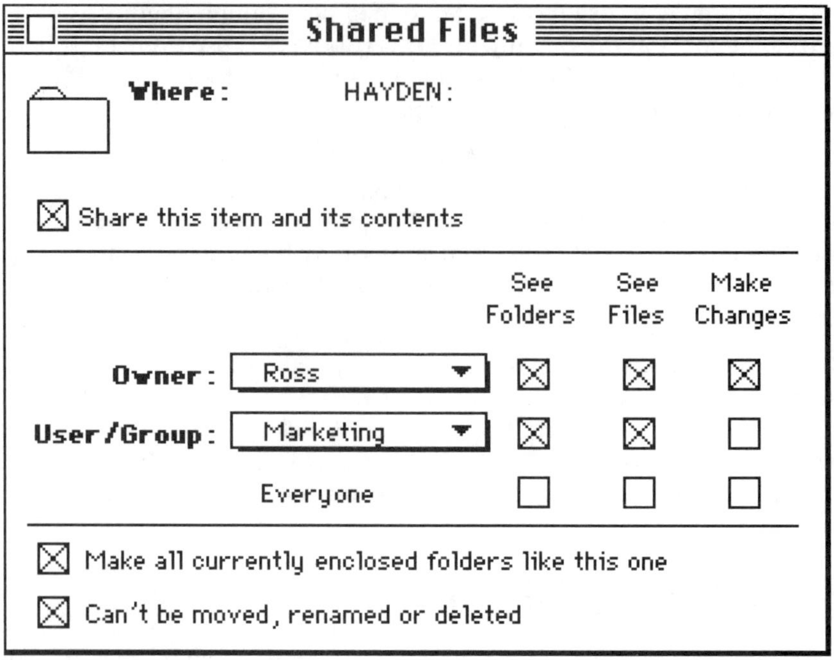

Fig. 2.9. File Sharing options.

If you try to shut down while people are accessing your Mac, your Mac automatically warns them before it shuts down.

Special Editions

Networks aren't the only places where communication thrives. System 7.0's farthest-reaching effect will be realized when applications exploit its capability enabling programs to talk to each other. The most immediate way this communication occurs is through Publish and Subscribe.

Publish and Subscribe are similar to Copy and Paste, and also appear in the Edit menu (see figure 2.10). The Edit menu in Microsoft Word 5.0 enables you to publish a selection or subscribe to selections published by other "System 7.0-savvy" applications. Instead of copying a selection, you publish it. Instead of pasting a selection, you subscribe to it. With Publish and Subscribe, changes you make to the original automatically apply to all copies. If, for example, your word processor

A Diminutive Desktop 2

subscribes to a spreadsheet chart, any changes you make to the spreadsheet automatically update the chart in the word processor. This automatic updating even can occur between two Macs over a network.

Fig. 2.10.
Publish and Subscribe options appear in the edit menu.

```
Edit
Can't Undo        ⌘Z
Repeat            ⌘Y

Cut               ⌘X
Copy              ⌘C
Paste             ⌘V
Paste Special...
Clear
Select All        ⌘A

Find...           ⌘F
Replace...        ⌘H
Go To...          ⌘G
Glossary...       ⌘K

Create Publisher...
Subscribe To...
Link Options...
Edit Object...
```

Publish and Subscribe are examples of Inter-Application Communication (IAC), which will eventually let you control IAC-aware programs from other programs through scripts similar to HyperCard scripts. For example, you could have Software Ventures' MicroPhone II 4.0 download data to your Claris Resolve spreadsheet without ever leaving the Resolve application.

As attractive as System 7.0 features are, a few dark realities cloud System 7.0's rosy success on your PowerBook.

RAM Cram

First—and most significant to PowerBook owners—System 7.0's new functionality exacts a large chunk of hard disk space and RAM. System 7.0 requires 3M of disk space and more than 1M of RAM just to arrive at the desktop. The PowerBook 100 can run on System 6.0, which requires less RAM and less disk space, although Apple neither recommends nor supports this configuration.

Furthermore, using System 6.0 precludes you from using the remote access and power management software written specifically for PowerBooks. These features require System 7.0, and they are about as easy to live without as a keyboard.

Apple provides some relief with an extension package called System 7 TuneUp. One of the programs in System 7 TuneUp is System 7 Tuner, an extension that helps manage memory in low-RAM situations. System 7 TuneUp allows more free RAM under certain conditions when using System 7.0.1. The extension places a bullet next to the system software version when you choose "About This Macintosh" in the Finder (see figure 2.11).

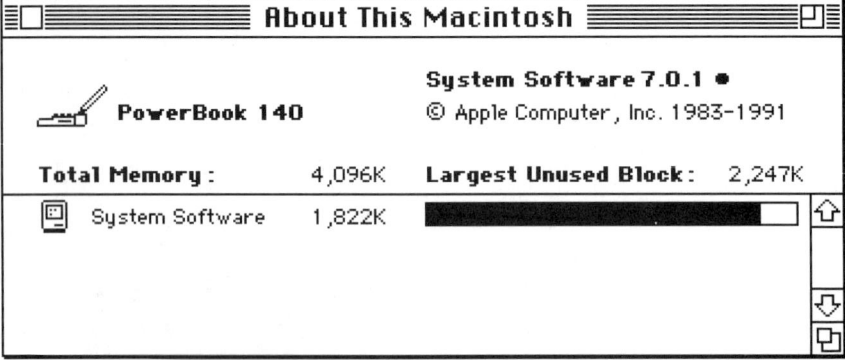

Fig. 2.11. System 7 Tuner places a bullet next to the system version.

For better or worse, your PowerBook is married to System 7.0. Eventually, the latter's features will probably convince you it's for the better, but you should realize the price of System 7.0's power. Since the advent of MultiFinder in 1987—which enabled Mac users to "multitask" (run more than one program at a time)—many users take for granted the ability to switch among open applications. This juggling act is practically impossible on a PowerBook with only 2M of RAM.

A Diminutive Desktop 2

To get the feel of multitasking without upgrading your RAM, you are confined to using an integrated software package which may not be as well-suited to your tasks (see Chapter 3, "Application Software"). Even integrated programs—although usually efficient—are so cramped for space in a 2M System 7.0 configuration that you can forget about adding such comforts as virus detection, screen sharing, and macro programs.

In essence, if you want to perform multitasking on a PowerBook, you must purchase a memory upgrade from Apple or a third party to increase the RAM to at least 4M.

Seven Can Wait?

Most Macintosh applications—even games—by now are compatible with System 7.0, even in 32-bit mode. However, relatively few applications take advantage of its features, and not all programs that include the features have implemented them well.

Most applications, for example, can take advantage of the expanded memory, high quality fonts, and flexible file placement System 7.0 offers. But to use context-sensitive help system and inter-application features, you must upgrade many applications to make them "System 7.0-savvy."

Almost all major programs have System 7.0-savvy versions on the drawing board, but such programs have been disappointingly slow to arrive. In fact, the savvy versions of some popular programs haven't even been announced yet.

The System 7.0-savvy programs that have arrived aren't always fulfilling, either. Some applications do not make good use of Balloon Help, or cannot publish and subscribe. So, if you're on the edge of your seat waiting to use all that System 7.0 offers, you may need a comfortable seat cushion until your software comes up to speed.

7.0.1 for the Road

System 7.0.1 contains all the features of System 7.0 plus bonuses for PowerBook owners. Perhaps to make the fast Macintosh Quadras seem even faster, System 7.0.1 improves the standard way that programs handle math functions when a math coprocessor is present. The only PowerBook that benefits from this boost is the 170, because it's the only PowerBook with a math coprocessor. Apart from that general enhancement, System 7.0.1 incorporates several features especially for the PowerBooks.

Caps Lock

The PowerBook keyboard strongly resembles the Mac Classic keyboard with at least one notable exception: The Caps Lock key does not remain pressed when you activate it. In addition, the PowerBook keyboard has no status light (unlike the Apple Extended Keyboard) to indicate that Caps Lock is active. With no indication of an active Caps Lock, "hunt-and-peck" typists can go mad after discovering they have mistakenly typed an entire paragraph in upper case.

Fortunately, the Caps Lock extension included in System 7.0.1 places the ever-popular universal Caps Lock symbol (almost as recognizable as the universal choking symbol) in the menu bar, just to the left of the Balloon Help icon (see figure 2.12). If you find that the Caps Lock symbol conflicts with other programs that use that part of the menu bar, you may want to remove the Caps Lock extension from the Extensions folder.

Fig. 2.12.
The Caps Lock symbol in the menu bar.

RAM Disk

A RAM Disk is the opposite of virtual memory. Virtual memory makes a Mac treat hard disk space as RAM; a RAM disk makes a Mac treat RAM as hard disk space. RAM disks are much faster than even the fastest hard disks and—unlike accessing virtual memory—accessing RAM disks does not diminish battery time.

Although software to create RAM disks on desktop Macs has been available for quite some time, this software has been slightly less advantageous because you lose the contents of the RAM disks when you shut down or restart. Newer programs can back up the contents of the RAM disk to the hard disk, but backing up can be a time-consuming process.

A Diminutive Desktop 2

The RAM disk portion of the Memory control panel enables you to set aside a portion of RAM as a very fast disk. Because of the nature of PowerBook RAM, though, a RAM disk's contents remain intact even when you shut down a PowerBook 100. You also can restart—or put to sleep—other PowerBook models without sacrificing the contents of their RAM disks. RAM disks represent a fast and energy-efficient means of permanent storage, despite a high cost per megabyte.

To create a RAM disk, open the Memory control panel (see figure 2.13) and set the amount of RAM you want to allocate to the disk. Remember, as the amount of RAM available for the RAM disk increases, the amount available for your applications decreases.

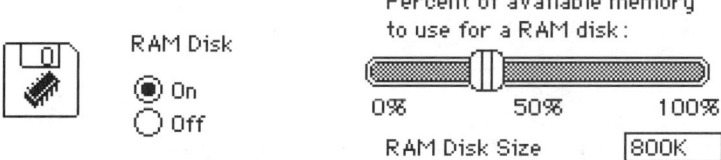

Fig. 2.13.
The RAM Disk portion of the Memory control panel.

Sleep Command

There are several ways to put a PowerBook to sleep (none of which will get you in trouble with the Humane Society). Perhaps the most obvious method is to select the Sleep command from the Finder's Special menu. The Sleep command shuts off the PowerBook's hard disk and screen, but saves any work you have open. Therefore, you don't need to save your work before putting a PowerBook in Sleep mode.

> *Tip:* You can also put a PowerBook to sleep with a shareware control panel called Siesta by Andrew Welch. Siesta enables you to assign any key combination to put your PowerBook to sleep. You still must contend, however, with AppleTalk warnings if AppleTalk is active. PowerSleep, a free alternative to Siesta by Urs Calibran, is an FKEY (a Command-Shift-number combination), which means you must install it with a program such as Suitcase II. When you press Command-Shift-0 with PowerSleep installed, the PowerBook goes immediately to sleep without warning you about losing network connections.

The Battery DA

The Battery desk accessory is a great example of the kinds of things Apple can do because the company controls both the hardware and the system software of a PowerBook. Although other portables merely beep when the battery is low, choosing Battery from the Apple menu provides a graphical display of the amount of juice you have left (see figure 2.14).

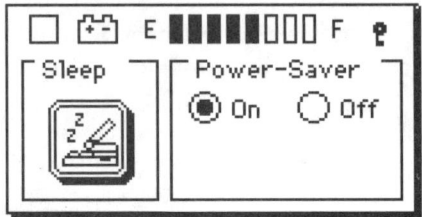

Fig. 2.14. The Battery DA displays a juice guage.

The Battery DA can operate in either expanded or collapsed mode; it uses a toggle control like the Alarm Clock DA. In collapsed mode, the Battery DA displays the battery icon and a fuel gauge similar to an automobile's gas gauge. The battery icon displays a lightning bolt through the icon when the battery is recharging.

Clicking Battery's toggle switch reveals a sleep button that puts the PowerBook to sleep. As usual, the PowerBook warns you that network communications may be interrupted unless you deactivate AppleTalk in the Chooser. If you have a 170, you also can activate or deactivate the 170's special Power-Saver mode (see Chapter 1, "Portable Power") in the expanded DA. Changes to the Power-Saver mode take effect after restarting.

Tip: The Battery DA is rife with shortcuts. Option-clicking the battery icon puts the PowerBook to sleep. If AppleTalk is active and you want to skip the usual warning about losing network services, Option-Shift-click the battery icon.

A Diminutive Desktop 2

Portable Control Panel

You access and configure the Portable control panel like other control panels. The Portable control panel has several components that vary depending on which PowerBook model you own. The upper control, System Sleep, determines the number of minutes the PowerBook waits before automatically going to sleep.

The lower slide control determines the period of inactivity after which the hard disk stops spinning. The screen, however, remains on. Any action that requires hard disk access causes the hard disk to spin up again; there is a slight delay in response until it's running at full speed.

Sleep extends the amount of time you can work without recharging your batteries. However, sleep is a tad inconvenient because you must wait for your PowerBook to wake up after it has taken its automatic nap. That's why you may want to have your PowerBook go without sleep if you have it plugged in. To keep your PowerBook awake, select the Stay Awake When Plugged In checkbox in the Portable control panel.

> ***Tip:*** Selecting the Stay Awake When Plugged In checkbox presents a dialog box warning that leaving the PowerBook without sleep for more than 24 hours may damage the screen. If you want to prevent system sleep to preserve AppleTalk connections or save time spent while waking up, you may want to use a screen saver on your PowerBook. Consider a program such as QuickTools' Sunset that can invert a normal screen saver image to produce a "white" background (see Chapter 6, "Productivity Enhancers").

One power-saving feature that you normally don't notice is System Rest. This feature automatically slows down the PowerBook when it detects no user interaction. This feature may interfere with certain background operations, such as long spreadsheet calculations. Option-clicking Minutes Until Automatic Sleep reveals a dialog box (see figure 2.15) enabling you to turn off System Rest. This means that applications that work unattended (such as spreadsheets performing large recalculations) do not slow down when you walk away from your machine. To turn off this rest feature, click Don't Rest. The Rest feature remains off until you restart your PowerBook.

Fig. 2.15.
The PowerBook's "Don't Rest" dialog box.

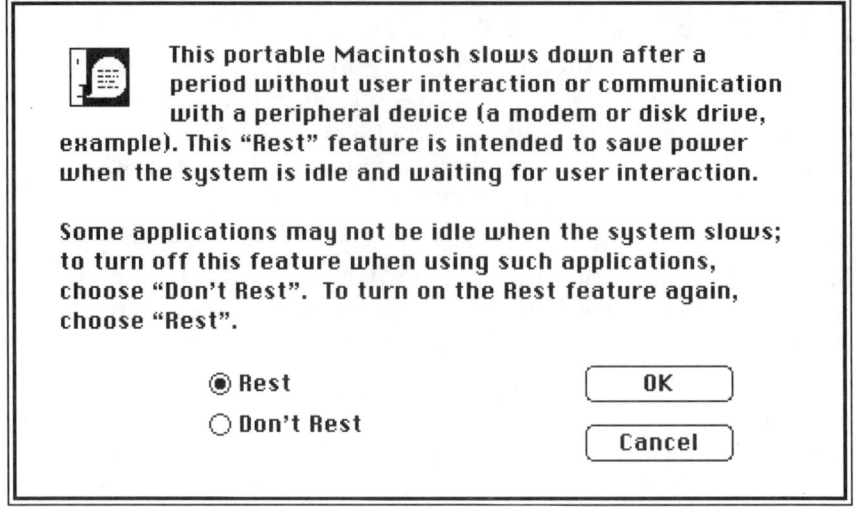

You can configure two special features of the PowerBook 100 through the Portable control panel. A SCSI Disk mode control facilitates the machine's ability to "SCSI-dock" to a desktop Mac (see Chapter 4). At the top of the control panel's window, select a number that does not match the SCSI ID of any device attached to your desktop Mac. This procedure avoids the danger of SCSI ID conflicts. And because a PowerBook 100 has no on/off switch, you can have the machine automatically wake from sleep by entering the time and date in the lower-left corner of the control panel.

If you use an Apple internal Fax/Data Modem with the 140 or 170, you can specify whether you're using an internal or external modem with the Portable control panel. As a result, your communications software knows where to look when you select the modem port. You also can have your PowerBook wake automatically if the internal modem senses an incoming call.

Off and Running

This chapter took a long look at the new capabilities in System 7.0, including some special features for PowerBook owners. As comprehensive as system software is, though, the system really is just a manager for the true stars of portable computing: the applications with which you do your work. The next chapter examines the types of software you may find appealing on the road, especially if you can't run your current applications comfortably.

Application Software

Before the Macintosh computer first appeared, Apple had a special group of employees called evangelists. Their mission was to convince major application vendors to create software for Apple's innovative new machine. That group must be proud to know that their efforts helped establish a huge and powerful Macintosh software library. This library contains thousands of programs ranging from scientific data analysis tools to games. The PowerBook provides the unique freedom to take your favorite Mac applications wherever you go.

Because PowerBooks are true Macs, they work with virtually all Macintosh software. Ideally, you can take the same applications that you use on your desktop Mac and use them on your PowerBook. In fact, some vendor licenses allow you to do just that—without buying another copy of the software (check your software license to be sure).

In spite of the consistency among all Mac applications, no one likes to invest the time required to become familiar with new programs. Unfortunately, though, the limited hard disk space and limited RAM of the PowerBooks (particularly the 100) may force you to sacrifice some memory-hungry applications in favor of ones with more modest computing demands.

If a PowerBook is your first Mac, you may want to choose software that lends itself well to portable computing. As a new user, you must wade through an even more bewildering array of choices in many software categories.

Integrated vs. Lean Applications

Integrated software programs accomplish a variety of tasks, typically combining word processing, spreadsheet, database, graphics, and communications modules.

Integrated software generally is easy to use because it's designed for beginners. Many of these programs, however, offer more advanced capabilities when you are ready for them. Consider whether the software offers a growth path. In other words, can you easily pick up a stand-alone program without having to relearn the basics?

By the nature of Macintosh software, it is relatively easy to pick up another program after you learn the first one, but some companies go an extra step to ensure that the modules of their integrated packages resemble their popular stand-alone programs. For example, the database component of ClarisWorks mimics Claris' popular stand-alone database FileMaker Pro.

PowerBooks introduce integrated software to a new class of people. Experienced users who may feel comfortable using a variety of applications on the road might be dismayed to find that with the limited capacity of the stock PowerBook 100 or 140, favorite high-end applications may not easily fit on their hard disk. Even if you purchase a PowerBook 170, which has all the horsepower of a Mac IIci, you find that RAM and hard disk upgrade options for the IIci are more varied and less expensive than their 170 counterparts, and will continue to be so in the near future.

An important consideration for experienced users is how much you sacrifice by using integrated software. Perhaps less than you think. Traditionally, integrated software packages have been branded as hacks-of-all-trades, masters of none. But though stand-alone programs always boast features that integrated programs lack, integrated packages are improving. Some integrated packages offer features not found in popular stand-alone programs.

Application Software 3

Experienced users also may be interested in a different kind of growth path: a downward-compatible one. If you are a MacWrite II wizard, you probably feel comfortable with many of MacWrite II's keyboard equivalent commands. You therefore would be more productive if keyboard equivalents (such as those for aligning and formatting text) were consistent with the integrated program you must live with on the road.

> *Tip:* If you have a difficult time adjusting to different keyboard commands, consider one of the task automation utilities described in Chapter 5, "Managing Time and Contacts." Some programs (such as WordPerfect and Excel) have built-in macro languages that enable you to assign new keyboard equivalents. Microsoft Word also allows you to do this, through the Commands menu item.

Attractive as integrated programs are, they aren't the only programs well-suited to PowerBook owners. Stand-alone applications accomplish a specific purpose (such as word processing or charting). These programs already come close to Apple's vision of future Macintosh software—small, focused programs that work well together—giving you the best of all worlds.

The main advantage of lean programs in the Macintosh environment is that you can combine them to suit your individual needs. If you need only word processing and spreadsheet capabilities, you can choose the packages that best fit that need.

If you want to multitask on your PowerBook or if you insist on bringing a full suite of extensions on the road, lean programs may be your ticket. Lean applications demand less RAM than many programs, but it still is difficult to run more than two lean applications on a stock PowerBook 100. To their credit, however, because lean programs address a specific task, they generally run faster and consume less disk space than integrated packages.

The missing link in this utopia is inter-application communication (IAC). Programs such as BeagleWorks—which can dynamically update information stored in separate frames—will retain certain advantages until smaller, more specific applications support Publish and Subscribe.

This chapter discusses several integrated software packages as well as several lean applications well-suited for use on a PowerBook.

Integrated Software

From modest personal organizers like the Sharp Wizard to powerful minicomputers like Digital Equipment Corporation's VAX, almost all computer platforms have some sort of integrated software available. Integrated software combines the functions of several different programs into one convenient, cost-effective program.

Integrated software falls into two categories. "Mini-MultiFinder" programs treat their components as separate applications, as if you ran four or five different programs simultaneously. Microsoft Works and GreatWorks fall into this category. The modules in these two programs exchange data primarily through the Clipboard, although it probably won't be long until the modules start to share data dynamically through AppleEvents.

"Frame-based" programs typically start out with a blank page and enable you to create boxes on the screen. You then can use these boxes for word processing, spreadsheets, or graphics. ClarisWorks, HandiWorks, and BeagleWorks take this approach.

The breadth of integrated packages prevents discussion of each individual product in great detail. However, the following summaries should help you decide which software to investigate.

Microsoft Works

Microsoft Works, the "mother of all integrated software," defined the standard for its category: compact, easy-to-use (the box even says "No experience necessary"), and communicative. Microsoft Works also defined the five categories most integrated packages share: word processing, spreadsheet, database, communications, and graphics (see figure 3.1). Unfortunately, the program failed to innovatively uphold its standards. For too long, it was the best choice, because—after silencing Lotus Jazz forever in 1986—Microsoft Works was the only choice.

Today, though, Microsoft Works lags behind its competitors. One hallmark of modern integrated programs is a consistent user interface among modules that goes even deeper than the consistency normally found among Mac programs. For example, all Mac applications share the Apple, File, and Edit menus, but the modules of integrated programs may share four or five menu titles and scrupulously ensure that keyboard combinations remain consistent throughout all modules.

Application Software 3

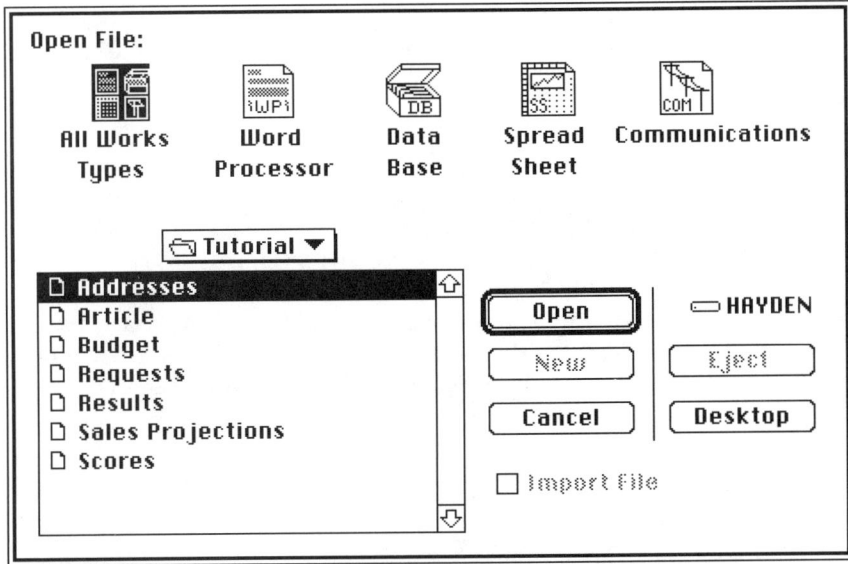

Fig. 3.1.
Microsoft Works modules.

This is not the case in Microsoft Works. Pressing Command-R in the word processing module activates the Replace command, yet pressing the same keystroke-combination in the spreadsheet module activates the Fill Right command. You must get used to the logic of Works before you can start being productive, especially in the abysmal database module. In short, Microsoft Works is about as tightly integrated as the former Soviet Union.

Essentially, the program retains a vintage 1986 flavor; while Works operates fine under System 7.0, it contains no System 7.0-specific features—not even Balloon Help. Although Works isn't a memory hog, other packages give you more per megabyte. This is one software classic in dire need of an overhaul.

GreatWorks

If most were best, GreatWorks would be the best with eight different application modules to its credit. No other company considers spreadsheet and charting to be different applications, and Symantec alone boasts an outstanding outlining module—an advantage that proves invaluable for organizing thoughts on the road.

Philosophically, GreatWorks improves upon the Microsoft model, providing a better interface that is consistent among modules. The menus are brief and straightforward and the program does include Balloon Help.

The communications modules of GreatWorks, ClarisWorks, and BeagleWorks—vital to transferring information with other types of computers—are nearly indistinguishable. The modules all are based on Apple's Communications Toolbox (see figure 3.2), which provides a consistent way to specify communication settings such as baud rate (transmission speed) and terminal emulation (the type of character-based screen the Mac should imitate). The extensible Toolbox will be able to take advantage of advanced protocols such as Zmodem once the protocols are released as communications extensions.

Fig. 3.2. The Communications Toolbox.

Some minor annoyances blemish GreatWorks' otherwise smooth operation. The slickly designed Open… box fails to dim the New button if no document type is selected. The database palette could be more interactive. The palettes should tear off. Surprisingly, there is no Preferences command to let you customize aspects of the program's behavior.

GreatWorks' memory requirements may exclude the program from use on PowerBooks with only 2M of RAM. Caught between chaotic Microsoft Works and ambitious ClarisWorks, the workaday modules of GreatWorks betray its moniker somewhat, but this solid performer packs useful, easy-to-use tools.

Application Software 3

ClarisWorks

Claris Corporation, Apple's software subsidiary, consistently produces well-designed and easy-to-use software, even if that software is often unfashionably late to market. Foremost, ClarisWorks serves as a teaser for the company's full line of mainstream products. The word processing, spreadsheet, database, and drawing modules have generic names, but Claris could have named them MacWrite, Jr., Son of Resolve, FileMaker Lite, and MacDraw Classic.

If you already use several Claris applications, you will feel right at home with ClarisWorks. If you are a new user, ClarisWorks provides a clear growth path. GreatWorks, though, follows so many Claris conventions, such as Hypertext Help, XTND, and a FileMaker-inspired database module, that you probably could adapt easily to that program as well.

ClarisWorks glides more easily between modules than any of its competitors. In the Claris tradition, a palette glued to the left side of the window houses tear-off fill and line palettes (see figure 3.3), as well as all the tools for the word processor, spreadsheet, and drawing modules. Including the database tool might have alienated users familiar with FileMaker Pro's robust interface.

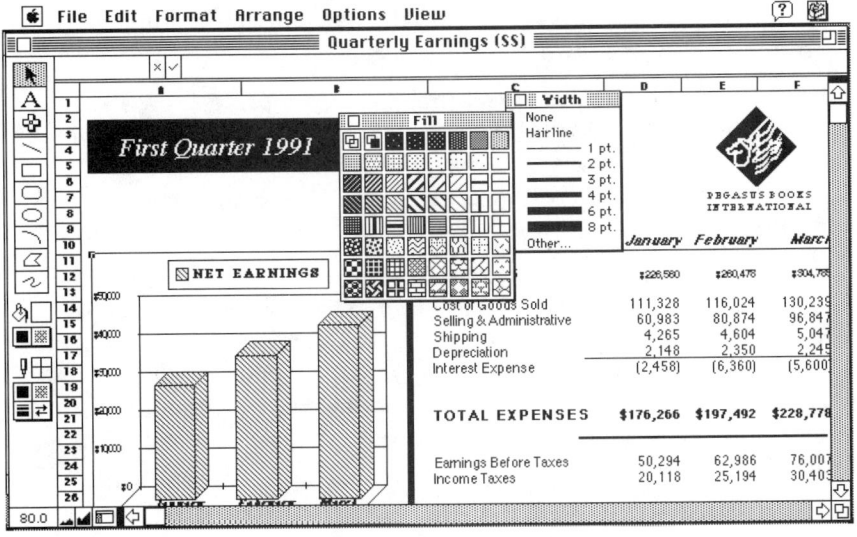

Fig. 3.3. ClarisWorks' tear-off palettes.

Like BeagleWorks, different types of documents can coexist in frames on the page, but Claris' method of choosing the frame type before drawing the frame is more intuitive. The ClarisWorks drawing module

dissolves into the other modules as ever-present tools, whereas you must make a new frame for any drawing in BeagleWorks. Like Microsoft Works, ClarisWorks incorporates macros that enable you to streamline repetitive tasks, saving time and therefore battery life.

The ClarisWorks word processor follows MacWrite II's interface and keyboard conventions, adding split bars and custom magnification levels slated for eagerly awaited MacWrite Pro. The word processor exclusively includes footnotes. Mail merges, well-implemented in MacWrite II, are easy here as well. And you can link text boxes, making ClarisWorks a desktop publishing program of last resort.

ClarisWorks doesn't yet take advantage of special System 7.0 features such as Publish and Subscribe, but it is an efficient application. Weighing in at under 600K of disk space and requiring a mere 900K of RAM, ClarisWorks can run on a stock PowerBook 100. (Just make sure you don't use many extensions like those described in Chapter 6, "Productivity Enhancers.") Most users won't soon outgrow ClarisWorks, but those who do will find a comfortable home in the Claris family of applications.

BeagleWorks

Beagle Bros.' slogan, "The True Meaning of Integration," is no marketing hype. BeagleWorks is—literally—the best-integrated integrated software for the Macintosh.

Like ClarisWorks, BeagleWorks is frame-based, but BeagleWorks extends the concept further than ClarisWorks. In BeagleWorks, you can create virtually any type of frame within any document. This liberating design facilitates the creation of complex documents that incorporate words, pictures, and numbers.

Without any models to follow in stand-alone products, Beagle Bros. wisely explored interfaces used in other Mac programs. The most extraordinary interface asset BeagleWorks borrowed is a QuarkXPress-like interactive toolbar. The toolbar—actually a palette—floats over your documents. Its controls vary depending on which module you select. You can format text with a few button clicks, and color lies a tear-off menu away.

Beagle Bros. went the extra mile in most of its modules. The word processor features paragraph styles and a word count feature, and the program can wrap text around irregular graphics. The spreadsheet features in-cell editing like Lotus 1-2-3 for Macintosh and an automatic summation button like that found in Microsoft Excel. The BeagleWorks communications module even includes a phone book. Attention to

Application Software 3

detail is apparent in a hierarchical File menu that enables you to specify the types of new documents without using a dialog box.

BeagleWorks fully exploits System 7.0. It can publish and subscribe to data and communicate with other applications under System 7.0. It even can generate dynamic links between its internal modules under System 6.0. With debugging code in the pre-release version tested, the entire BeagleWorks program fits on a high-density floppy disk, but the program may not run on a PowerBook with only 2M of RAM.

HandiWorks

Although Claris and Beagle Bros. love to show spreadsheets embedded in their word processors, that's an old trick for RagTime. RagTime is MacVonk's high-end desktop publishing/spreadsheet tour de force.

MacVonk originally marketed a low-end version of RagTime—RagTime Classic—to cater to Apple's low-cost Macs. MacVonk replaced RagTime with HandiWorks. Geared toward PowerBook owners, HandiWorks earnestly addresses complaints about RagTime Classic's lack of file import capability via XTND, Claris' file translation technology (see Chapter 4, "Yakety Mac"). To quell the critics, MacVonk bundles DataViz' MacLink/Plus Translators, which can work with XTND to seamlessly import many MS-DOS formats.

HandiWorks is a frame-based package that includes word processing and spreadsheet capabilities. It also includes an address and phone book DA that is surprisingly well-integrated with the rest of the package (see figure 3.4) as well as accessible from within any other software package. HandiWorks performs some neat tricks, such as automatic addressing of faxes and other documents. Its marketing folks, however, may have outshone its programmers in pricing HandiWorks below the list price of competing products.

Lean Applications

The advanced capabilities of BeagleWorks and ClarisWorks raised the standards of integrated packages. However, their individual modules still lack many bells and whistles of stand-alone programs. Even though some integrated packages run on a PowerBook with only 2M of RAM, you literally must take the programs for all they're worth. For example, even if you only need BeagleWorks' word processing and spreadsheet modules, you must carry along all the extra database, drawing, and painting baggage when you drag the BeagleWorks icon onto your PowerBook's hard disk.

3   Hayden's PowerBook Power Book

Fig. 3.4.
The HandiWorks address book DA.

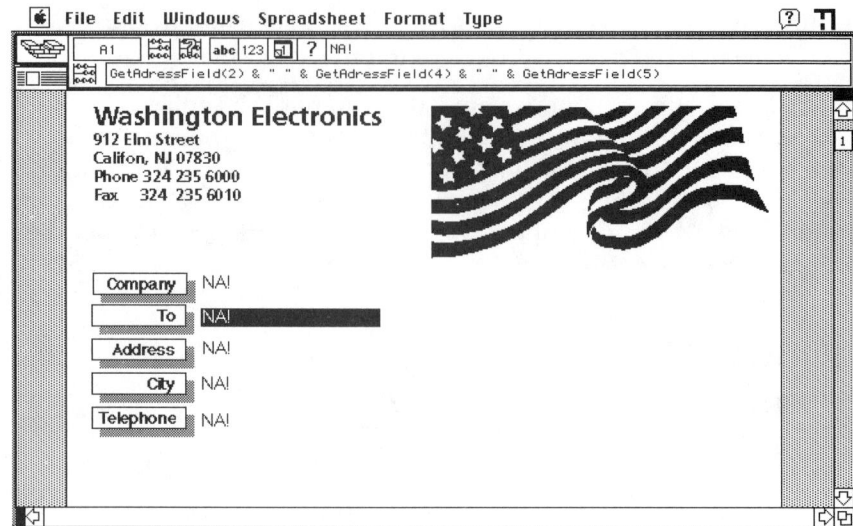

The following lean applications provide alternatives to the integrated packages. The lean application's results often surpass what their counterpart modules offer, yet the applications leave enough RAM to open another program. You won't find any offering from Microsoft, Claris, Aldus, or Adobe here. After several years of playing leapfrog (during which competing programs scrambled to add more features than their competitors), lean applications have become an endangered species. Apple's cry for smaller, focused, System 7.0-savvy applications, however, may increase the number of lean applications.

Word Processing

At its introduction, many considered T/Maker's WriteNow to be a middle-of-the-road word processor, somewhere between MacWrite (the Mac's first word processor) and Microsoft Word (which now dominates the advanced word processor market). WriteNow lacks the useful XTND architecture implemented in integrated packages and its main competitor, MacWrite II. Regardless, WriteNow's meager RAM requirements, sprightly processing pace, uninhibiting interface, and well-chosen feature set make the program attractive for the portable environment.

WriteNow lacks conventional paragraph styles that facilitate formatting text to custom settings. However, the program compensates by providing two methods for reformatting paragraphs. One method uses the Shift and Option keys while changing margin and tab settings for

Application Software 3

multiple paragraphs you selected. The other method comprises using Copy, Paste Ruler, and character settings commands, thus enabling you to format paragraphs conveniently (see figure 3.5). Although style sheets (coming soon in WriteNow 3.0) are more useful for longer documents, copying and pasting rulers is much faster than setting up a style. Even powerhouses such as Microsoft Word and QuarkXPress would benefit from this feature.

Fig. 3.5. Formatting characters in WriteNow.

Although WriteNow may appear to be the mainstream word processor most accommodating to PowerBook owners, Nisus Compact is the first word processor specifically engineered for those owners. One of the best-kept secrets in Macintosh word processing, Paragon Concepts' Nisus is an unusually swift high-end word processor. Nisus features a drawing module, an outrageously flexible macro language and one of the most advanced search-and-replace features available in a word processor.

In a bid to become the word processor of choice for PowerBook users, Paragon Concepts shaved off advanced features, reduced Nisus' RAM requirements to less than 400K, and dubbed the impressive result Nisus Compact. Nisus Compact uses the same file format as its more full-featured sibling, so you can do more with your Nisus Compact files when you bring them back to your desktop computer.

Nisus Compact takes extra steps to avoid battery-sapping disk access. In addition, the program provides a File Clerk feature that can reach out to files via AppleTalk Remote Access (see Chapter 4, "Yakety Mac"). Nisus Compact provides a thicker I-beam cursor to facilitate working with hard-to-read screens (see figure 3.6), and the program also leaves behind some of the complexity of Nisus' search command. Nisus Compact's search command, however, does retain the unique capability to select all occurrences of a found word at once, and the program even adds a "fuzzy find" feature that can search for words you may have misspelled. Nisus Compact also supports XTND for easy access to other file formats.

Fig. 3.6. Nisus Compact's special features.

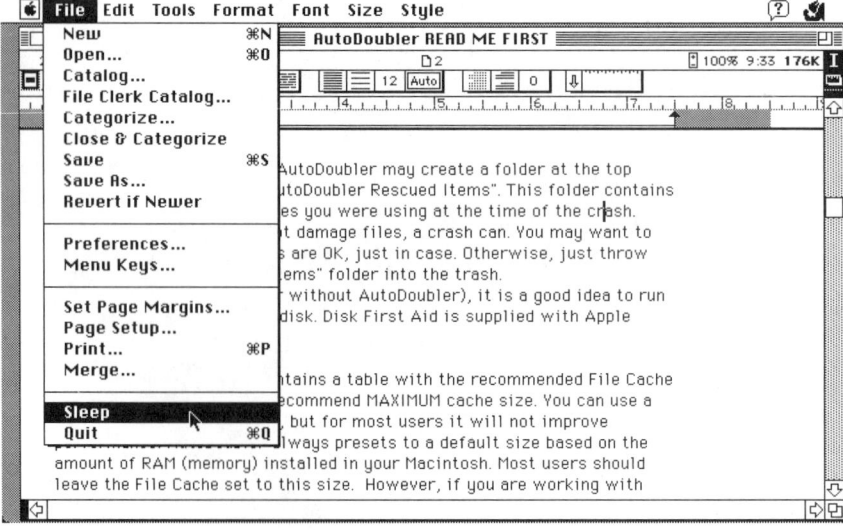

Despite these advanced features, Paragon Concepts ironically removed the spell checker and thesaurus from Nisus Compact in order to conserve RAM. The company, however, offers these and other features (such as macros and Balloon Help) as add-on modules, bringing the functionality of Nisus Compact closer to Nisus.

Application Software 3

Tip: Turn off auto-saving options in WordPerfect and other word processors to conserve battery life.

Spreadsheets

There is something about spreadsheets that breeds machismo. It's as if the market has said, "Don't bother us with these wimpy low-RAM number-nibblers! Give us the Excels, 1-2-3s, and Wingz of the world that eat all our RAM and compute the world GNP until the year 2346!"

Fortunately, there is hope for those of us who only occasionally want to compute some expenses while using most of their RAM somewhere else.

Bravo Technologies' MacCalc provides the basic features of a spreadsheet without the expense or bulk of a mainstream spreadsheet program. The program is ideal for quick computations or for models that don't require advanced graphing capabilities or a macro language. 1-Shot Worksheet by Baseline Publishing feels like a forms package, yet the program can draw upon a rich selection of spreadsheet-like operators (see figure 3.7). 1-Shot's Equation Editor enables you to define fields with a wide variety of formula-building operators.

Fig. 3.7. 1-Shot Worksheet contains a wealth of spreadsheet-like operators.

Databases

Tip: If all you're looking for is a program to manage names, addresses, and phone numbers, a number of excellent contact managers may better suit your needs (See Chapter 5 "Managing Time and Contacts").

Exodus Software's Retriever II is a flat-file database that uses just 512K in a simple interface. The program presents your data in a spreadsheet-like grid accompanied by a well-designed icon bar that provides fast access to common features (see figure 3.8). Retriever II shows its desk-accessory roots by allowing you to open only one database at a time. The nimble design, however, makes the program a winner for quick data management.

Fig. 3.8. Exodus Software's Retriever II.

Rec	✓	Agent	Price	Sq Ft	Cost/Sq ft	Community	Style	Address	#BR	
1		Jean	65000	1600	40.62	Norwood	Ranch	1557 Race	3	
2		Joe	75000	1700	44.12	Norwood	2 story	1008 Fleece	3	
3		Bill	79900	1670	47.84	Cincinnati	Ranch	9876 Peabody	4	
4		Joe	85500	1700	50.29	Cincinnati	Ranch	10 Neff	4	
5		Joe	87000	1700	51.18	Cincinnati	2 story	8177 Applewood	3	
6		Penny	98000	1850	52.97	Cincinnati	3 story	333 Toadvine	3	
7		Jean	100000	1950	51.28	Cincinnati	Split-level	1234 May	3	
8		Penny	102000	1700	60.00	Evendale	Tri level	1156 Neumann	3	
9		Bill	114000	2000	57.00	Wyoming	Split level	7000 Main	3	
10		Bill	127000	1750	72.57	Wyoming	2 story	778 Niedermann	4	
11		Joe	136800	2100	65.14	Wyoming	Ranch	118 Booklin	4	
12		Jean	152000	2200	69.09	Cincinnati	2 story	14 Fedder	5	
13		Jean	162300	1950	83.23	Cincinnati	2 story	1445 Vine	3	
14		Bill	208000	2300	90.43	Cincinnati	Ranch	955 Johnson	5	
15		Jean	225000	2750	81.82	Cincinnati	Ranch	5490 Yancy	4	3 f

DAtabase by Baseline Publishing is a desk accessory alternative that provides more versatile viewing. This flat-file wizard is ideal for classifying information that does not lend itself well to the advanced address managers.

Application Software 3

> ***Tip:*** If you're one of the lucky ones whose PowerBook has gobs of RAM, you may want to look at Panorama II. This flexible spreadsheet-like database includes a great data-entry feature called clairvoyance. If Panorama recognizes a word you are typing, the program finishes typing the word for you! Panorama also is extremely fast because it loads itself into RAM, minimizing disk access.

Graphics

Zedcor has a history of packing the functionality of applications into desk accessories. This history provided great advantages for System 6.0 users who avoided MultiFinder. Instead of opening another program and fiddling with memory allocations, users could access advanced capabilities with a single menu choice from the Apple menu. Zedcor based an entire integrated software package on this approach and called the package DESK.

With System 7.0., Zedcor's strategy backfired somewhat. System 7.0 facilitates multitasking and features an Apple menu that can list any item on your hard disk. Many of Zedcor's DESK applications are hefty, considering their capabilities; several applications need 1M or more to run. But two of the package's brightest jewels are DeskPaint and DeskDraw, which Zedcor sells together in one package. Under System 7.0, both DeskPaint and DeskDraw work as applications, rather than as DAs.

A full-featured painting program, DeskPaint includes full-color capabilities, but its black-and-white features are still impressive. You can work at any resolution, from 72 dots per inch (screen resolution) to the quality of imagesetters (an incredibly tedious, RAM-demanding endeavor). DeskPaint asks for 2M of RAM, but the program is far less demanding when working with low-resolution, monochrome images.

DeskDraw perfectly complements word processors that lack graphics capabilities. You can access DeskDraw's MacDraw-like tools using less than 400K of RAM (see figure 3.9). In addition, DeskDraw's clean, simple interface doesn't clutter the screen with palettes.

Fig. 3.9.
Zedcor's
DeskDraw.

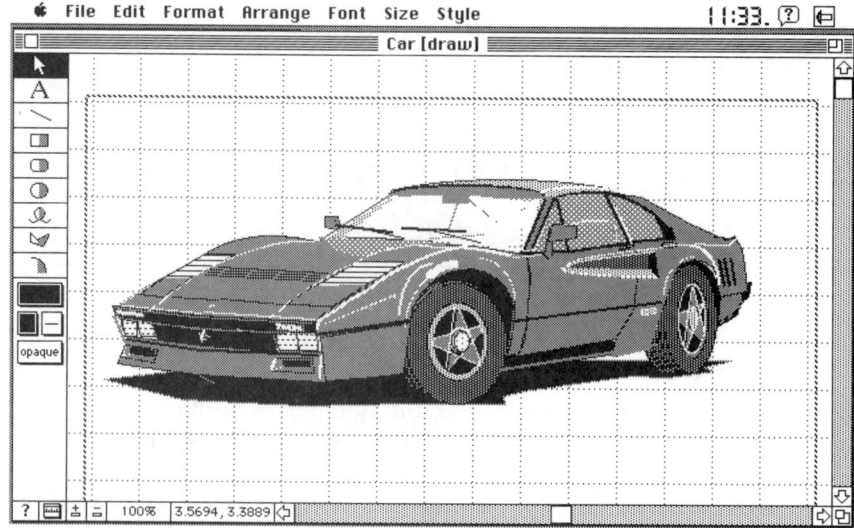

CE Software's Amazing Paint now holds the dubious distinction of ruler of the black-and-white paint programs in the MacPaint tradition. Owing much to the success of the Macintosh LC, low-cost color paint programs flourish, while black-and-white programs flounder. Amazing Paint offers a quick method for creating bit-map art for HyperCard stacks or for low-resolution printers such as the ImageWriter.

Communications

In contrast to full-blown communications programs such as MicroPhone II (which comes on three disks), Dave Alverson's ZTerm is a small (144K) program that requires a scant 300K of RAM. ZTerm's price is also fairly small: a $30 shareware fee. Several substantial differences distinguish ZTerm from bare-bones communications offerings, but the wondrous Zmodem protocol really sets ZTerm apart (see figure 3.10).

When two computers exchange files with communications software, you must choose a protocol (a set of rules) for how the files transfer. The most popular protocol is Xmodem. It's safe to assume that any communications program that can send files can use Xmodem. Zmodem transfers files faster than Xmodem, and Zmodem can start receiving files automatically without the user manually opening a menu and choosing Receive File.

Application Software 3

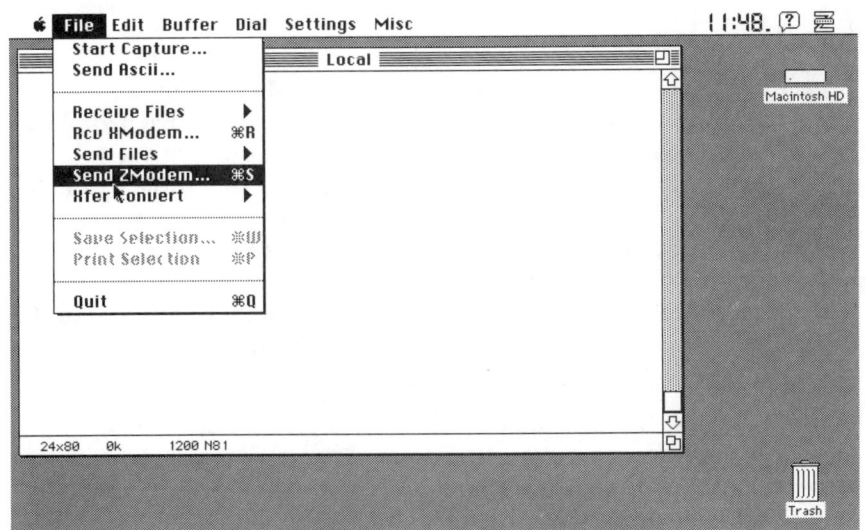

Fig. 3.10.
ZTerm's Zmodem protocol.

Zmodem miraculously can resume transfers interrupted by modems disconnected because of poor phone connections (provided you don't move the temporary files Zmodem creates). Imagine a three-hour transfer becoming interrupted with five minutes remaining in the transfer. Without Zmodem, you probably would be forced to send the entire file again!

Outliners

The startup screen of Symmetry Software's Acta 7 describes Acta as "The Indispensable Productivity Tool." Actually, Acta 7 is the System 7.0-savvy version of a popular outlining program that lets you organize thoughts and plan agendas and projects.

Acta's unusual terminology of sisters, daughters, and aunts may take some time to understand, but its unobtrusive design helps you develop thoughts to flesh out later using your word processor. The ideal method for achieving this organization is through System 7.0's Publish and Subscribe feature. Unfortunately, relatively few word processors currently can subscribe to data, although many word processors promise to start subscribing soon (perhaps they need one of those thoughtful postcards that drop out of magazines).

Conclusions

GreatWorks, ClarisWorks, and BeagleWorks stand out as modern integrated products that meet 85% of most users' needs. Each application features a consistent user interface among modules, a spell-checker, and a thesaurus. The three programs also use Apple's Communication Toolbox and XTND technology. This makes the programs easily adaptable to new communications and file translation tools important for PowerBook users. HandiWorks slickly integrates names and addresses into documents in an economical RAM partition, but the program has no communications module and no method for managing other types of data.

ClarisWorks and BeagleWorks facilitate the mixing of different document types on the same page. However, users more comfortable with Microsoft's "mini-application" model can find a modern alternative in GreatWorks, an application with few unnecessary and distracting tools. BeagleWorks outshines its competitors in many respects, but ClarisWorks is a compact, capable program with a clear growth path into a strong family of applications.

If you don't need all the features of an integrated package, or if the features seem too confining, lean applications provide efficient solutions for specialized needs. Lack of AppleEvent support, however, currently hampers many lean applications. If you don't mind that your desktop applications don't leave much RAM for anything else—or if you're willing to pay the steep prices for PowerBook RAM—indulge yourself.

Reaching Out

When it comes to sharing your work, no universal file format can compare to paper, but printers often are not available on the road. The convenience and speed of electronic communications make it an appealing alternative to overnight couriers. The next chapter thoroughly explores how you can share your data with other computers from here to Timbuktu.

Yakety Mac 4

Although other platforms have begun to approach its ease of use, the Macintosh family remains unique. Many people forget that the Macintosh family remains the only broad family of personal computers that users can network (link together to share files and resources) without the need for additional hardware. (Apple co-founder Steve Jobs created a notable exception—high-speed networking in his NeXT computers.) Apple continued this tradition by including faster networking ports on the blazing-fast Macintosh Quadra 700 and Quadra 900.

Alas, the majority of computers in the world are not Macs. Although there are ways to get Macs and PCs talking, many concerns about logistics and compatibility must be overcome when dealing with different types of computers.

This chapter discusses how you can use your PowerBook to communicate with other Macs, other types of computers, online services, and even fax machines.

The PowerBook's Portals

The PowerBook's printer port, modem port, SCSI port, expansion port, and floppy disk drive are the machine's doors to the outside world.

The printer port and modem port are serial ports. Most computers have at least one serial port. With a serial port, you can attach devices such as printers, modems, and digitizing tablets, and you can exchange information with other computers.

The printer port is especially important because it is a LocalTalk port. LocalTalk is Apple's original cabling scheme. In a LocalTalk network, small connector boxes plugged into each Mac's printer ports are connected to each other with LocalTalk (also called shielded twisted-pair) cables available from Apple. This type of network is called a daisy chain. If you have ever hooked a Mac to an Apple LaserWriter, technically, you have installed a network.

Although LocalTalk is easy to set up, it is not very flexible. Historically, LocalTalk cabling was expensive and not readily available. In 1985, Farallon shipped PhoneNET, which could do everything LocalTalk could do. Unlike LocalTalk, however, PhoneNET worked on unshielded twisted-pair cabling, better known as "phone wire." Now, instead of a trip to your Apple dealer, all you need to hook up Macs is a trip to your local electronics store. PhoneNET also has other advantages over LocalTalk when used in large, sophisticated networks.

When connected through the printer port, PhoneNET moves data at LocalTalk's speed of 230K per second (several times slower than even a slow hard disk). This speed is adequate for most printing and light file transfer needs, but transfers of large files over the network require faster alternatives. One of the most popular transfer alternatives for Macs is Ethernet, which theoretically can transfer data 40 times faster than LocalTalk, although the actual improvement is only about four times as fast.

Although LocalTalk is built into PowerBooks, PowerBooks must rely on third parties to connect to an Ethernet network directly. You can avoid purchasing an Ethernet adapter for your PowerBook if the network to which you are connecting has a router such as Liaison (see "Dialing Up").

PowerBook modem ports probably won't see much action, especially on the 170, which comes standard with an internal fax modem. Many fine portable external modems exist (any external modem works with the PowerBook as long as the modem has the right cable), but none of the external modems can match the convenience of an internal modem (see Chapter 1, "Portable Power").

Of course, because many external modems are battery-powered, they reduce the drain on your PowerBook's main battery. This leaves you a free slot in the unlikely event someone devises a different type of card that uses the modem port.

Yakety Mac 4

Stock Exchanges

Normally, there are four ways for two Macs to share files: via floppy disk, serial cable, modem, and network. The PowerBook 100 introduces a fifth way: via SCSI cable. You can use floppy disk and cable transfers when your PowerBook is close to another Mac (although you can risk mailing floppy disks), but modem and network transfers can occur between two Macs half a world apart.

Flipping Floppies

Floppy disks are convenient and therefore often are the default medium of file transfer. The main advantage to using a floppy disk to transfer files is that the two machines do not have to be physically linked. Instead, both machines must have floppy disk drives (which may be an issue if you're toting a PowerBook 100 without an external floppy drive).

Transferring files via floppy disk is faster than transferring files via modem. However, the floppy disk method is laborious because you must copy everything twice—once to the floppy and once from the floppy. Every time you access the floppy, you're draining battery power. Add to that time for potential virus scans. Another disadvantage is that you are limited to the size of the floppy disk, which is 1.4M at best. If you're using an original Mac II, older Mac SE, or Mac Plus, you're limited to a mere 800K.

Ready, Willing, and Cable

One of the slickest features of the PowerBook 100 is "SCSI-docking." Because SCSI-docking uses the very fast SCSI bus for file transfer, it's the fastest method of transferring large files between a PowerBook 100 and a desktop Mac.

The SCSI port is the widest port on the lower back of the Mac. On a PowerBook, the SCSI port is reshaped into a square to conserve space. The SCSI port is one of the Mac's most versatile ports, accommodating hard disks, CD-ROMs, optical drives, scanners, and even certain printers. And, using a special cable, the port can accommodate a PowerBook 100.

To dock a PowerBook 100, make sure to turn off both the PowerBook and the desktop Mac. Turn off a PowerBook 100 by pressing the Reset and Interrupt buttons simultaneously. To be safe, you also should

remove all other devices from the desktop Mac's SCSI port. The data you need to transfer may be on an external hard drive attached to the desktop Mac. If so, you can plug that external hard drive into the PowerBook using another type of cable with 30 pins on the PowerBook end and 50 pins on the external hard drive end. Using the Portable control panel on the PowerBook 100, set the SCSI ID to a number not being used by any other SCSI device (see figure 4.1). Turn on the PowerBook first, and then the desktop Mac.

Fig. 4.1. Setting the SCSI ID.

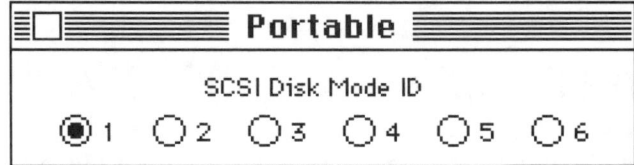

Tip: Each device in a chain linked together by SCSI cables must have a unique identification number from 1 to 6 (0 is the Mac's internal hard disk and 7 is the desktop Mac itself). You can set the IDs of most SCSI devices through a switch on the back of the device.

A docked PowerBook internal hard disk shows up as another disk on the Finder of the desktop Mac. Using the desktop machine, you can access and copy files between the two hard disks. While the PowerBook is docked, using its keyboard and trackball has no effect. The screen displays only a floating universal SCSI symbol, which looks like a diamond with a horizontal line through the right corner.

If you need to transfer files across a network or send them to a file server, you can use a LocalTalk or PhoneNET connector (the kind used to connect most LaserWriter IIs). Plug the connector into your printer port and log on to a file server or shared folder by selecting AppleShare from the Chooser. (Of course, you should check with your network administrator before you start unplugging network connectors from machines or printers.)

If you have an all-Ethernet network, the only way to connect the network is with an external SCSI Ethernet adapter, available from Dayna, Asante, and Nuvotech. For more information on these devices, see Chapter 1, "Portable Power."

Yakety Mac 4

When transferring files via a network, it doesn't matter which file-sharing software you use, as long as the software uses the AppleTalk Filing Protocol (AFP). All AFP-compliant servers enable you to access servers from the Chooser by selecting the AppleShare icon. Popular file-sharing systems that work in this manner include AppleShare, System 7.0, Novell NetWare, Banyan VINES, and Microsoft LAN Manager. If you want to connect with these networks remotely, see "Remote Controls" in the next section.

Perhaps you have a small, mixed-platform, or non-System 7.0 network that still uses the once-popular MacTOPS (formerly just "TOPS") network. To communicate with others on the network, you need to upgrade to MacTOPS 3.1 or later. Earlier versions of MacTOPS do not work with System 7.0 and, therefore, don't run on a PowerBook.

> *Tip:* MacTOPS uses several hundred K of RAM, so activate it only when you need to communicate.

Remote Controls

PowerBooks come with AppleTalk Remote Access (ARA)—a control panel and application that enable your Mac to access any modem-equipped Mac that uses System 7.0.1 or later. If you've ever used System 7.0's file sharing capability, you know almost everything you need to know about using ARA. ARA does more than just let you share files, it enables you to access network services.

To access ARA, double-click on the Remote Access application icon and enter your user name, network password, and the phone number you want to dial (see figure 4.2). Remote Access tells you how long you've been connected or displays the status in another window. The desktop Mac must be on and also running ARA. Because it requires System 7.0, ARA can run in the background. As a result, if someone is using the desktop Mac, that person can continue working. (Just hope his or her machine doesn't crash, because if it goes, so do you.)

After you click on Connect, ARA informs you that you're connected and starts timing your call (a nice touch for long-distance expense reporting). Nothing will seem different, though. So, where's the magic? To find out, select the Chooser from the Apple menu.

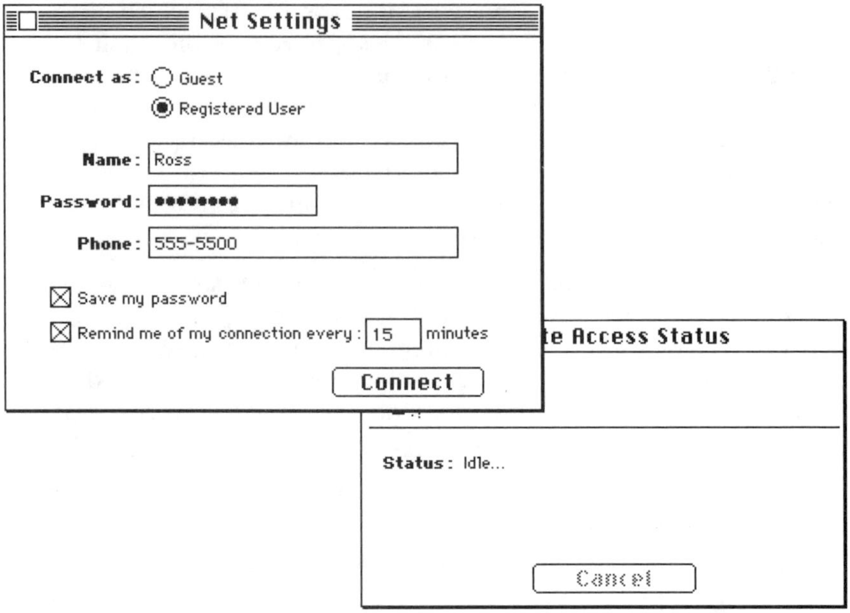

4 Hayden's PowerBook Power Book

Fig. 4.2.
ARA needs only your name, password, and a number to dial.

If the desktop Mac is attached to a network broken up into zones, the zones appear below the Chooser's list of devices. If a zone listing appears, scroll to select a zone containing a file server and click the AppleShare icon. You see a list of shared folders or file servers normally accessible from the network Mac. If you log on to one of the shared folders or file servers, the icon of that item appears in the Finder. You then can copy files back and forth from the shared folder or file server as if it were another disk.

Click on LaserWriter. You now can print to any networkable LaserWriter. With ARA, you can send a report to the intended recipient before you arrive—without the quality degradation of a fax machine. Other types of network services, ranging from electronic mail and file servers to programs that facilitate group exchange like MacVonk's Inforum and Pacer Software's PacerForum, also are available when you are connected via ARA.

Apple considered the security risks of having outsiders dial into your Mac (see figure 4.3). Within ARA, you can designate passwords, limit the amount of connect time, and instruct the Call Back Security option to call you at a specified number to ensure that you made the call. If you're at a desktop Mac and don't want people dialing into your shared folders, open the Users and Groups control panel and double-click on names of users you don't want to be able to call-in. Deselect

Yakety Mac 4

the Allow Remote Access checkbox if it is selected. If you want users to have access but would rather call them back at predefined numbers for security's sake, select the checkbox marked "Call Back At #:." Then enter the number at which you can reach the caller.

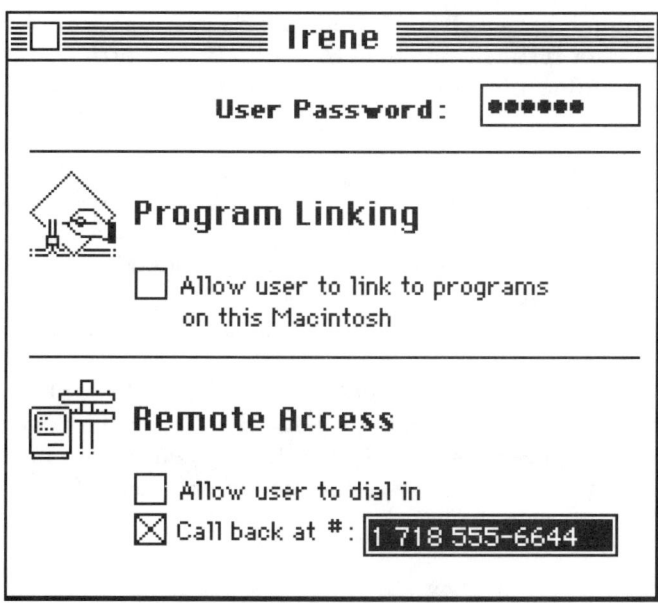

Fig. 4.3. Securing remote access.

You also can control the network resources to which people have access by using the Remote Access Setup. Clicking either the "entire network" or "this Macintosh only" button determines the machines with which the caller can communicate. You must select "entire network" to successfully access LaserWriter NTs and other shared resources. However, if your printer is a non-network printer, such as a Personal LaserWriter LS or StyleWriter, you can select "this Macintosh only."

> *Tip:* To share a printer that you normally cannot access over a network (such as a StyleWriter or LaserWriter LS), you may want to investigate ShadowWriter from Gizmo Technologies. This program enables a Mac attached to a non-network printer to print files from other machines on the network, including those machines that dial in.

ARA is an elegant (not to mention free) tool that comes with every PowerBook. However, ARA has some limitations. First of all—and this applies to any file-sharing software—you may find that dialing in at 2400 baud (the speed of Apple's internal fax modem) to be slow. In fact, 2400 baud is so cumbersome that if you have several megabytes to transfer, you might as well send it on disk via overnight courier. You get much better results using the 9600-baud PowerPort/v.32 by Global Village Communications or the tiny external QBlazer by Telebit.

> *Tip:* ARA employs its own error-checking process that automatically turns off some advanced error-checking file transfer protocols. ARA does, however, take advantage of v.32 and v.32bis modems. These modems can transfer data at speeds of 9600 and 14,400 bits per second.

Second, document exchange limitations still apply. If your PowerBook doesn't have the proper fonts to display a document, the document won't appear properly formatted when it is copied to your machine. To get around this limitation, see the section entitled "XTNDing Yourself" later in this chapter.

Building Bridges

If you dial into a Mac that is not running System 7.0, you cannot use ARA. You can, however, achieve similar results using Farallon's Liaison program. Like ARA, Liaison can run in the background on a desktop Mac. On a PowerBook, Liaison appears as a Chooser extension. To use Liaison, you select the Chooser from the Apple menu and then select the Liaison icon. Liaison dials the remote Mac. When you log in, you can access files and printers just as you can with ARA.

You may not want to dedicate a Mac to handling dial-ins. You also may not want to risk the slowdowns and potential crashes of using ARA or Liaison on a Mac that's in use. In that situation, consider a special hardware device such as Shiva's Telebridge or NetModem. NetModem also provides an economic way for people on a network to share a modem.

Sharing Alike

With the exception of being a Red Sox fan, few things demand more patience than trying to explain a screenful of information over the telephone. This is particularly nightmarish in the Mac's dynamic

Yakety Mac 4

universe of floating windows, small screen elements ("Click in *what little box?*"), and multitasking environment.

In contrast to ARA and Liaison—which let you log on to the shared folders and hard disks of other machines—two programs enable you to observe and actually control other machines: Timbuktu and Carbon Copy Mac.

Farallon's Timbuktu and Timbuktu/Remote both let you view and control screens across a network. Timbuktu/Remote enables you to do the same with Macs connected via modem. Timbuktu is a desk accessory; you activate it from the Apple menu. When you select Timbuktu, you see a list of other Macs on the network running Timbuktu. Select one of the other Macs and wait for the Timbuktu window to appear. Depending on the size of the screen and the speed of the network, it might take a while for the Timbuktu window to appear.

Timbuktu exclusively enables you to have multiple windows open simultaneously and view them in color (although the latter feature is about as useful to a PowerBook owner as a mouse pad). In any case, these features move at a snail's pace, even over a fast network such as Ethernet. If you try to use multiple windows over LocalTalk, your patience might expire. If you try showing color through a 2400-baud modem, you might expire.

Timbuktu also has comprehensive security controls governing who can do what on your Mac when you connect to other Macs (see figure 4.4). Both Timbuktu and Carbon Copy enable you to control remote Macs, but flexible security is one reason why Timbuktu costs more.

Ordinarily, Farallon recommends Timbuktu/Remote for modem access, but given the ease with which you can connect to a network using ARA, Farallon ships Timbuktu in Farallon's PowerBook bundle. Although Timbuktu provides features not available in Timbuktu/Remote, remember that the desktop Mac must be running System 7.0, as well as either ARA or Liaison, to use Timbuktu. If you have just one Mac with which you will be connecting, or if your network is running System 6.0, buy Timbuktu/Remote instead.

>
>
> *Tip:* You may need at some point to transfer just a paragraph or two from a very large file. To do so, use Timbuktu's handy Clipboard Exchange feature. Open the document on the remote Mac and select the text you need. Click the Get Clipboard icon. The contents of the remote clipboard transfer to your clipboard, and you can paste the contents into whatever file you are working on.

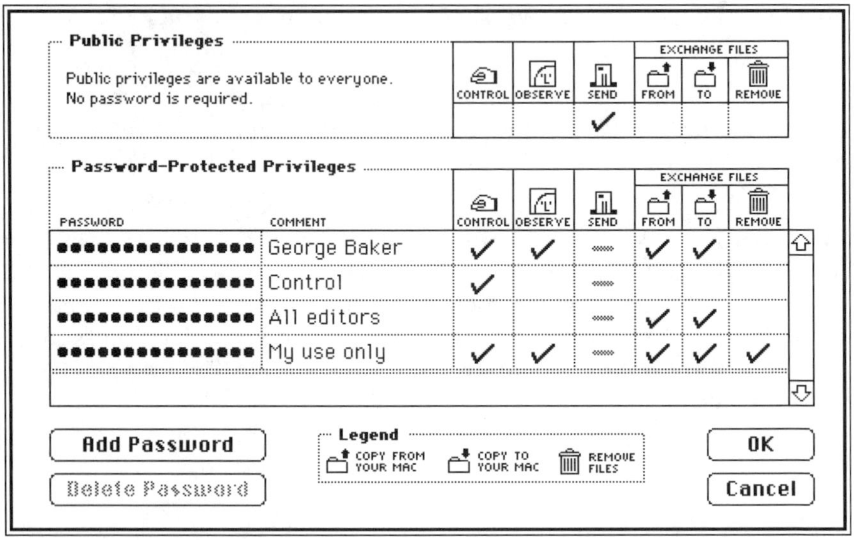

Fig. 4.4.
Timbuktu offers flexible security.

Carbon Copy Mac is Microcom's counterpart to its popular Carbon Copy Plus on the PC. Despite the company's DOS experience, Farallon is poised to lengthen its lead in the features race. Farallon plans to do this by releasing a version that enables Mac users and Microsoft Windows users to share screens for the first time. Carbon Copy's most convenient asset is its diversity—you can use the same program over the network or through a modem without using ARA. The program's most remarkable asset, however, is its price. At less than $200 for a version that allows an unlimited number of users in a network zone, Microcom is practically giving the program away.

File Groupies

If you communicate routinely with someone else's Mac, you may consider purchasing Baseline Publishing's DoubleTalk, a terminal emulation program written with the Mac in mind. Baseline is kind enough to provide two copies of DoubleTalk—one for the PowerBook and one for the obsolete Mac you bought two weeks ago. With DoubleTalk, a user can leave batches of files for a caller to receive. In other words, if someone knows you're going to call to receive files, DoubleTalk can have those files ready when you call. You simply connect using DoubleTalk on the PowerBook, grab the files you need, and disconnect.

Yakety Mac 4

In addition, with DoubleTalk you can send and receive files simultaneously. This feature—combined with DoubleTalk's already optimized file transfer protocols—drastically reduces long distance time if you have files going back and forth. Not only that, with DoubleTalk you can type a message to the person at the other end while you transfer a file. (As a result, you can gloat about how you get to travel with a PowerBook while your office mate does not.) The program features an easy-to-use, customizable interface that enables you to trade groups of files and "chat" at the same time (see figure 4.5). DoubleTalk enables you to get up to speed faster than most terminal emulation programs.

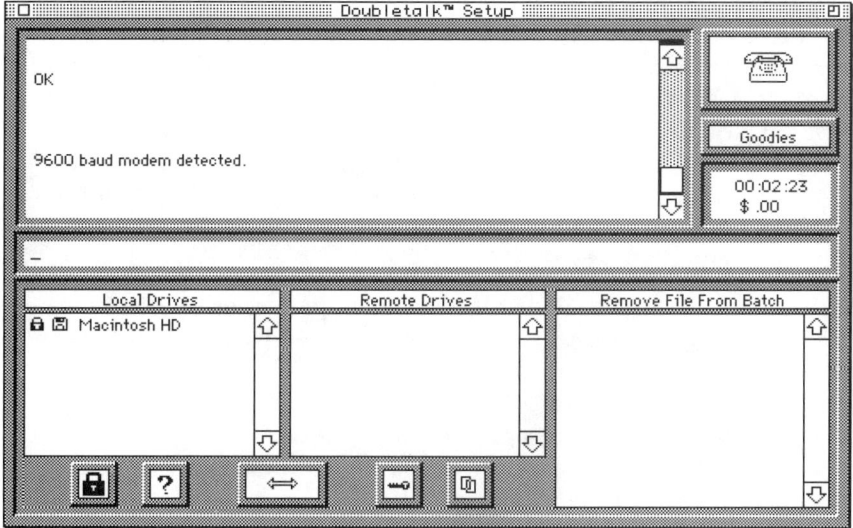

Fig. 4.5. With DoubleTalk you can trade files and "chat" simultaneously.

Conversation PCs

In addition to overcoming the hurdles normally associated with file transfers, additional considerations hamper dealing with IBM PC-compatibles. PCs can't take advantage of the built-in file sharing in System 7.0 and they were not designed with network software in mind. As a result, ARA does not work. Macs and PCs also have different methods of formatting 3 1/2-inch floppy disks, so once you've used a 3 1/2-inch floppy disk in a PC, it's a DOS disk. The only way you can turn it into a Mac disk is by erasing it.

Furthermore, Mac and PC users often use different software to accomplish the same tasks. If you think the Mac has plenty of software to choose from, you're right. However, it is just a foothill compared to the mountain of DOS software available. As someone once said, "Eight million DOS users can't be wrong, and even if they are, you have to humor them."

There are, however, four ways to get Macs and PCs talking: via floppy disk, serial cable, modem, and network.

Se Habla "DOS"

Introduced on the Macintosh IIx and available on all PowerBooks, Apple's newer type of floppy disk drive not only holds more data, but also can read MS-DOS, OS/2 (IBM's still-evolving advanced operating system), and ProDOS (Apple II's operating system) disks. The most important of these formats for most people is MS-DOS, which nearly every IBM PC-compatible uses. Technically, even Microsoft Windows users are still running DOS, but Windows has a friendlier face and fewer limitations.

Although the PowerBook drives, dubbed SuperDrives or FDHDs (Floppy disks, high-density), physically can read DOS disks, even System 7.0 is unprepared for such disks. Therefore, be careful not to pop a DOS floppy disk into your Mac disk drive, or the dreaded, "This disk is unreadable…" message will appear. If this occurs, click Eject. Clicking Initialize irrevocably erases all the DOS data on the disk and reformats the disk as a Macintosh disk.

If you occasionally need to read data from a DOS disk, you can use Apple File Exchange (AFE), included with System 7.0. After launching AFE, you insert the DOS disk in the floppy drive. The disk's files will appear in the file list (see figure 4.6). Using the familiar but nonetheless abysmal Font/DA Mover method, which presents two lists of files and a button to move files between them, select the files on the floppy disk by Shift-clicking or dragging through the list. Then click the Translate button to transfer those files to your hard disk.

You must use Apple File Exchange to read DOS disks unless you purchase a "DOS disk reader" from Dayna, Insignia, or Argosy. All three disk readers handle file exchange more elegantly than AFE. Slow and cumbersome, AFE remains ill-matched to the wide variety of DOS file formats. Although DataViz provides a set of translators that you can use with AFE, opening AFE with the entire set of translators results in a disk-bashing, battery-wasting waiting period as the program reads every format. This is no reflection on the excellent set of translators, which you can use more productively (see "XTNDing Yourself").

Yakety Mac 4

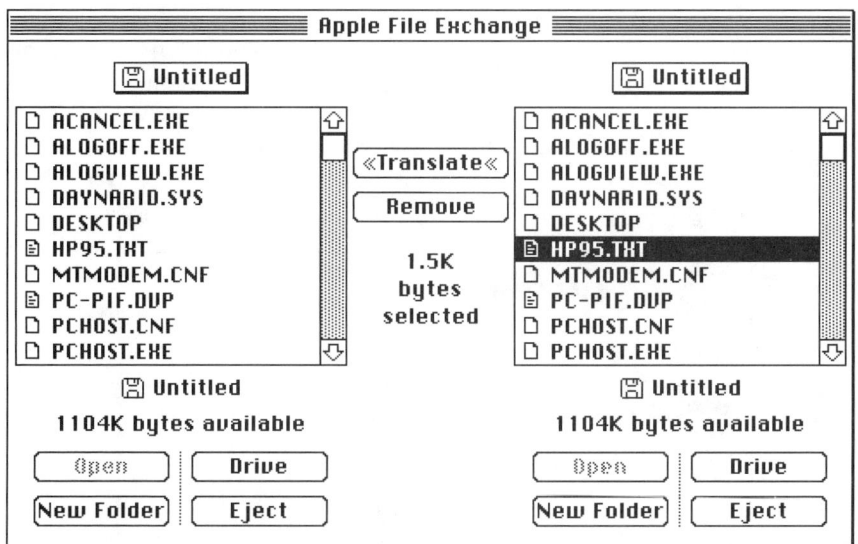

Fig. 4.6.
Using Apple File Exchange to read DOS disks.

Easy DOS It

Insignia Solutions' AccessPC, Dayna's DOS Mounter, and Argosy Software's MountPC offer a better way to access DOS disks. These control panels enable the Mac to do what should come naturally: access DOS disks from the Finder and from within Open dialog boxes. These products operate transparently. Inserting a DOS disk when one of these programs is active makes the PowerBook treat the DOS disk as if it were a Mac disk. This trick always impresses Mac-illiterate DOS users.

Another benefit of using one of these programs is extension mapping (see figure 4.7). Extension mapping is a process in which DOS filenames become linked to a Macintosh application. Even when DOS disks are made available to the Finder, the disks appear as generic document icons. In other words, the disk icons appear as plain rectangles with dog-eared corners; double-clicking on the disk "icons" results in an "application not found" message. This occurs because DOS uses a different (and less reliable) means of associating documents with the programs that created them. Not to be confused with Macintosh extensions, which add functionality when dragged to the System Folder, DOS extensions are the three letters that follow the period in DOS and Windows filenames.

Examples of common extensions include ".WK1" for Lotus 1-2-3, ".DOC" for Microsoft Word, and ".XLS" for Excel for Windows. Extension mapping enables you to open your choice of Mac programs when you double-click on files with certain extensions. For example,

double-clicking on the DOS WordPerfect file "REPORT.WP" can launch the Macintosh WordPerfect application, which can read files created by its DOS counterpart. DOS Mounter 3.0, in fact, enables you to use special characters in extensions so that double-clicking on files with similar extensions can launch the same Mac application.

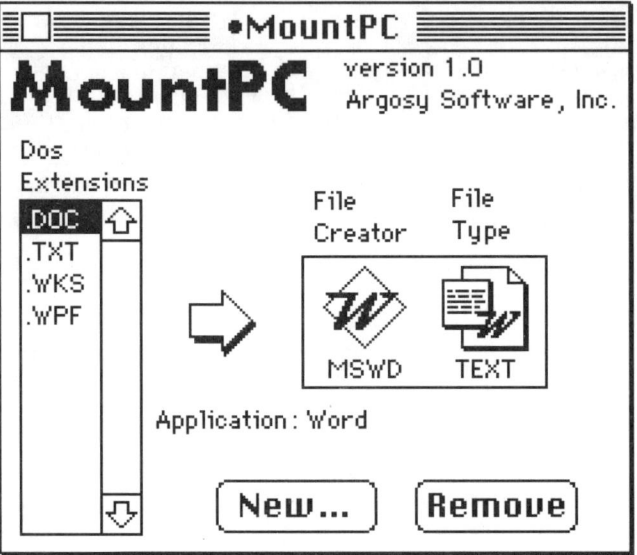

Fig. 4.7. Argosy's MountPC links DOS files to Macintosh applications.

Programs such as WordPerfect that are file-format compatible across platforms benefit greatly from extension mapping. Other Macintosh programs that can read files created by their DOS or Windows counterparts include Aldus PageMaker, Lotus 1-2-3, Microsoft Word (be sure to save WinWord files as "RTF") and Microsoft Excel. Before 1-2-3 was on the Macintosh (and that was a long time), Excel could read DOS-based Lotus 1-2-3 files, so you still can specify files with a .WK1 extension to launch Excel.

XTNDing Yourself

Many DOS programs, most notably word processors, still don't have Mac counterparts. Examples of such programs are MultiMate, OfficeWriter, Professional Write, Amí Pro (although a Mac version is slated for release in late 1992) and XyWrite III. But extension mapping still can work for these programs if you use a translator set and a Mac word processor that supports XTND (pronounced "extend").

Yakety Mac 4

XTND is a seamless file-format translation system developed and licensed by Claris. XTND enables ClarisWorks, for example, to open and save files in different popular word processor file formats. All programs that support XTND can use the same set of translators. Typically, you implement XTND through the Open and Save dialog boxes of your programs, where a File Format pop-up menu appears below the file list (see figure 4.8). Pressing and holding the mouse button while pointing to this menu reveals a variety of file formats the program can read or save its files as. This list typically includes at least five or six popular file formats.

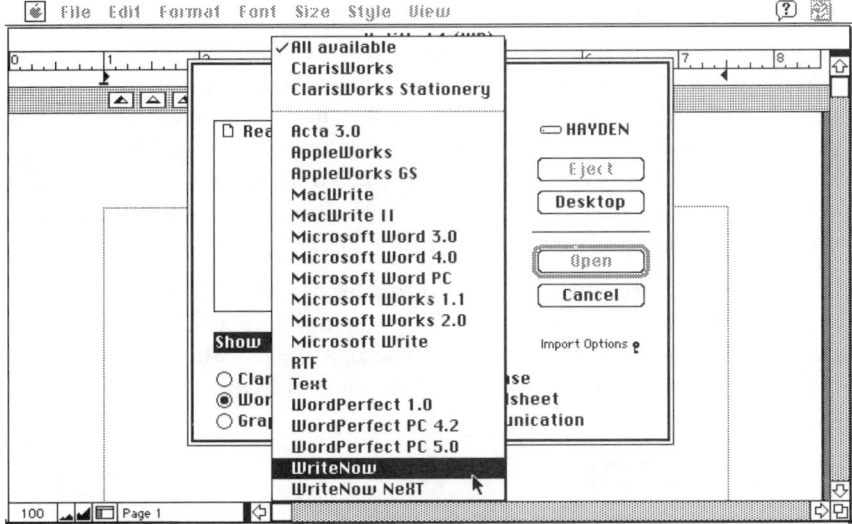

Fig. 4.8. The XTND file format translation system.

One of XTND's greatest strengths, however, is that it can work with third-party file translators. Therefore, you do not have to depend on the supplier of the software to write specialized translators. When used with specialized translator programs, your programs may be able to read and write 30 or 40 different file formats! Two of the three major file format translation programs for the Mac, MacLink/Plus and Mastersoft's Word for Word, now include or will soon include bridges. As a result, their translators may be used within the growing ranks of Mac programs that use XTND. Some of the programs that use XTND include MacWrite II, MacDraw Pro, ClarisWorks, BeagleWorks, HandiWorks, Taste, WordPerfect, GreatWorks, On Location, RagTime, Instant Update, and In Control.

4 Hayden's PowerBook Power Book

> *Tip:* The flexibility of MacLink/Plus Translators keeps the translators popular among applications. For example, Apple File Exchange prefers MacLink/Plus Translators to be in the Apple File Exchange folder, although programs that use XTND want the translators to be in the Claris Translators folder within the Claris folder in the System Folder (whew!). You can use aliases to keep the translators wherever programs need them.

XTND's greatest advantage is that it leaves you free to choose the programs you want to use without worrying about whether the programs have compatible DOS counterparts. After all, while on the road you incur a greater chance of having to share information with other people without knowing which programs they use. Sticking to the few popular file formats already supported by most Mac word processors saves you the expense and hard disk space of storing a comprehensive set of translators. If, however, your PowerBook must deal with different formats frequently, it helps to be prepared.

Unfortunately, although XTND and third-party translators continually improve, the differences among programs may prevent a perfect translation. For example, you may have trouble translating advanced features such as math equations, tables, and indexes.

ASCII Jumps

Although file translation programs support a dizzying array of options, some applications remain unsupported. For these applications, your last resort may be to save files in ASCII format (sometimes called DOS files or text-only files). Virtually all programs can interpret plain ASCII files.

Compatibility has its price: all formatting is stripped from your document. Apple and other major vendors are working toward a promising new interchange format called RXTX. For the next few years, however, ASCII is the best you can do.

Graphic Contents

No ASCII equivalent exists for graphics. There are, however, several popular formats that you can transfer across platforms. If a format is

not popular on both the PC and the Mac—such as TIFF or EPS formats—you first should try MacLink/Plus, which offers some graphics support. If the file format is obscure, check out FGM's PICTure This, which can convert many different file formats to PICT. (Almost all Mac programs can read PICT files.)

Sending a Cable

The problem of linking Macs to PCs is not new. The difficulty existed long before Macs even had SuperDrives. Fortunately, two companies provide proven solutions for overcoming the physical and practical differences between Macs and PCs. The products of these companies are especially useful to PowerBook owners.

Traveling Software's LapLink Mac III and DataViz' MacLink/Plus both provide complete solutions for transferring files to a PC via serial cable (included with both packages) or modem. The two applications also operate similarly. You install the file transfer software on both the PowerBook and the PC and begin the connection from either machine. If you use serial cable, the connection is immediate. Over a modem, of course, you first must dial a phone number. Once connected, you can select files on either machine and copy the files to the other computer. You also have the option to translate the files to a suitable file format as they travel.

Both LapLink and MacLink/Plus have bonus features. LapLink doubles as a capable file-sharing system that can send files across a network. MacLink/Plus includes Dayna's DOS Mounter, which provides desktop support and extension-mapping features. MacLink/Plus has a more complete set of translators, recognizes common file formats automatically, and provides automatic recognition of different file formats' slick drag-and-drop features under System 7.0. Either program, however, is a fine solution to a perennial problem.

C> Shells

If you want to control a DOS machine remotely the same way you control a Mac remotely with Timbuktu, a good choice is Argosy Software's RunPC/Remote. With RunPC/Remote you can type on the remote machine, open programs, and even cut and paste between windows. However, RunPC is a one-way ticket; the DOS machine cannot control your PowerBook. RunPC also does not support Microsoft Windows yet. It will be interesting to see whether Argosy can beat Timbuktu to the gate with an upgrade that enables you to run Windows from your PowerBook. RunPC/Remote includes MountPC, as well as Software Bridge/Mac, an accurate set of translators that focuses on word processing formats.

Incidentally, you will experience better performance when you control a DOS machine than when you control another Mac (especially when using color). This occurs because with a DOS machine you only have to transfer screens full of characters across the network instead of transferring bitmapped Macintosh screens.

Big Blue in a Box

Long before there was Lotus 1-2-3 and WordPerfect for Macintosh, people wished they could run these software packages on their Macs to retain compatibility. The best solution was to purchase the equivalent application available for the Mac or a program that reliably imported and exported the application's file formats. For example, FoxBase+/Mac can read database code created by FoxBase+ for DOS, or code created by the phenomenally popular dBASE III Plus.

Not all DOS developers are as enlightened as Microsoft, WordPerfect, and, most recently, Lotus. Computers can accomodate most file formats either directly or through translation. However, some programs (notably the DOS program Paradox) have no Macintosh counterpart. There also are custom software programs developed for DOS that somehow escaped Mac translation. That's why Insignia created SoftPC.

If you have seen Apple ads claiming that PowerBooks can run DOS software, you may not have noticed a small asterisk. SoftPC is the reason for that asterisk. SoftPC is a Macintosh application that works a bit of magic by emulating an IBM PC-compatible (see figure 4.9). Sure enough, when you double-click on the SoftPC icon, the SoftPC window turns black and you hear the familiar grinding sound of a PC starting up. Internal memory ticks off and you are treated to the legendary "C>" prompt that has long had DOS users yearning for a Mac environment.

SoftPC performs some impressive stunts. Because the PowerBook's floppy disk drive (or the external disk drive on a PowerBook 100) is already capable of reading DOS disks, SoftPC enables you to use the drive as a DOS A: drive. With SoftPC's unique file-sharing architecture, you can designate a Mac folder as an E: drive. Any file you drag into the Mac folder is available to DOS applications that search the E: drive. Folders appear as directories. If you also have Insignia's AccessPC, you can treat a SoftPC-created hard disk just like a Mac hard disk on your desktop.

Yakety Mac 4

Fig. 4.9.
SoftPC enables your Mac to work like an IBM PC-compatible.

```
                           SoftPC
NLSFUNC   EXE     3029    2-03-88    2:31p
PRINT     COM     8995    2-03-88    2:31p
RECOVER   COM     4268    2-03-88    2:31p
SELECT    COM     4132    2-03-88    2:31p
SORT      EXE     1946    2-03-88    2:31p
SUBST     EXE    10552    2-03-88    2:31p
SYS       COM     4725    2-03-88    2:31p
BACKUP    COM    29976    2-03-88    2:31p
DEBUG     COM    15866    2-03-88    2:31p
EGA       CPI    49065    2-03-88    2:31p
GWBASIC   EXE    80592    2-03-88    2:31p
KEYBOARD  SYS    19735    2-03-88    2:31p
LCD       CPI    10752    2-03-88    2:31p
LINK      EXE    39172    2-03-88    2:31p
PRINTER   SYS    13559    2-03-88    2:31p
RAMDRIVE  SYS     6481    2-03-88    2:31p
REPLACE   EXE    13234    2-03-88    2:31p
RESTORE   COM    35650    2-03-88    2:31p
SHARE     EXE     8608    2-03-88    2:31p
TREE      COM     3540    2-03-88    2:31p
XCOPY     EXE    11216    2-03-88    2:31p
FC        EXE    15974   12-15-89   12:57p
       51 File(s)   1028096 bytes free

C:\DOS>_
```

SoftPC is an ambitious product. It isn't easy to emulate an IBM PC-compatible using only software. When it comes to speed, however, SoftPC is a dog, and not even a greyhound at that. The basic version of SoftPC emulates an IBM PC XT-class machine with a CGA (low resolution) monitor. Insignia also sells a SoftAT version that emulates a 80286-class machine (approximately the equivalent of a Mac Classic) with a matching 80287 math coprocessor, improved graphics capability, and expanded memory capabilities. Even with all these enhancements, though, a real 286 flies by a PowerBook 170 running SoftAT.

Overpowering RAM requirements diminish SoftPC's advantage for most PowerBooks. SoftAT requires about 2.5M of RAM just to run. To make more memory available to your DOS applications, you must allocate more memory to the SoftAT application. To designate the full 4M of RAM that SoftPC can use, you must wait until 6M RAM upgrades are available for the PowerBook. Although SoftPC provides an answer to the cross-platform needs of many PowerBook owners, it is much slower than an "equivalent" PC.

Normally, SoftPC provides two methods of activating the function keys that are so important in DOS software. One method is to use the function keys on the Apple Extended Keyboard. The other method is to hold down the Command key as you press numbers on the keypad.

4 Hayden's PowerBook Power Book

> *Tip:* Because a PowerBook has neither a keypad nor function keys, the latest version of SoftPC enables you to enter "function key mode" by pressing Command-F. Typing a number then activates the corresponding function key. For example, if you are using DOS WordPerfect and press Command-F and then 2, WordPerfect's help screens appear because F2 activates Help in that program.

If you're ever strapped for a function key, you can attach an ADB keyboard to the PowerBook. Don't leave the keyboard attached too long, however, because it uses more juice than a football team out of Gatorade.

Look Who's Talking Too

Because no Finder interface is available on other computers (except the cosmetically similar Apple IIGS), and because MS-DOS machines outnumber Macs, PowerBook users must resort to a character-based terminal emulation program. A terminal emulation program provides a common ground for transferring text and files between different types of computers. So even if you need to transfer data to an Apple II, Commodore Amiga, or an Atari ST, you always can communicate via a terminal emulation program. Some online services require that you have a terminal emulation program in order to log on.

Because terminal emulation programs are so generalized, you need to determine some obscure parameters before sending files. You need to know parameters such as bits per character, stop bits, and parity. If you don't know which settings you should use, a safe bet is 8 bits, 1 stop bit, and no parity (sometimes abbreviated as "8,1,N").

Many communications programs now incorporate Apple's Communications Toolbox, which provides a consistent, extensible method for setting parameters (see figure 4.10). The advantage is that once you know how to set parameters for one Macintosh communications program, you know how to set parameters in all of them. The Apple Modem tool, for example, enables you to choose baud rate, parity, and stop bits.

Many fine terminal emulation programs enable you to reach out to character-based systems. Three of the most popular programs are

Yakety Mac 4

Software Ventures' MicroPhone II, Hayes' SmartCom II, and Freesoft's White Knight. SmartCom II and MicroPhone II feature easy-to-use interfaces, but MicroPhone II boasts a powerful scripting environment that can automate the accessing of online services. As a bonus, MicroPhone II has a Windows version that shares a similar interface.

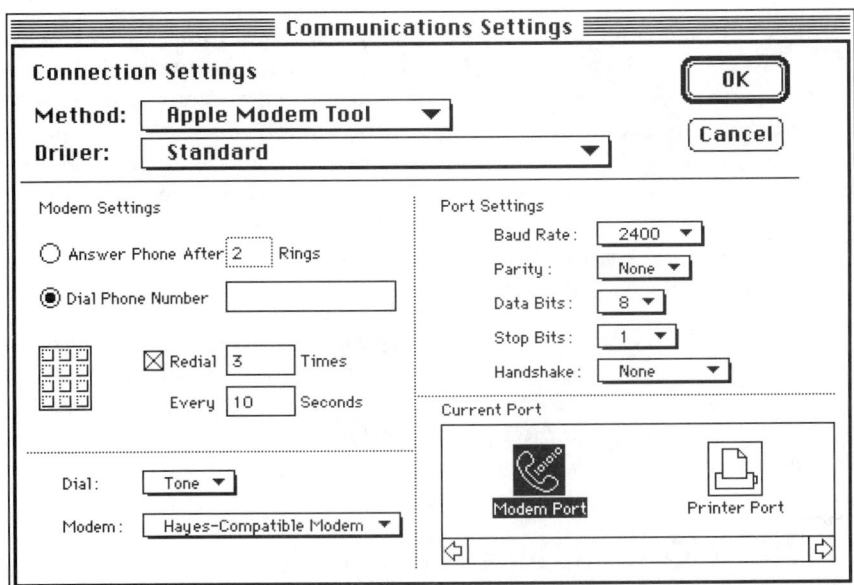

Fig. 4.10. Apple's Communications Toolbox.

FreeSoft's White Knight may have even more robust scripting features than MicroPhone. White Knight's interface is not as straightforward, but White Knight itself is a fantastic bargain at half of MicroPhone's price. Most integrated software programs include a bare-bones communications module which you can use if you don't need the advanced features of these terminal-emulation powerhouses.

Net Worth

As mentioned earlier in the Mac "Network Transfers" section, many popular PC networks, including Novell NetWare and Banyan Vines, support AppleTalk Filing Protocol. As a result, accessing these networks is identical to accessing a Mac file server, although you still must deal with file format issues discussed in "Se Habla DOS."

Wired to the World

With a communications powerhouse in your briefcase, you have access to some of the most useful, entertaining, and expensive online services the world has to offer. Connecting to an online service is, in principle, similar to connecting to any other type of computer.

Online services often are run from massive minicomputers that can tie into vast databases worldwide. Each of these dial-in services gladly sends you information about why you should spend your online time with them. The literature often covers the wealth of services you find online, including forums, files, shopping, electronic mail, "live" chats, and vendor support. The services, however, often are generalized because virtually any modem-equipped computer using terminal-emulation software must be able to access the services. Some services, however, require special software.

Following, then, is a brief summary describing how to access various online services through a PowerBook, and what you might gain from the services. By the way, if you want to contact me online, feel free to do so. You can reach me on America Online (Ross Rubin) or CompuServe (72137,2627).

America Online

Few and disciplined are the Macintosh users who can resist America Online. America Online provides free software enabling you to access its services. The services boast outstanding chat and file libraries, stock quotes, and forums. America Online replaces archaic navigation commands in favor of windows, folders, and HyperCard-like buttons. America Online's QuickFinder feature makes finding files in any category a breeze. The most notable (though not unique) feature of America Online is that it works like any Mac program. You access commands via menus and navigate through folders similar to the Finder's folders and buttons (see figure 4.11).

America Online makes extensive use of sound. It greets you by saying (literally) "Welcome!" and, perhaps, "You've got mail!" In the chat rooms, you can designate sounds to play on another person's Mac if the sounds are on that user's hard disk. When you leave the service, the program says "Goodbye!" Be forewarned, however. Because America Online is a graphical program, a slower Mac updates the screen more slowly, and, as a result, there is more billable online time.

Yakety Mac 4

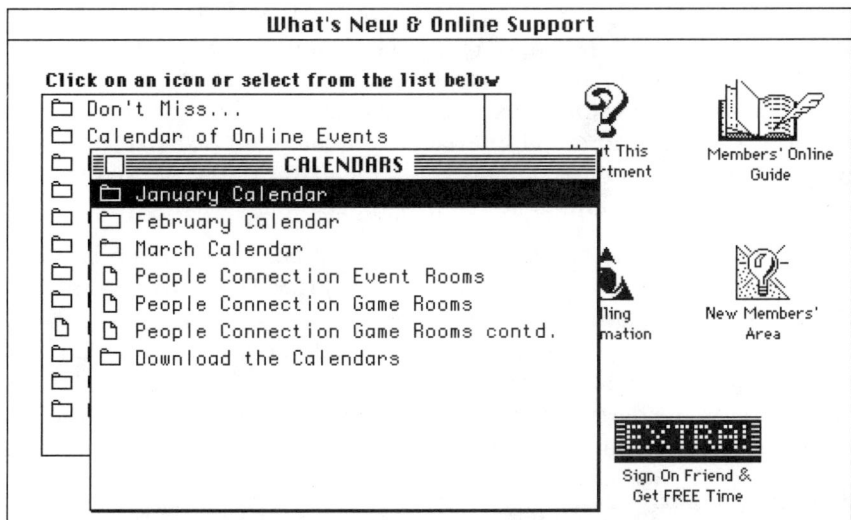

Fig. 4.11.
America Online works like any other Mac program.

Tip: To conserve battery life, keep your speaker's volume level set to zero. Each time the speaker is used, it draws a charge from the battery. Of course, if your PowerBook is plugged in, by all means, feast your ears.

America Online could benefit from several additional features. Given the number of files uploaded each day, forums should have a "New files since last visit" option. Batch downloading (the ability to retrieve several files consecutively without interaction), as well as background downloading, also would be welcome features. In addition, it's often difficult to follow forum topics because the topics lack threads—that is, you can't read a reply to a reply. America Online 2.0 is due soon, though, and should address at least some vocal users' requests, as well as offer online drawing, extended font support, and other goodies.

CompuServe

The CompuServe Information Service (CIS) is one of the oldest and largest online services in the world. Prodigy is catching up quickly in its own membership ranks, but it cannot approach the tremendous depth of games, databases, files, forums, and other services found on CompuServe. Several thick tomes are available that are dedicated to describing what you can find online.

CompuServe's Mac forums, collectively known as MAUG (Micronetworked Apple Users' Group) boast some of the most active and knowledgeable members of the Macintosh community. It rarely takes more than a day for an expert to answer even the thorniest question. MAUG's traditional interface is anything but Mac-like. To its credit, though, the service has answered most Mac users' prayers in the form of two complementary access programs.

CompuServe Information Manager (CIM) is an excellent choice for the new CompuServe user. CIM replaces many of CIS' DOS-like prompts with icons, menus, and dialog boxes (see figure 4.12). Like most graphical front-ends, CIM's leisurely pace might annoy you, but you are more likely to feel frustrated by CIM's incompleteness. You still must access many parts of CIS—such as the File Find section—in the character-based terminal mode.

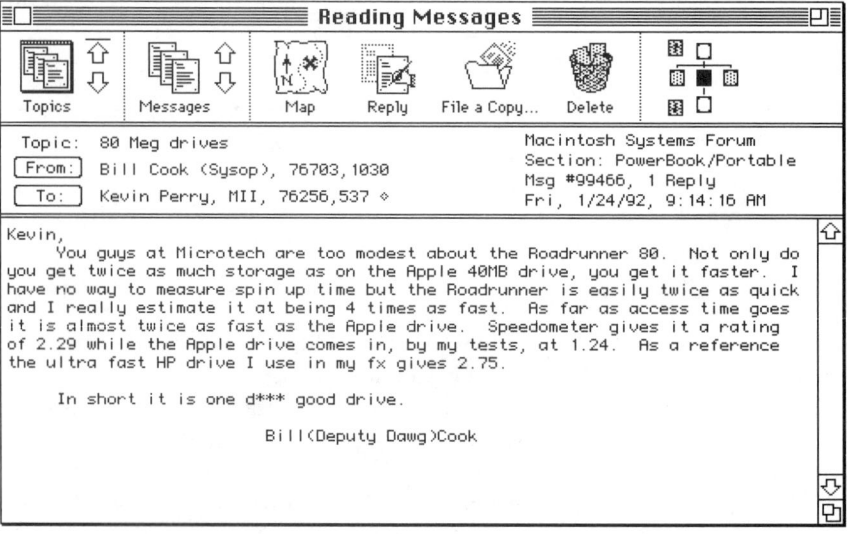

Fig. 4.12. CIM is CompuServe "for the rest of us."

CompuServe Navigator lacks CIM's intuitive approach, catering more to the needs of the advanced user. With Navigator, you can graphically compose scripts that make the most of your online time. You also can access new electronic mail and forum messages automatically. You then can read the messages at your leisure—when CompuServe's billing clock isn't running. You also can compose messages offline and stay online just long enough to send the reply. Navigator costs more than CIM, but if you are a power CIS user who performs a variety of routine tasks online, Navigator offers a speedy return on your investment.

Yakety Mac 4

Both CompuServe Information Manager and CompuServe Navigator are inexpensive (CIM is practically given away through routine promotions), yet both applications make it easy to navigate CIS' riches in a familiar way. If you'd rather save your hard disk space, or if you already know your way around CompuServe, you always can access the service through a terminal emulation program.

CONNECT

CONNECT (formerly MacNet) is a business communications forum that companies sometimes use in place of a worldwide electronic mail system. CONNECT features a well-designed Macintosh interface that preceded America Online's. The similarity, however, ends at the interface. If you're looking to have fun online, spend your dollars elsewhere. CONNECT emphasizes stock quotes and professional forums. Among this forum's advantages are high-speed modem access and a Windows client that operates similarly to CONNECT's Mac counterpart.

GEnie and Delphi

GEnie and Delphi are two smaller and less-expensive CompuServe alternatives with supportive and vocal Macintosh sections. You can access these services by using traditional terminal emulation programs. GEnie, in particular, offers a variety of access plans including free electronic mail. In other words, you are not charged for time online when using electronic mail (unless you send files with your mail).

GEnie has a Navigator-like access program called Aladdin that automates connect sessions for the PC. The makers of Aladdin have promised a Mac version of Aladdin, but this is one GEnie that has been slow to answer a Mac owner's wishes. When the Mac version of Aladdin appears, GEnie will represent a great bargain in online services for Mac users.

Prodigy

Prodigy—a service born of a partnership between IBM and Sears—is one of the best bargains in online services. At just over $12.95 per month (less if you pay in advance), you can access Prodigy's electronic mail, extensive shopping services, and even order groceries (in selected areas). Subsidized by advertisers whose ads take up a fourth of each screen, the service has defended its right to limit electronic mail use and refuse posts and letters considered offensive to any of Prodigy's members or advertisers.

Although Prodigy offers its own access software for the Mac, Prodigy doesn't act like any other Mac program. There are no pull-down menus, you must double-click buttons, and you nearly have to jump through hoops just to save information to a disk.

> *Tip:* To save Prodigy files, you must obtain a copy of a DA called "*P* to disk" and print the information. Ironically, you can't get the DA online from Prodigy, because Prodigy is the only major service that lacks file libraries.

All the Fax

In business, fax machines have become almost as common a communications tool as the telephone itself—the tool on which the fax machine relies. Although you also can use a modem to transfer either data or faxes, the data takes a different form on the receiving end.

To send a fax, the PowerBook converts each page to a graphic image. The PowerBook then transfers the graphic images to the remote fax machine, which acts as a medium-resolution non-PostScript printer. The resolution of a fax machine is approximately 200 dots per inch, higher than an ImageWriter II but not nearly as high as a LaserWriter or StyleWriter. And, unlike LaserWriters, faxes lack Adobe PostScript for producing high-quality graphics. To get professional-looking text on the receiving end, you must use TrueType or Adobe Type Manager.

To send a fax using Apple's fax software, install the fax software using the installer program that comes with the PowerBook 170, or use the Apple Fax/Data Modem if you have the fax software installed on a different PowerBook model.

Apple's fax software includes a Chooser driver, a fax monitor application, and a Fax Cover application that streamlines cover sheet design. Once you have entered all your relevant contact information, select Fax Sender from the Chooser and select Print from your application's File menu. From the Print dialog box, you can designate new recipients or drag existing recipients from your phone book into the recipients' list. After you confirm that all your settings are to your liking, click OK to start the fax.

When you click OK, you can monitor the status of your fax with the Fax Monitor application. This application notifies you of progress and maintains a log of your faxing attempts that you can review at any time.

Yakety Mac 4

> *Tip:* To send just one fax with Apple's fax software, hold down the Control and Shift keys as you select Print from the File menu. This action temporarily selects the Fax Sender software and returns you to your normal printer the next time you select Print.

If you choose a third-party internal fax modem, the functionality of the fax software may differ from—and in many cases be superior to—Apple's software. For example, with the PSI PowerModem you can create a sophisticated distribution list that sends a fax to a group of people with just one command. The PowerModem also includes a Quickfax desk accessory that enables you to fax short notes without having to open a word processor (see figure 4.13). PSI's PowerModem software has several features that Apple's software lacks, including a QuickFax desk accessory and the ability to receive faxes and create distribution groups.

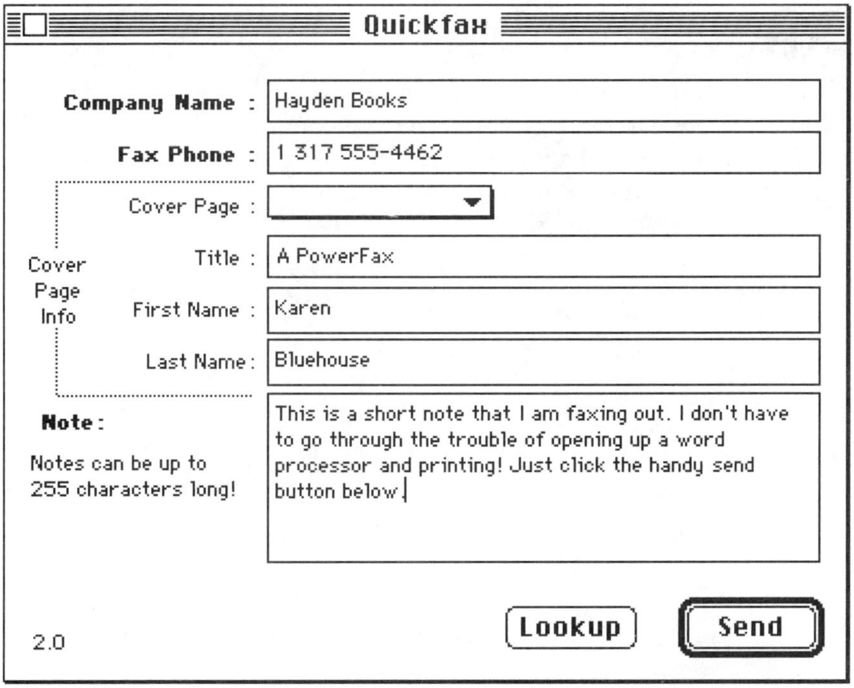

Fig. 4.13. QuickFax can fax a note without using a word processor.

Tips for Sending Faxes:

- Use the Send Later feature of your fax software to send faxes when telephone rates are lower.

- Use a nice, legible typeface such as Lucida from Adobe (and don't make the type too small).

- Use TrueType fonts or Adobe Type Manager. This ensures that text in the fax looks good regardless of the size of the type.

- Avoid Encapsulated PostScript (EPS) Images. Faxes are not PostScript devices, so EPS images fax poorly. Also avoid grayscale and color images. Fax machines act as black-and-white printers.

- Avoid bitmap images such as those created in MacPaint and HyperCard. PICT, or object-oriented graphics, transfer much better at fax resolution.

Reaching Out

Your communications tools provide the means to keep in touch, but you'll still need to manage your time and contacts in order to work with other people. Chapter 5, "Managing Time and Contacts," describes a plethora of programs that can help you get to people you need to see at the time you need to see them.

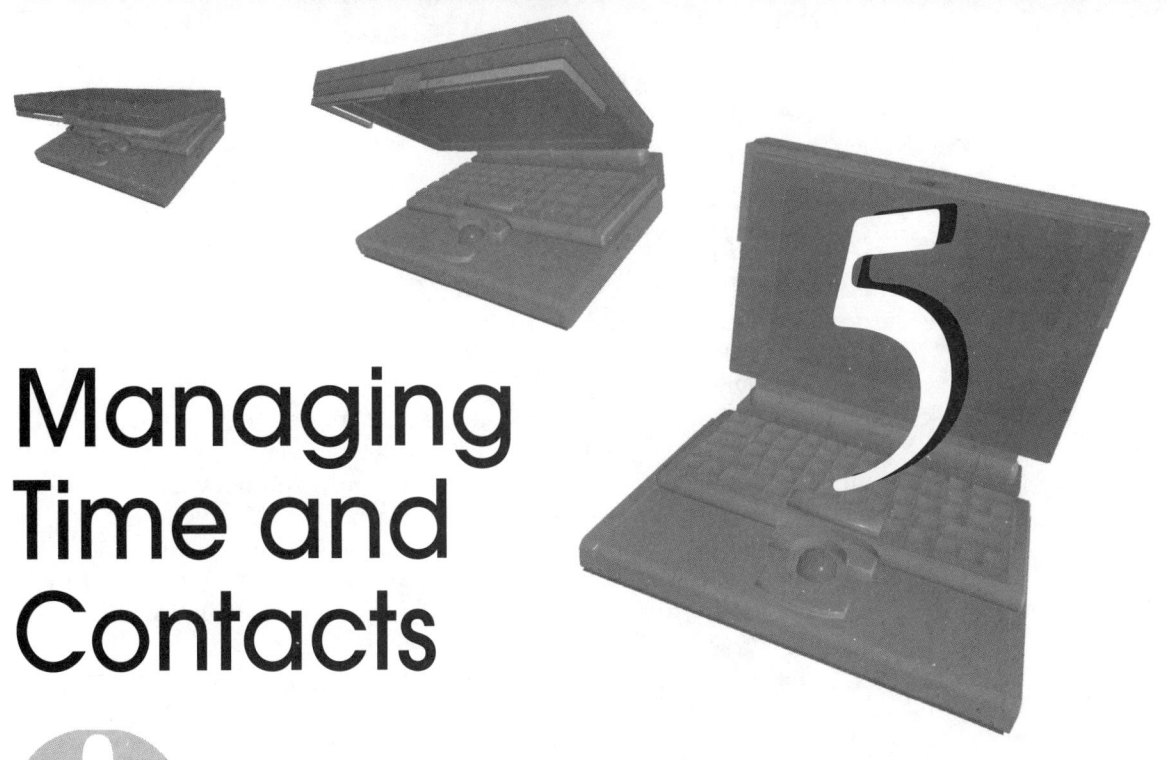

Managing Time and Contacts

O f the thousands of tasks a PowerBook can handle, one of the more mundane yet valuable capabilities is managing time and contacts on the road. The small and lightweight PowerBook 100 in particular, lends itself to keeping in touch when you're away from the home or office. The very announcement of the PowerBook created a surge in the number of products that can act as your personal traveling secretary.

Time and contact managers are sometimes called Personal Information Managers (PIMs). Ideally, a PIM should help you manage time and contacts, but very few applications actually do this. Instead, most Mac software concentrates on either time *or* contacts, providing a rich variety of choices to manage what you need.

Forget-Me-Nots

The first reminder program for the Mac was the Alarm Clock DA. Alarm Clock enabled you to set an alarm that sent your Apple menu flashing. This often incited panic in new users who had a tough time figuring out how to turn off the alarm. Today's less mysterious reminder programs sport enhancements such as a postpone or snooze feature and a choice of alert sounds.

Smart Alarms and Appointment Diary

JAM Software's Smart Alarms was the first commercial reminder program, and it remains among the most configurable. Smart Alarms places two desk accessories in the Apple menu: Smart Alarms (the reminder DA/extension) and Appointments (the scheduling DA). You can convert appointments to Smart Alarms reminders using just a menu selection. JAM Software sells a multi-user version of Appointments Diary which enables you to set common and personal reminders. Reminders also can invoke a macro created with QuicKeys 2 or other macro programs. The pioneering Smart Alarms enables quick data entry in its disorienting window, and with Smart Alarms you can link a reminder to a macro by clicking a checkbox (see figure 5.1).

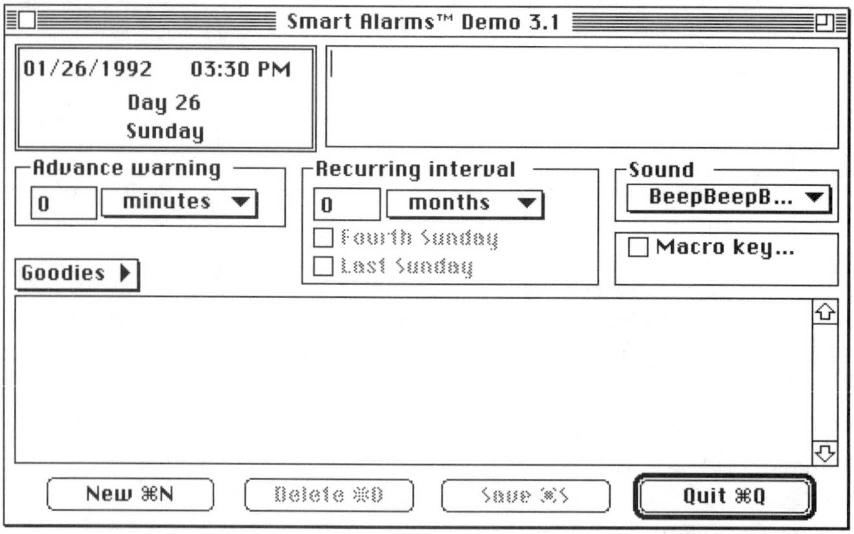

Fig. 5.1.
With Smart Alarms you can link a reminder to a macro.

The Smart Alarms Preferences dialog box is somewhat verbose. For example, the Preferences dialog box enables you to designate applications in which the reminder dialogs should not appear because the dialogs themselves might interrupt time-critical work.

Although Smart Alarms retains one of the speediest reminder entry procedures, some parts of its interface are inconsistent. Smart Alarms has kept up with the pack and includes new features. The latest version even can send text to pagers via Ex Machina's Notify program. All in all, Smart Alarms is a solid choice.

Managing Time and Contacts 5

Alarming Events

As the producer of QuickMail, CE Software has the distinction of being the Macintosh electronic mail (E-mail) leader, edging out Microsoft Mail. But CE Software has an eclectic catalog ranging from applications such as the black-and-white Amazing Paint to utilities such as QuicKeys 2 and Tiles. CE Software's Alarming Events takes a more integrated approach to reminding than Smart Alarms does.

Alarming Events' main calendar window displays an entire year or just a few months, depending on how you resize the window (see figure 5.2). Pressing Return while the main calendar window is open presents the Single Day window, which enables you to enter reminders for a given day. The Single Day window displays a monochrome tree as the default graphic. You can replace the tree, however, with any less environmentally conscious picture of your choice.

Fig. 5.2. The Alarming Events notification window.

Data entry in Alarming Events should be simplified. Five fields and three pop-up menus constantly force you to switch between the trackball and the keyboard. The group of fields and menus doesn't even include another pop-up menu from which to choose from five potential appointment statuses: pop-up alarm, flashing alarm, timed event, to do, and done. The distinctions among the reminder types are based on the types of notification given—you easily can remove the distinctions with a notification method preference. A forthcoming Version 1.1 should help streamline entering reminders.

When Alarming Events notifies you with a dialog box or window, the program presents the text in a hard-to-read font (CE provides an alternative font). Although the window can display a detailed description of the reminder, the window also displays seven icons so small and cryptic that one of the icons is devoted to explaining the other six!

Alarming Events does have a few nice touches. The program tracks the number of days overdue To Do items are. Procrastinating PowerBook owners, however, might like a way to turn off this feature (perhaps

they can write to the company when they get around to it). Alarming Events can print formatted schedules (but not in pocket-organizer form), integrates well with CE's CalendarMaker program, and can specify the duration of reminders (although it provides no graphical display of these durations).

When compared to innovative CE Software titles such as QuicKeys 2 and QuickMail, Alarming Events is slightly disappointing. Its needlessly complicated data entry method and reminder responses discourage daily use.

Easy Alarms

Essential Software is a latecomer to the traditional DA reminder program game. Like scheduling software, Essential Software's Easy Alarms can have multiple calendars open simultaneously. Unfortunately, though, there is no easy way to move reminders between programs. Easy Alarms also operates as an application under System 7.0.

You can send reminders, with their included sounds, across a network to other Easy Alarms users. However, the lack of a server that can hold reminders limits Easy Alarms' networking features for PowerBook owners. If you're not logged on to the network when the reminder is sent, you cannot receive it.

Easy Alarms' New Reminder dialog box facilitates data entry with pop-up menus for month and date. The superior Edit Remember window facilitates rapid entry of appointments with an intelligent tab order and hybrid fields/pop-up menus (see figure 5.3). You can enter time through pop-up menus that double as data-entry fields.

This streamlined approach may confuse new users, but it is a worthwhile innovation. Easy Alarms' calendar window can zoom to occupy the whole screen, but this feature doesn't take advantage of the available space compared to Now Up-to-Date. Although adding Balloon Help would provide clarification for the tiny buttons at the bottom of each calendar, it would be nice to have bigger icons or improved icon labels to provide better clarity.

Notwithstanding, the recently released Version 1.5 of Easy Alarms is poised to become the Ferrari of reminder programs. Version 1.5's exemplary handling of To Do items appeals to people whose tasks are not always time-sensitive. But Easy Alarms' true power comes from its user-scripting language. Easy Alarms may be the first time management program for the Mac that not only reminds you to do something, but actually performs the task for you.

Managing Time and Contacts 5

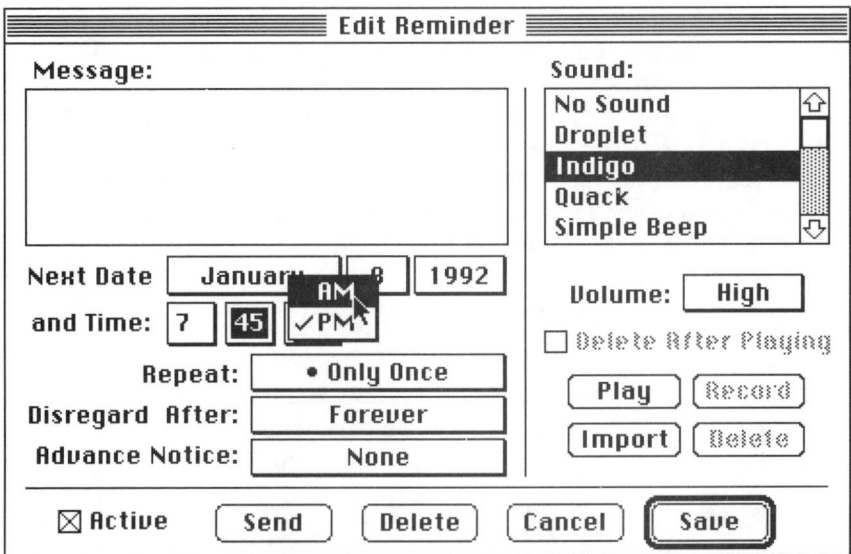

Fig. 5.3.
The Easy Alarms Edit Remember window.

Using AppleEvents, Easy Alarms can tell your backup program to start a backup or your communications program to log on to a certain service. Of course, this facility depends on the availability of programs that support AppleEvents, which continues to grow slowly. Like Smart Alarms, Easy Alarms can send text to a personal pager.

Some reminder programs are small pieces in a larger catalog, whereas Essential understands the Mac market and is committed to Easy Alarms as its centerpiece. With a user-scripting language, Essential already is taking Easy Alarms places no other reminders programs tread.

First Things First

Visionary Software's First Things First (FTF) takes a novel approach to setting reminders. FTF appears as a 1-inch square clock icon that you can move anywhere on the screen. Using its preferences dialog box, you can select either an analog or digital display. Unlike normal Finder icons or palettes that are specific to applications, FTF's clock floats above all applications.

First Things First also conveniently turns itself into a menu bar clock when you drag it into the menu bar or when you Shift-click the First Things First icon. You can't specify the digital clock font as you can with other menu bar clocks. You can, however, drag the clock anywhere in the menu bar, leaving plenty of room for the Balloon Help menu and Caps Lock symbol.

5 Hayden's PowerBook Power Book

Double-clicking the First Things First clock opens a dialog box that enables you to set reminders and preferences. The program can manage both a To Do list and reminders in categories you specify. Using this combination, you can view a particular category of tasks. The dialog box also enables you to set the usual preferences for a reminders program, such as the sound that the reminder triggers. In addition, you can set unique preferences, such as whether you want to see a digital or analog clock. With First Things First's split Preference dialog box, you can choose a default among First Things First's categories and priorities. You also can choose the type of floating clock that appears. (see figure 5.4).

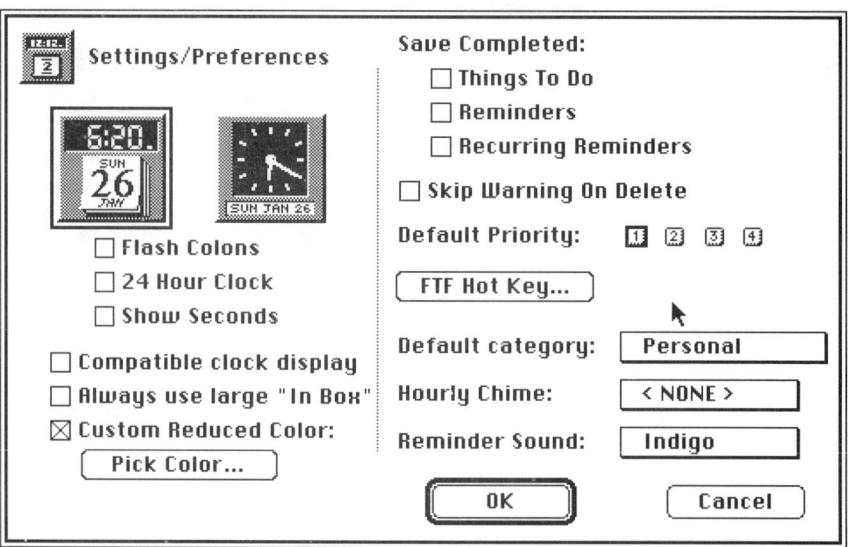

Fig. 5.4. First Things First's split Preferences dialog box.

Already sporting an interface that provided for immediate access via hot key or double click, Visionary bolstered the power of FTF with Version 2.0. The enhancements include prioritized To Do lists, which enable you to assign one of four priority levels to your To Dos. FTF now can create a custom group in which you can combine viewing criteria and provides a "compatibility mode" which confines the program to the menu bar. Although you probably won't experience compatibility problems with this mode turned off, you may prefer to have notifications appear in the menu bar.

PowerBook users should appreciate FTF's convenience and new flexibility. Users may spend some time using the program's new merge utility that enables users to import appointments from more traditional reminder programs. The merge utility also provides what the company

Managing Time and Contacts 5

calls a "merge and purge" method for reconciling two FTF data files. By enabling you to merge reminder files that you modified on the go with reminder files on your home Mac, FTF addresses an important concern of PowerBook users.

The fresh and flexible approach of First Things First probably will win you over. The program's ability to stay quietly in the menu bar not only makes First Things First accessible, it cleverly eliminates the need for another program. Hats off to Visionary for an inspired answer to an ancient software challenge.

> *Tip:* Remember? is a $20 combination desk accessory and extension by Dave Warker that can provide basic reminders. Among its features are multiple calendars that you can use to designate different types of reminders.

Right on Schedule

Originally, scheduling programs were better suited to planning itineraries than reminder programs were. Instead of notifying you about isolated appointments, scheduling programs enable you to map out your entire month at one sitting. That system of scheduling has changed dramatically with the latest batch of programs. New applications enable you to scan the programs' calendar files for items that you mark for reminding. Now a superset of reminder programs, some schedulers remain more complex than simpler reminder programs, but are redefining what people expect from time management programs.

DayMaker

Pastel Development's DayMaker sets a new standard for flexibility in a beautifully designed time manager. Any item you enter in DayMaker becomes either a calendar item or a note item. Calendar items can have different characteristics, such as start and end times, "Done" status, an advance reminder, and even a Gantt chart display. You can include all of these characteristics in multiple columns to which you may have to scroll to gain access. (Pastel should include "panes"—like those in Microsoft Excel—to ease the viewing of columns that are far apart.) DayMaker includes a bare-bones reminder extension that reminds you of specified appointments.

You can enter start and end times using a unique pop-up menu that enables you to select AM or PM, hours, and minutes all at once. One of DayMaker's views of your personal data reflects a traditional calendar. The one-step Time pop-up menu and the Taps pop-up menu enable you to classify appointments quickly (see figure 5.5). It may take some time adapting to DayMaker's strange behavior. However, this approach enables you to change times quickly, undoubtedly a common occurrence for the power scheduler who would find DayMaker appealing.

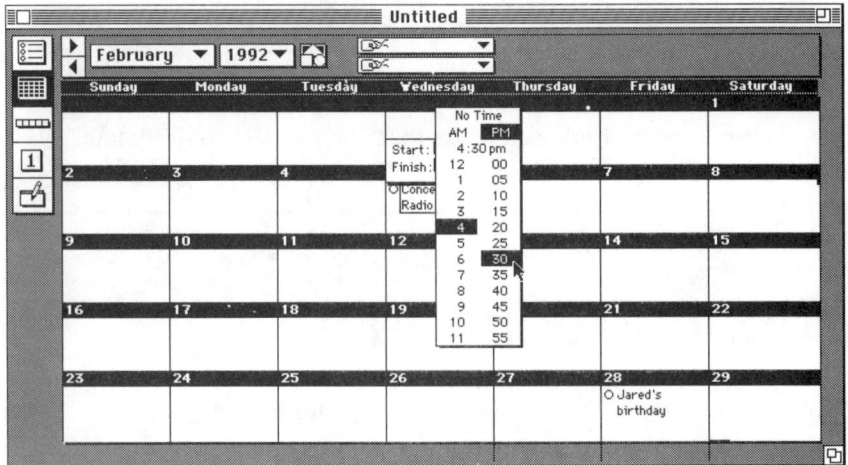

Fig. 5.5. DayMaker enables you to classify appointments quickly.

Items stay in collections marked by tags that specify how the items relate to one another. Tags can be hierarchical, so notes containing inquiry phone numbers for your credit cards and utility bills can have unique tags, but also share the parent tag "Billing." You can round up these items by means of a comprehensive Find command that can search on any characteristic or tag.

Despite a well-designed interface and rare support for Balloon Help, DayMaker is not very intuitive. Actually, the purpose of many of DayMaker's features is not obvious until you begin to rely on the program. Pastel should rename certain menu titles and include task-specific online help like that found in In Control. If your schedule is so diverse that you need to visualize it with Gantt charts or filter schedule items by applying multiple tags, DayMaker is in a class by itself. Despite DayMaker's ease of use, it is not approachable. This makes DayMaker the only product in its category with a learning curve.

Managing Time and Contacts 5

Even if DayMaker's alluring breadth of features entices you, keep in mind that this Cadillac of schedulers needs a sizable garage. DayMaker really shines when you have constant access to it, and its RAM requirement of 700K approaches the requirement of entire integrated software packages.

In Control

In contrast to DayMaker—the abundant features of which can tame even the most unwieldy itinerary—Attain Software's In Control fills what has long been a painful void in Macintosh software: a flexible To Do list manager. The authors of the original FileMaker, a database that evolved into one of the best-selling Macintosh databases, have bound the flexibility of outliners to the easy navigation of spreadsheets to create an easy and useful organizing tool. In Control is one of the few programs with an understandable tool bar (see figure 5.6). The outline/spreadsheet combination falls between simple list programs and project managers. At first glance, the program may appear to be a competitor of Acta 7, a dedicated outlining tool, but both programs deserve a place on your hard disk.

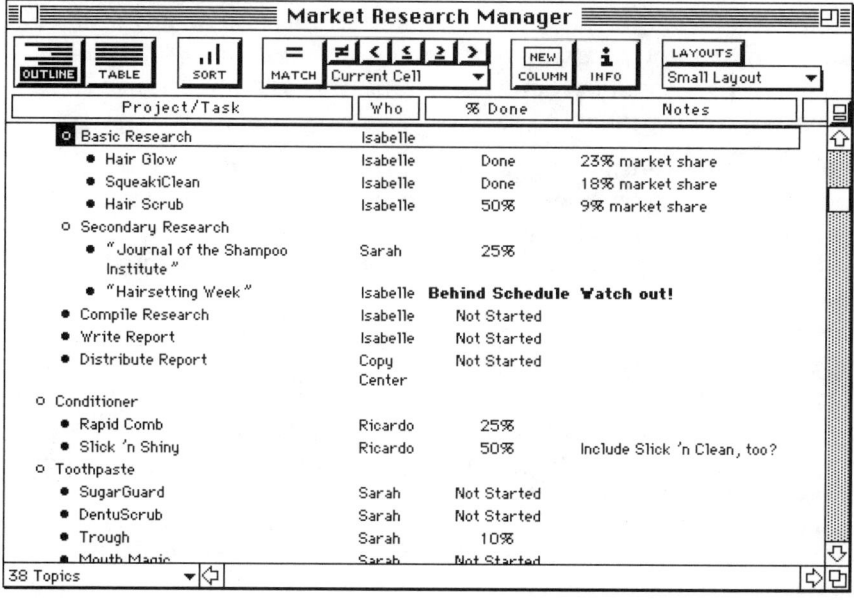

Fig. 5.6. In Control is one of the few programs with an understandable tool bar.

If you've used outliners and spreadsheets, you know how to use In Control. You can view your To Do list in outline form, with minor items indented under major items. Users who dislike outlines can, instead, view the list as a spreadsheet-like table without the gridlines.

Each item in the list has its own row. But unlike Acta 7, which remains ideal for organizing writing, In Control enables you to add aspects to each item in the list through new columns that can list date due, priority, or person responsible. You can sort, switch, or resize all columns, and you can set up data entry shortcuts for repetitive entries.

In Control is a rare gem, but it is not a perfect one. Many applications have been slow to adopt Publish and Subscribe, but these two features are missed in In Control. Otherwise, the focus and compactness of In Control make it a model System 7.0 application. Although it supports a multitude of import and export formats via Claris' XTND technology (see Chapter 4, "Yakety Mac"), this flexibility is no substitute for live data links.

For example, In Control would be much more powerful if it could subscribe to a list of names in a database and change assignments in a project based on changes to the database. Although its freeform listing of items is liberating, it would be helpful to assign steps to the To Do list without making a specific column just for this task. It also would be helpful to have the program perform time calculations or set up task relationships without becoming as overbearing as a project management program or spreadsheet.

This polish notwithstanding, In Control is a handy program that takes a fresh look at task management. Users that rely on the power of MacProject II may see In Control as simplistic. But In Control handles its purpose handily and simply. It is the task manager "for the rest of us."

AgentDA

Many programs provide a variety of views of your time, but none are as versatile as AgentDA. With AgentDA, you can view a window containing two to seven days in a row, and two to five weeks in a column. You quickly can choose the number of weeks or days by clicking the appropriate number in the lower right corner of the window. Shortcut icons that serve as navigational aids are new to Version 2.0. Instead of scrolling through the weeks using the scroll bar, a pop-up menu enables you to drag through the weeks to a particular day. The icon below the menu jumps to the current date.

Managing Time and Contacts 5

These aids are especially helpful because AgentDA does not follow a traditional calendar metaphor: months blend into one another. With AgentDA, Team Building Technologies created a scheduler that is in touch with how most people plan their lives: by the week. The way the program works does take some getting used to. However, AgentDA's design challenges traditional scheduler programs that become awkward when switching between the end of one month and the beginning of the next month.

AgentDA also provides two main views of your schedule: list and grid. The list view usually is the more readable view because it presents appointments in chronological order. The grid view breaks the day into half-hour segments, thus giving you a more graphical picture of how busy your day looks. AgentDA can display up to five weeks of your schedule at once. The program works well with PowerBooks, but it really shines on large screens (see figure 5.7).

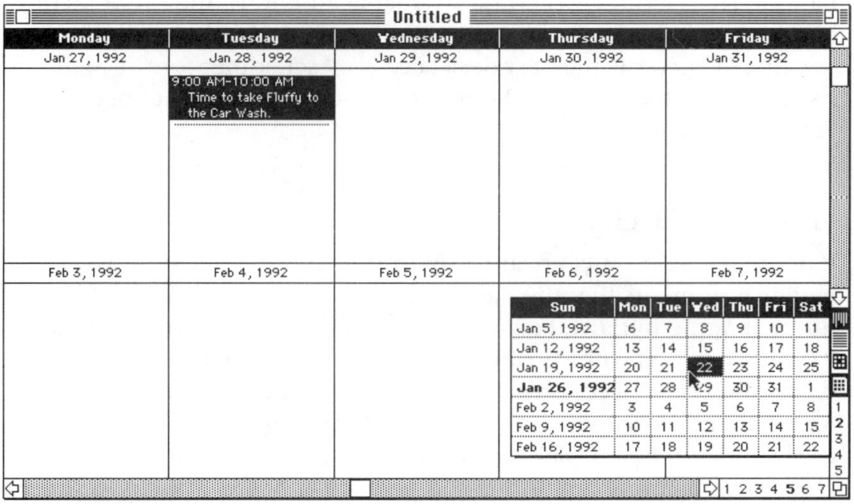

Fig. 5.7.
AgentDA's list view.

AgentDA pioneered a data entry system that embraces the Macintosh interface. To create an appointment, you need only drag from the appointment's start time to its end time. You reschedule appointments by dragging the appointment to the desired day. You can duplicate appointments by Option-dragging. Shift-clicking multiple appointments selects the appointments. Selecting an appointment and pressing Delete removes the appointment.

AgentDA claims it can handle To Do items, but it falls far short of In Control or even Andrew Welch's shareware desk accessory ToDo!. Essentially, in AgentDA, items you do not mark Done are designated as To Do items. There ought to be a way to post events that are not linked to a specific time—not everyone has his or her life pinned down in half-hour increments.

With one of AgentDA's most powerful (yet imperfectly implemented) features, you can copy appointments from one schedule to another. AgentDA does not seem to remember dates moving from one calendar to another—the program requires you to select the proper date in the schedule to which you are pasting. That's not so bad, but pasting events from multiple dates into another AgentDA window disappointingly lumps all the appointments into one date.

The artsy layout of AgentDA's instruction manual's is a bit distracting, but the manual is generously illustrated. Although AgentDA lacks Balloon Help (which would be a valuable addition), the program does have online help. Innovative, lean, fairly intuitive, and extremely flexible, AgentDA is the best desk accessory scheduler for the Mac. Its economy of size makes the program ideally suited to a busy PowerBook user.

Up-to-Date

If nothing else, Now Software's Up-to-Date may be one of most compelling arguments that the days of desk accessories are fading fast. It's not as if Apple outlawed or withdrew support for DAs. In fact, System 7.0 provides DAs with capabilities they never had before. But previously, you could access conveniently only desk accessories from the Apple menu. Now, you can access full-fledged applications just as easily. Indeed, Up-to-Date seems much more at home in the Apple menu than its more ambitious competitor DayMaker (discussed later) does.

Up-to-Date, however, is far more than an odd example among its competitors. The program is perhaps the finest personal scheduling tool for the Mac. Up-to-Date sports an elegant, straightforward interface that deftly handles tasks that other programs make tedious. Now Software obviously surveyed the field in designing Up-to-Date, "borrowing" many of the data entry shortcuts, such as draggable appointments, pioneered in AgentDA.

Managing Time and Contacts 5

Unlike AgentDA, though, Up-to-Date uses a traditional calendar metaphor that makes you feel right at home. With Up-to-Date you can set different types of calendar items. The "see-through months" option allows a peek into other months, if space is available on the calendar (see figure 5.8). This "see-through" feature helps compensate for lack of a perpetual calendar. Up-to-Date also adds thoughtful touches such as scalable date numbers within calendar boxes and banners that can identify events that last several days. It also can print your schedule in a wide variety of formats suitable for personal organizers.

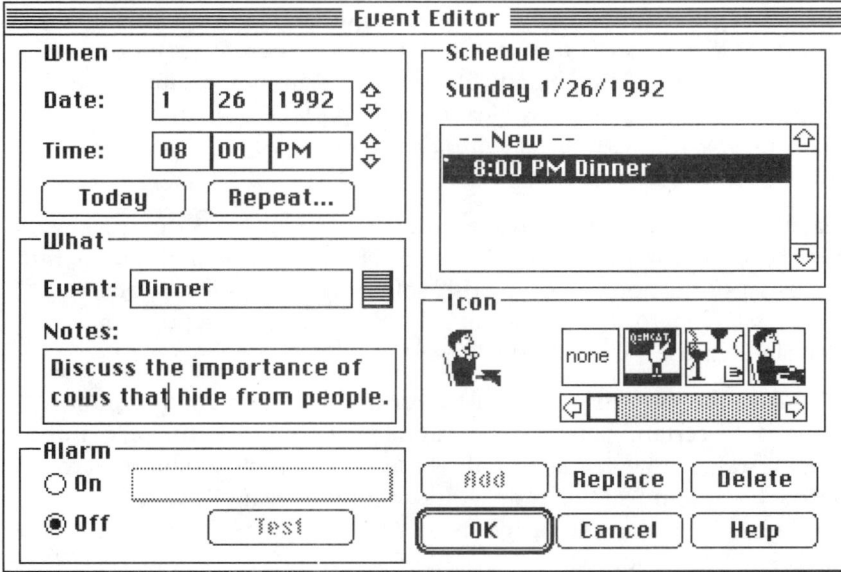

Fig. 5.8.
Up-to-Date's Event Editor.

Up-to-Date's most powerful capabilities are in its networking features. Any Mac running the application can act as a calendar server, to which people can post public events. Other workstations can subscribe to the calendar—the calendar then updates these workstations automatically at defined intervals. Best of all, you can view events from different calendars on the same screen, designated by different type styles.

With a few minor improvements, Up-to-Date would be more than up to par. It would be helpful if—for example—you could title and reduce floating notes to icons within certain calendar days. Better management of the to do list also would be welcome. With Up-to-Date's multiday option, you can view weekly events in a grid, like in AgentDA, but Up-to-Date's multiday option is not as flexible. Nevertheless, Up-to-Date is a convenient, versatile network scheduling program that does not sacrifice the needs of individuals on the network.

The Far Side Calendar

The Far Side Calendar from Amaze! Inc. boasts one feature no other calendar program offers: cartoonist Gary Larson's bizarre sense of humor. The calendar features a different cartoon for each day until the end of 1993. At that point, Amaze! presumably will offer a refill of snakes, cows, insects, cave people, scientists, and nerdy kids that have long populated the perverse comic strip.

Other aspects of the calendar complement Larson's wit. The program sometimes links cartoons to holidays. For example, on Halloween, 1991, a deer opens her apartment door to find trick-or-treaters dressed as hunters. Whenever you launch the program, there is a random chance that you will see equally funny animation. One example is a sequence in which a window cleaner gets splotched on your screen by a giant fly swatter, with the resulting mess being wiped away by another window cleaner.

What's more, Amaze! seems to have more calendar ideas up its sleeve. The Themes menu now lists "The Far Side" as the only menu item, but the design of the application lends itself to new modules. Soon, Amaze! will bring out a new set of calendars designed around the syndicated cartoon strip "Cathy."

If The Far Side were as capable as other calendars, its entertainment value would certainly make it the calendar of choice on the Mac. But a modal interface that seems to follow the least-common-denominator approach to support Microsoft Windows hinders The Far Side's usefulness. Certainly, the program is not a serious contender for a cross-platform standard.

The Far Side's most glaring omission is the lack of an extension to notify you of reminders when the calendar program isn't open. Because the program uses 512K, it is difficult to justify keeping the program open all the time, unless you intend to waste your battery time chuckling at the Far Sides of yesterday or seven months ago. On the other hand, the program provides a number of humorous animated icons that can serve as different types of reminders. The Far Side Calendar may not win awards for interface or features, but its sense of humor and animated icons make each event enjoyable (see figure 5.9).

With its humorous cartoons, amusing animation, and distracting icons eating several megabytes of hard disk space, The Far Side may be one of the least practical calendar programs for PowerBook. How could Larson have it any other way?

Managing Time and Contacts 5

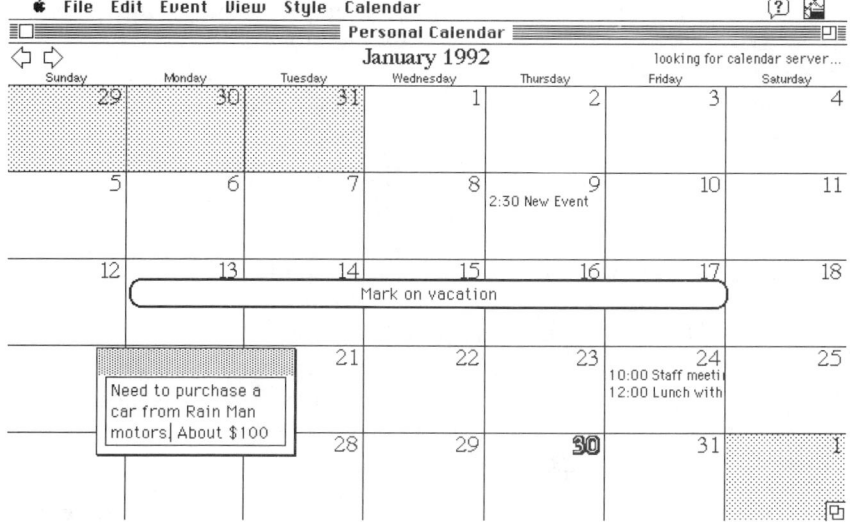

Fig. 5.9.
The Far Side Calendar contains animated icons for each event.

Jot Lag

If Alarm Clock was the Mac's first reminder program, Note Pad probably was the Mac's first address book. As a last resort, you always can grab this simple DA from the Apple menu and enter a name or number. For more sophisticated tasks, however, you may want to consider an address manager.

Address managers are specialized databases, a category of software that keeps track of information using fields and records. If you think of a Rolodex-like card file as a simple database, each individual card is a record and each piece of information on that card is a field.

In theory, an advanced database could handle the features that address managers offer if you had the inclination and expertise to create such a database. However, it would take a great deal of time and effort to replicate the convenience and power of address managers.

Address managers typically have fields already set up for names, addresses, and phone numbers. Some address managers contain special shortcuts that automatically format telephone numbers, saving you from typing those pesky parentheses. Many address managers also feature goodies such as dialing phone numbers, painless printing of envelopes, fax cover sheets, and paper-based personal organizers such as Filofax and DayRunner. Address managers fall into two categories: "free-form" and "structured."

Free-form address managers are well-suited to a quick jotting down of personal phone numbers. One of their most frustrating omissions is

lack of a Sort command. You cannot, for example, sort by address or zip code. The ability to sort, however, would at least encourage some consistency to files. Without this capability, it is easy for records to slip into random order. As a result, you must rely on the managers' rudimentary (albeit fast) Find command.

QuickDEX II

Casady & Greene's original QuickDEX program became a staple among Mac enthusiasts because of its lightning speed and free-form design. QuickDEX's sequel, QuickDEX II, continues the fine tradition of providing instant access to important information. Although QuickDEX II's layout remains among the simplest of all free-form address managers, Casady & Greene neglected some important features and interface traits.

QuickDEX II contains a window with two fields: one for data and one for search criteria. You can control the font and size of the data displayed. In addition, the window scrolls to accommodate long blocks of text. Most QuickDEX II commands appear in a menu that is so long it that it scrolls off the PowerBook screen. This is one desk accessory that would benefit from a Dynodex-like icon bar.

A major advantage that QuickDEX II retains is the capability of having multiple files ("card decks," in QuickDEX lingo) open at one time (see figure 5.10). In an astonishingly simple program, this masterstroke of flexibility enables you to keep several different categories of databases instantly available. This is a trick that some of the more advanced address databases cannot perform from their DA component. Casady & Greene capitalized on this advantage—you can switch between QuickDEX windows with a few predefined command keys.

QuickDEX II also boasts some of the most advanced dialing rules of any desk accessory. The program accommodates dialing credit card and local calls, and allows for exceptions when you are in certain area codes.

QuickDEX II has both an integrated approach to managing different databases and an unfettered Rolodex-inspired design. These two features make QuickDEX II a superior tool for managing bits of information that are not necessarily related to contacts.

Managing Time and Contacts 5

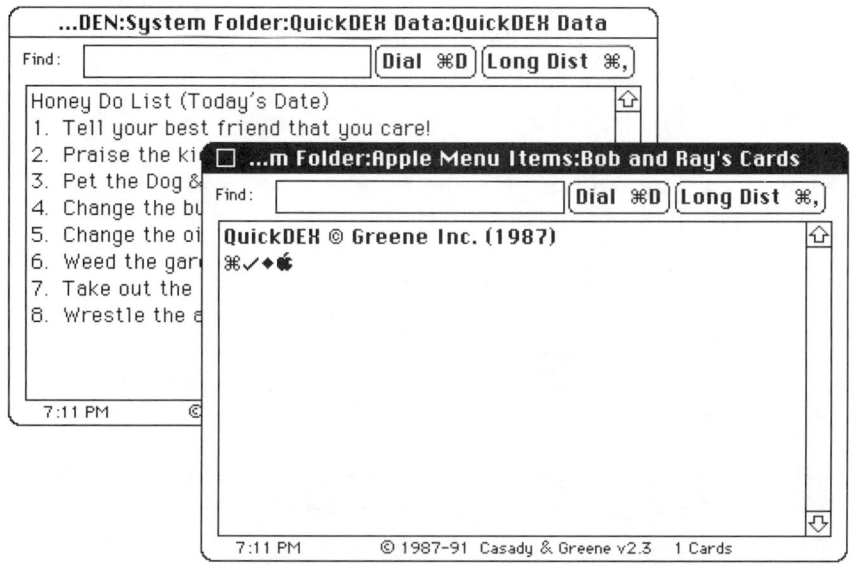

Fig. 5.10.
QuickDEX II enables you to have multiple card decks open at one time.

Unfortunately, QuickDEX II still lacks basic envelope-making capabilities. However, Casady & Greene is preparing to release an upgrade called SuperQuickDEX. SuperQuickDEX enhances the application's printing and envelope-making capabilities by adding two programs called Quickelope and PrintDEX II. This relatively expensive upgrade, however, probably won't match the integration already contained in INTouch.

INTouch

Advanced Software's INTouch stepped into the race before QuickDEX II in an attempt to court users frustrated with the long lag time before Casady & Greene shipped a worthy successor to QuickDEX. Like QuickDEX, INTouch doesn't store phone numbers, addresses, and fax numbers in separate fields. The program, however, does suggest more structure than QuickDEX.

INTouch's main window is divided. You are supposed to enter names and addresses in the left window and phone numbers in the right window. INTouch doesn't complain if you enter the phone number in the wrong field, but the program has a more difficult time dialing the number. Advanced Software designed the INTouch phone field as a place to take notes, and you can enlarge the field with a special zoom

box. QuickDEX's approach to having everything in a single field has its advantages, but the zoom box is an acceptable compromise that steers your eyes toward the data you need.

A number of on-screen buttons distribute INTouch's controls between a short, simple menu and the INTouch window. INTouch's main window separates addresses from phone numbers and notes. The DA can print envelopes and copy entire addresses with one mouse click (see figure 5.11). Navigational arrows enable you to move from record to record, and a camera button captures all the address information you need to paste into a letter in your word processor. In one revealing comparison, QuickDEX's manual lists 12 steps you must perform to make a card the default card; INTouch can revert automatically to the last card you selected.

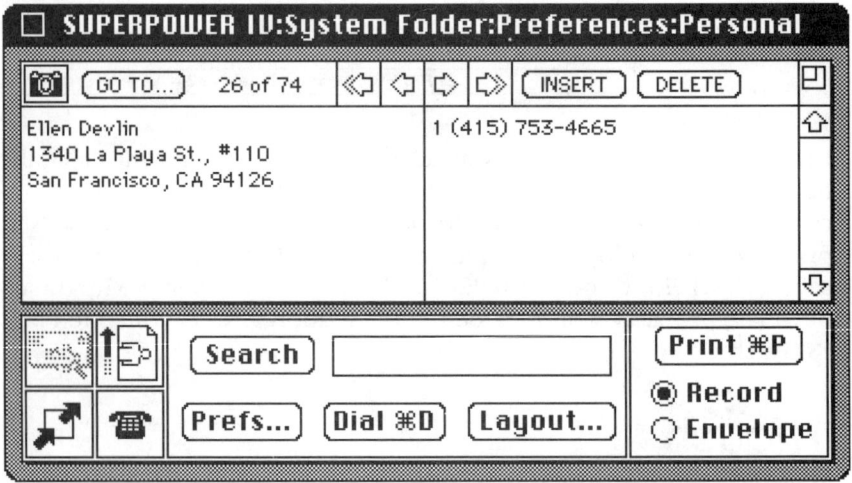

Fig. 5.11. INTouch prints envelopes and copies entire addresses with one mouse click.

With another button click, you can use INTouch's flexible envelope editor, complete with multiple return addresses and print preview. You can further enhance the envelope editor with Snap. Snap is a bundled control panel with which you can automatically paste address information into INTouch without opening the DA and pasting manually. Some users may question the importance of being able to print envelopes on the road. However, it is nice that you don't have to import contacts into another database when you arrive home.

INTouch and QuickDEX II both have speedy search commands. However, INTouch's more intuitive keyboard navigation commands

Managing Time and Contacts 5

(QuickDEX does not use the arrow keys) and Go To button facilitate moving among records. This is why the lack of a Sort command is an unfortunate omission for INTouch. Such a command would make for more effective browsing in an INTouch file. To its credit, though, INTouch does enable you to export data to a database that can sort.

Another quibble is that INTouch stubbornly prevents you from deleting, moving, or even exempting from export the first record. The first record contains information on how to contact Advanced Software. Although this information is handy, the program could store the information in the otherwise uninformative About box. Insisting on keeping the information in the database itself forces cleanup if you ever need to export INTouch's database for eventual use in a mail merge of other lists.

INTouch is network-aware, meaning you can place INTouch data files on a server and retain access to the data files through separately sold copies of INTouch. When someone modifies the record you are viewing, you see a small padlock in the window. This notifies you that the record you see is in use and you cannot modify it until it is available. This feature makes INTouch attractive as a central location for storing informal contacts such as local suppliers of food and office supplies. At under 200K of disk space, INTouch is much lighter than the Yellow Pages.

Playing the Fields

Typically, structured address managers are combinations of applications and desk accessories that quickly can search on any criterion from telex to car phone. All advanced address managers structure little pieces of information into fields. Address Book Plus, for example, can designate more than nine different types of phone numbers in any of four phone number fields. Names are broken down into prefix (such as Dr. or Mrs.), first name, last name, and suffix (such as Jr. or D.D.S.).

This piecemeal breakdown of data offers several advantages over free-form databases. For example, you easily can sort your lists by last name, state, zip code, or any combination of these items. You can assign different categories to different people and easily export a subset of the list. You then can use the list for any purpose from party invitations to collection notices (or perhaps both, if you're genteel enough to bring up delinquency in an informal setting).

Dynodex and Address Book Plus

Portfolio System' Dynodex was the first structured address manager for the Mac. This company pioneered many features that Dynodex' competitors have since imitated. Shortcut keys for data entry, double-sided printing of popular portable address book formats, advanced sorting features, and performing multiple operations on a selection of records all appeared first in Portfolio System's product.

It seems, though, that Power Up's Address Book Plus has caught up with—and in some cases surpassed—Dynodex on a feature-by-feature basis. Both programs offer a plethora of printing, dialing, sorting, and selecting criteria. In addition, both programs offer two data entry shortcuts. Dynodex remains the speedier tool for most functions, but Address Book Plus enables you to dial directly any of a multitude of phone numbers with a single command key.

So Address Book Plus and Dynodex now are deadlocked in a rendition of "Anything you can do, I can do better." The more you use both programs, the more difficult it becomes to differentiate between them. This leaves you to assess the less-tangible features, such as aesthetics and company direction, to determine which program best fits your needs.

The compact design and blazing speed of Dynodex make the program almost as convenient as unstructured desk accessories. However, Dynodex' diverse printing capabilities far surpass those programs. Dynodex' main entry screen is smaller than the screens of its competitors, but the screen accommodates most items you would want to see at a glance. In what is becoming a trend in graphical software—particularly in the Microsoft Windows side of the world—Dynodex sports an icon bar with which you can activate frequently used functions. As is the case with other icon bars, the Dynodex icon bar contains some buttons that are not intuitive. The selection button, for example, looks as if it generates a pie graph (see figure 5.12).

Pokey and ungainly Address Book Plus boasts a wealth of automatic data-formatting options you can configure on the fly. If Dynodex' data entry screen is too small, though, Address Book Plus' screen is too big, eating up more than half of the screen (see figure 5.13). However, with Address Book Plus' bundled DA, you can browse records more economically. The interface and manual of Address Book Plus are more refined than the interface and manual of Dynodex, which are crammed with lots of helpful hints in a cluttered fashion. Both programs could use a layout editor to save time and space by helping you use only the fields you need.

Managing Time and Contacts 5

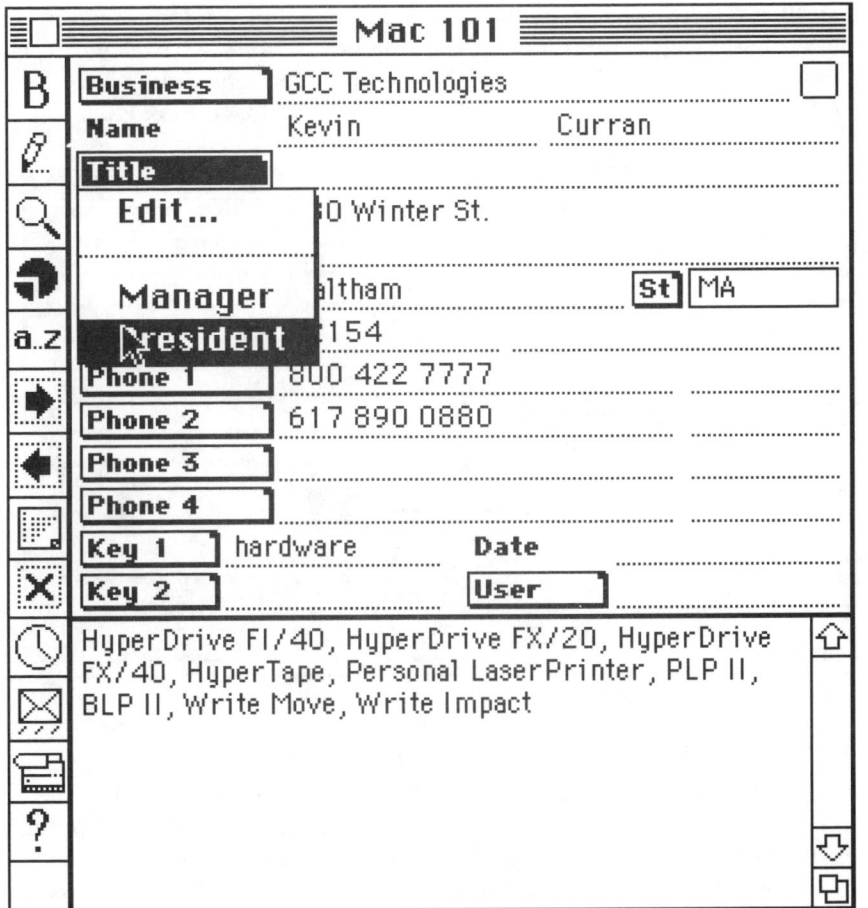

Fig. 5.12. Dynodex' icon bar contains both intuitive & non-intuitive icons.

Portfolio Systems seems focused on producing products that extend the concept of bridging computer and paper data. In addition to bundling custom laser printer paper with Dynodex, Portfolio Systems offers DynoPage, a printing utility that can output nearly any Macintosh file to the same types of personal organizers Dynodex supports. Portfolio Systems also is working to extend Dynodex' interaction with other utilities by means of AppleEvents support in the forthcoming Dynodex 3.0.

Power Up, on the other hand, has a formidable collection of DOS utilities as well as companion Macintosh utilities. Power Up capitalized on this collection by offering an easy method for combining Address Book data with Power Up's lean word processing desk accessory LetterWriter Plus. The pairing provides a very convenient way to handle a variety of tasks, including simple mail merges, for a fraction of the cost and RAM requirements of an integrated software package. The joining of DOS and Mac utilities also provides for some transportability of data between the Mac and DOS versions of Address Book Plus.

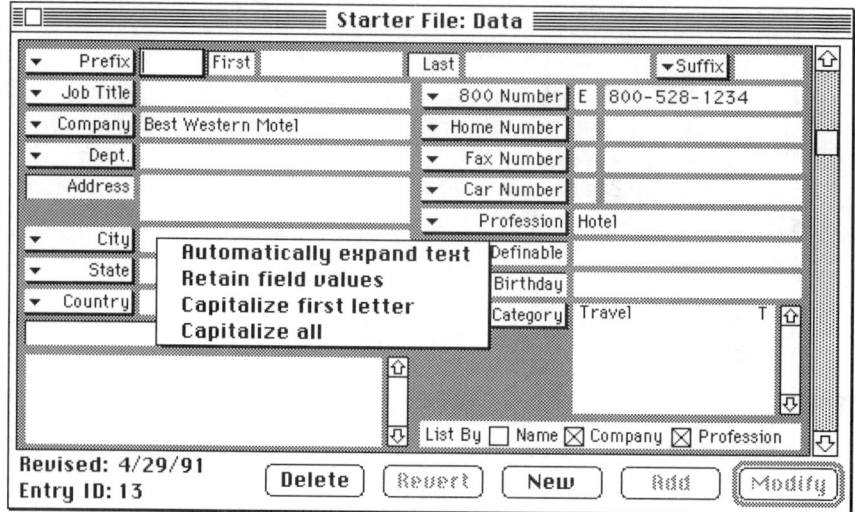

Fig. 5.13. Address Book Plus takes up more than half the screen.

TouchBASE

TouchBASE by After Hours Software has one of the most comfortable interfaces of the structured address managers. You control most of the customizing options of TouchBASE from a single menu at the top of the screen. Unlike Dynodex, TouchBASE has no vague buttons in its data entry screen. TouchBASE's window combines a compact layout with legibility. The label area combines several fields that enable you to copy addresses with a single menu choice. Unlike Address Book Plus, TouchBASE has no strange dialing codes that change with each record. Instead, TouchBASE's detail view shows three simple, self-explanatory buttons: New, Cancel, and Save (see figure 5.14). The tradeoff is that TouchBASE lacks some of its competitors' data-entry and dialing shortcuts.

Most of the time, you are working in one of two easy-to-read views, simply named "detail" and "list." Unlike Dynodex and Address Book Plus, TouchBASE prevents you from viewing both windows simultaneously. With TouchBASE, however, you can advance "frame by frame" in the detail view. In the list view, you see a spreadsheet-like grid with rows of records and columns of fields with such data as names, addresses, and phone numbers. Originally, you couldn't change the

Managing Time and Contacts 5

fields the list view displayed, but you have full control over this in Version 2.0. To change the fields, hold the mouse button down and a pop-up menu enables you to choose any field.

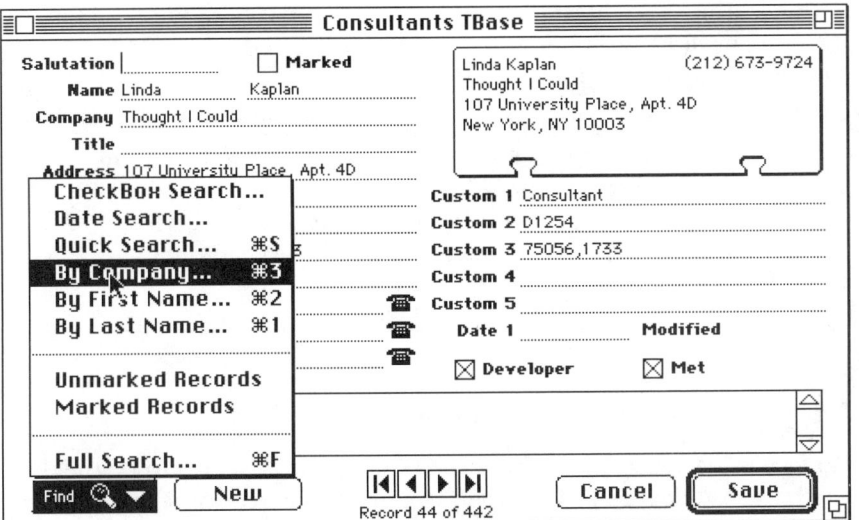

Fig. 5.14.
The TouchBASE window combines a compact layout with legibility.

Only TouchBASE can export data directly to a Sharp Wizard, a popular electronic data organizer that fits in your coat pocket. Address Book Plus can create text files to exchange with the Wizard or its main competitor, the Casio BOSS. However, you still must use separate—and sometimes clunky—file transfer software to transfer the data to the Wizard or BOSS.

Using TouchBASE, you simply connect the Wizard to your serial port and export away. The Wizard complements the PowerBook because the Wizard sacrifices versatility and compatibility for small size and long battery life. Compact as they are, personal organizers often are not as easy to use as your PowerBook. The ability to use TouchBASE as a front end is a clever and welcome feature that time management programs should adopt.

TouchBASE is the only structured address manager that supports network access. This means that several people can access a TouchBASE file at once, provided they all have a copy of TouchBASE on their Macs. Of course, because a PowerBook can access any network services using AppleTalk Remote Access, you can log in and view the file on the road as well. If a future version of TouchBASE can enable you to reconcile local and remote files automatically, TouchBASE could become the ideal workgroup contact manager.

117

TouchBASE is available only as a desk accessory, even under System 7.0. This prevents the DA from using System 7.0 features such as drag-and-drop opening and setting memory allocation. Ironically, though, TouchBASE is the only program to support Balloon Help at the time of this writing. TouchBASE compensates for the lack of file double-clicking by featuring a hierarchical Open command to which you can add frequently opened files.

> *Tip:* Jim Leitch's elegant $30 Address Book (not to be confused with the commercial Address Book Plus) may be all you need to keep track of names, addresses, and phone numbers. The shareware application and desk accessory even can track the length of phone calls.

Making Connections

On face value, Concentrix Software's Connections seems to be the answer to a disorganized person's dreams. Connections is the only product to combine a solid, structured address database with a flexible calendar, incorporating reminders and to-do lists. You can navigate through a resizeable tear-off palette. With Connections' elegant interface you can rearrange appointments by dragging time slots (see figure 5.15). Connections' palette connects you to other stacks in the collection. Connections is deep: With other programs you dial the phone through the Mac, whereas Connections maintains a call history with your notes on the call. You even can generate letters from within the program.

Connections' feature list goes on. The program can print schedules on personal organizers and—with some limitations—can notify you of changes made to a calendar shared over a network. If you want Connections to manage a particular task, modules can expand the program's functionality further. In fact, this well-conceived manager raises only one bone of contention, but this bone is big enough for a dinosaur skeleton.

Unlike other products available as applications or desk accessories, Connections was created in HyperTalk, the language used to customize HyperCard. A versatile application, HyperCard enables users to create databases incorporating words, numbers, and pictures by using HyperCard's built-in tools. HyperTalk's ease of learning and syntax management get your projects off the ground quickly, but the language's speed and power lag behind the more popular Pascal and C languages.

Managing Time and Contacts 5

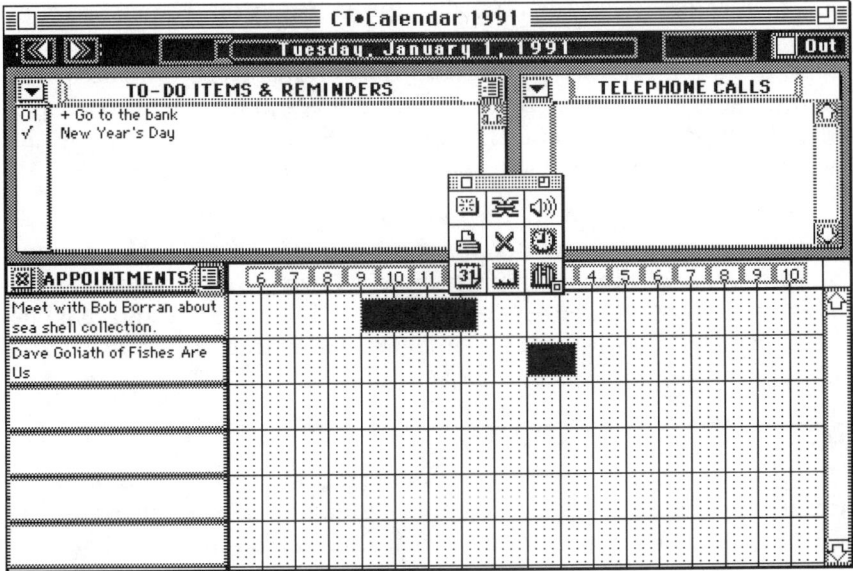

Fig. 5.15.
With Connections you can rearrange appointments by dragging their time slots.

As such, Connections soars and sags on the wings of HyperTalk. HyperCard's dynamic method of associating data facilitates integration among HyperCard's varied modules, but HyperCard's unique programming environment forces some interface compromises. For example, when changing the export order of fields, many programs enable you to drag fields into the fields' new export order. Because of HyperCard's weak dialog box support, though, you must rely on cumbersome Up and Down buttons to bring Connections' fields into the desired export order.

Connections is relatively easy to use considering its wealth of features. However, new users have to learn HyperCard conventions in addition to the standard Macintosh interface—the two are sometimes contradictory. For example, clicking an icon in the Finder selects that icon, and clicking a HyperCard icon opens that icon.

Connections' network and battery-saving features cater to PowerBooks. However, HyperCard's voracious RAM and hard disk requirements generally make HyperCard a candidate for the Trash on many PowerBooks. Even on a PowerBook 170, Connections is not especially speedy. In addition, you must allocate a whopping 1.2M of RAM and 4M of disk space to run the Connections program. You easily can run a beefy calendar and contacts management program in a fraction of that space.

Hayden's PowerBook Power Book

Potential errors in the HyperCard scripts expose Connections users to double jeopardy. Users first must worry about bugs in HyperCard's code and then worry about bugs in Connections' HyperCard scripts. In addition, information management programs should be approachable. The last thing new users need to see is hundreds of lines of HyperTalk when they click Debug in response to a HyperTalk error message.

Connections may be one of the most ambitious collections of HyperCard stacks ever written. Experienced HyperCard hackers will find a boundless and eminently customizable tool in Connections. For most users, though, Connections' RAM, hard disk, speed, and reliability concerns point toward a less integrated solution.

Selling the Dream

Connections is reminiscent of another category of software geared toward PowerBook, but that category's breadth and specialized purpose preclude it from in-depth discussion. Lead management programs such as Westware's Contact Ease and SuperOffice combine databases with mail merge and time management. Primarily, however, these types of applications are intended for sales professionals. If you purchased your PowerBook to help you with your sales career, one of these specialized programs may suit you better than a combination of the tools discussed in this chapter.

On the Horizon

The high tide of products vying for PowerBook owners' attention continues to inspire PIMs that integrate time and contact management. Late in 1992, Contact Software International plans to release its long-anticipated Macintosh version of its popular DOS program ACT!. The integration of ACT! may set new standards for Macintosh PIMs. ProAct Software soon will release TimeBook, another time and contact manager. TimeBook conserves screen space by using a traditional personal organizer interface while allowing the use of additional plug-in modules.

After Hours Software, makers of the popular TouchBASE desk accessory, will complement that product with DateBook, an application integrated with its contacts DA. In addition, ASD Software will introduce a new version of Active Memory, a flexible time manager that uses lists as opposed to the calendar to manage a variety of time management tasks.

Managing Time and Contacts 5

Conclusions

It makes sense to keep your scheduling and contact information in the same program. However—except for the HyperCard-based Connections program—no Mac program handles both scheduling and contact information well. As a result, you should select the application on either side that best suits your needs.

If all you need is a simple reminders program, Visionary's accessible First Things First combines a slick interface with basic scheduling capabilities. Having different categories of reminders greatly eases reminder management. Feature-packed Easy Alarms is ideal both for users more comfortable with a calendar interface for reminders, as well as users who like to plan computing activities around reminders.

On the other hand, users with demanding schedules will delight in dragging their appointment days all over the screen with AgentDA. Now Up-to-Date makes you wish AgentDA used a more traditional calendar metaphor, but AgentDA's easily modifiable schedule views offer more flexibility. If you have the RAM, get Now Up-to-Date. And if you have a need for group scheduling, get the RAM. Up-to-Date's thoughtful design make it a product you'll love to use.

If you're the type of person whose day is more task-driven than time-driven, In Control may win you over. Although it would be unpleasant to see the product become yet another scheduler, additional time management controls would broaden In Control's appeal.

The leapfrogging features game in the fiercely competitive contact management field leaves little to distinguish products. For formal contact management, TouchBASE's pleasing interface and networking features put it a notch above the speedy Dynodex and the flexible Address Book Plus. Users who need only to jot down names and phone numbers will find a handy tool in INTouch, which also can share files over a network.

Productivity Enhancers

Back home, you wish for more storage bays in your Quadra 900, but on the road you must settle for a PowerBook 170 with a 100M hard disk, 8M of RAM, cellular v.32bis fax modem, and enough battery power to make a DieHard jealous.

This is the chapter for power users.

This chapter discusses some of the best Mac utilities and software add-ons no Mac junkie would be without. Most of these programs come in the form of extensions and control panels, relatively small programs that provide new functionality when you drag them into the System Folder.

Although you wouldn't think twice about using many of these fine programs on your desktop Macs, you should weigh heavily the ramifications for souping up your PowerBook software. Especially in a low-RAM environment, the system memory used by extensions quickly adds up, perhaps not leaving enough memory to run your applications. This limitation is especially apparent in 2M configurations that don't leave much RAM for necessities, much less frills. Experienced users express frustration at being unable to customize their portable computing environment the way they can at home.

System extensions faithfully adhere to the law of diminishing returns. Although each extension enables you to accomplish routines with more finesse, extensions sometimes conflict with each other and with application software. Even with good diagnostic tools, you can go mad trying to decipher the combination of extensions that is making your PowerBook act strangely. And keeping up with frequent updates that fix obscure bugs and adding new features to stay competitive has become a nontrivial pursuit.

Conflicting extensions often cause system errors and other anomalies. If you usually have people by your side to hold your hand, those people might not be available remotely. Programs such as Timbuktu and Carbon Copy (see Chapter 4, "Yakety Mac") sometimes can help when you're isolated. On the other hand, because programs such as Timbuktu and Carbon Copy are extensions themselves, they sometimes can complicate the picture. Such programs also lose much of their usefulness when you must restart frequently, as is often the case when you diagnose extension conflicts.

In short, support services available to you at home probably cannot travel with you, so it's often safer to forego the use of unnecessary extensions on the road. On the other hand, if none of these caveats worries you and you're ready to throw caution to the wind to make your PowerBook sail through mundane tasks, prepare to explore the best ways to juice the machine's real power.

Power Launch

Although the Finder provides an excellent structure for file organization, it traditionally has been weak when opening files buried deep within layers of folders. File launchers have become less important in the System 7.0 era. In System 7.0, aliases and the configurable Apple menu provide most of their original benefits, but these utilities have evolved to offer new advantages and extend System 7.0's capabilities. There are two types of file launchers: those that create their own launch menu (such as Icom Simulations' On Cue II), and those that create hierarchical menus within the Apple menu (such as Microseeds' HAM).

Three popular launchers that create their own menu are On Cue II, Connectix' HandOff II, and Now Utilities' MultiMaster. All three programs place a menu at the extreme right or left of the menu bar. You can place your favorite programs and documents in this menu. On Cue II and HandOff II enable you to group related files in folders and

Productivity Enhancers 6

launch multiple files with one menu selection. For users whose flying fingers can't stand to leave the keyboard, MultiMaster provides keyboard activation along with the standard launch menu. MultiMaster enables you to launch files using a window that provides a variation on its menu (see figure 6.1).

Fig. 6.1. Launching files with MultiMaster.

MultiMaster and HandOff II enable you to hide windows automatically as you move among programs, a useful feature under System 7.0; HandOff II and On Cue II enable you to assign default options for applications. For example, On Cue II can specify default folders for programs; that is, whenever you open MacDraw and choose Open or Save, you see the "MacDraw Files" folder. HandOff II can specify default sound levels and colors for applications, which are two less important options for PowerBook owners.

HandOff II comes with SuperMenu, an extension that causes Apple menu items to appear in a hierarchy. When you drag folders into the Apple Menu Items folder, the folders become hierarchical menu items that enable you to directly launch folder contents from submenus. In addition to MultiMaster, Now Utilities includes NowMenus, which performs a similar function, described later. The field of competition grew even larger when AlSoft recently released MenuExtend as part of its AlSoft Power Utilities collection.

Nevertheless, the Cadillac of Apple menu managers is Microseeds' HAM (Hierarchical Apple Menu). HAM enables you to control the order of the Apple menu items listing, as well as deactivate individual Apple menu items. The program also provides a Recent Items menu that enables you to select file folders, files, and even file servers that you recently accessed (see figure 6.2).

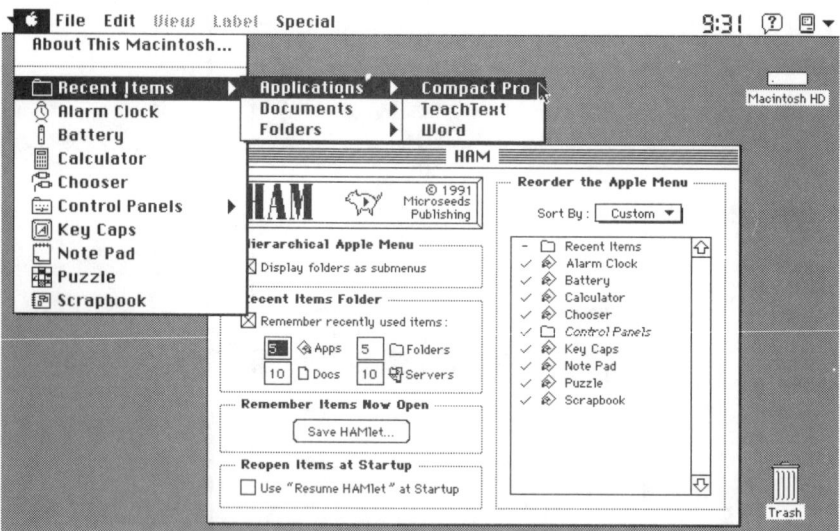

Fig. 6.2.
HAM's Recent Items menu feature.

Recent File Servers works well with remote access, saving you the hassle of using the Chooser to select file servers you last accessed. However, because the program causes your PowerBook to access the hard disk every time you open a folder or file, you may want to avoid this battery drainer. In addition, HAM uniquely enables you to assign groups of documents and applications that you can open with one menu selection, called a "HAMlet."

Two shareware control panels provide the basic functionality of hierarchical Apple Menu makers: BeHierarchic by Fabien Octave and

Productivity Enhancers 6

Menu Choice by Kerry Clendinning. Each control panel contains features not found in the commercial offerings. *Note:* If you come across a utility called Magic Apple, it may appear to offer similar functions, but Magic Apple is a buggy prerelease version of SuperMenu that you should avoid.

Although the positioning of the PowerBook's trackball makes it more accessible than on any other portable, programs that allow keyboard access retain an advantage on the road. Icom Simulations' On Cue II and Now's MultiMaster stand out because they enable you to open files from the keyboard.

You do not have to configure On Cue II's keyboard-launching functions or configure groups of files to open together. On Cue II's QuickFinder desk accessory excels at rounding up similar files spread out among many folders. These features, combined with On Cue II's considerable RAM appetite, make On Cue II well-suited only for PowerBook users with RAM to burn. However, the program can't be justified if you already use MultiMaster in the recommended Now Utilities (discussed later).

Nailing Files

CE Software's DiskTop and Fifth Generations' DiskTools (a component of Fifth Generation Systems' File Director) have long been file-juggling standards for users who wanted to avoid returning to the Finder. The two programs operate as more flexible versions of the Open dialog box, providing a list view of files and folders that you can sort by name, size, or date. Finder 7.0—which is always active—has made many of DiskTop's and DiskTools' features redundant. The programs, however, can copy and move files completely through the keyboard, which Finder 7.0 cannot.

A noteworthy addition to this genre is On Disk, part of On Cue II. On Disk can move almost any group of items or their aliases to nine folders that are significant in System 7.0. Like older utilities, On Disk provides list views of your files, but it features enhancements expressly for System 7.0. One such feature is a "Move to Special Folders" command that can move files directly to the Apple Menu Items folder for easy access (see figure 6.3). On Disk also follows Finder 7.0 conventions for moving through the Desktop layer and enables you to view privileges for any folder easily. On Disk's Find command is so fast that it can scan the entire PowerBook hard drive in a fraction of a second.

6 Hayden's PowerBook Power Book

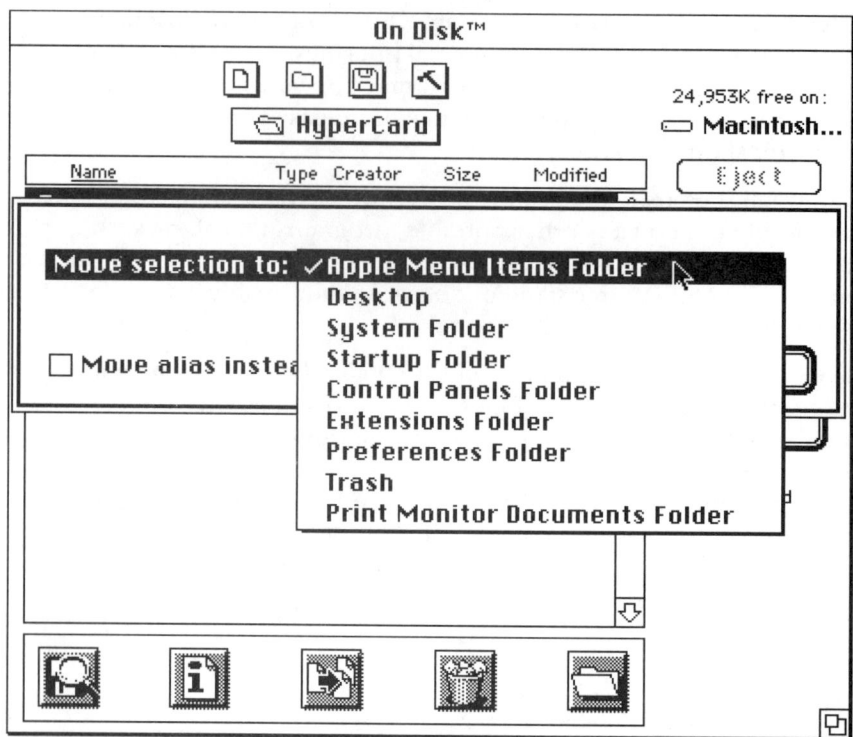

Fig. 6.3. On Disk's "Move to Special Folders" command.

Another advantage of On Disk is that the program is accessible from where you often need it most—from an application's Open and Save dialog boxes. Other programs such as Now Utilities' SuperBoomerang and Aladdin Systems' ShortCut also operate from the standard Open and Save dialog boxes, but only On Disk provides the same features whether you access the program from the Apple menu or from within a dialog box.

On Technologies' On Location can copy, move, and delete files just like other utilities, but these capabilities are side shows to its main performance as an extremely fast file finder. Like On Disk, On Location can find files that match certain criteria in the blink of an eye, but the program also can find files based on the files' contents (see figure 6.4). For example, On Location can search for all files that contain the words "love" or "money." On Location also can search floppy disks that are not in the PowerBook by memorizing their contents. Using On Location, you can index files on a floppy and keep the index on your hard drive, saving a lot of battery draining and time wasting associated with floppy disk swapping.

Productivity Enhancers 6

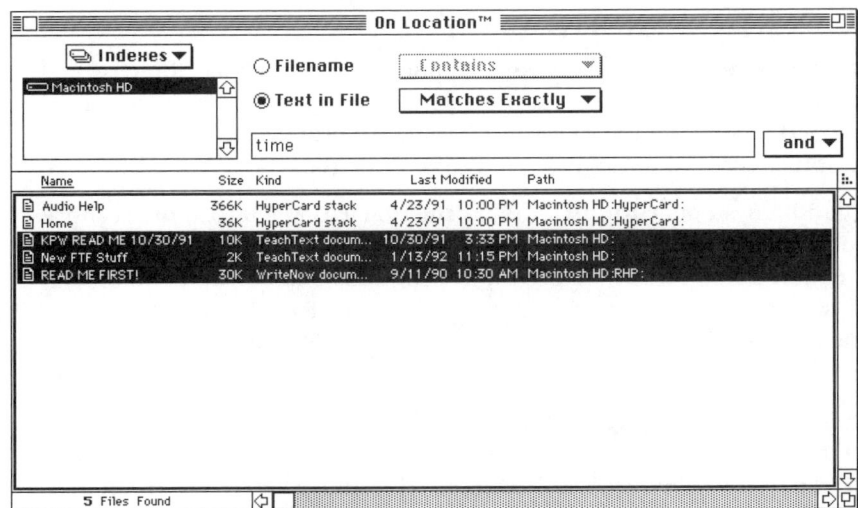

Fig. 6.4.
On Location's specialized search function.

To keep up with the ever-changing contents of your files and to maintain speedy searches, On Location employs background indexing. Like a screen saver that kicks in when you walk away from your Mac, On Location starts chugging at your disk whenever your machine is idle. For your battery's sake, you should turn off background indexing and endure the wait as On Location updates its indexes.

The Squeeze Play

Another class of utilities doesn't necessarily enable you to perform tasks more quickly. In fact, such programs may slow down your operation slightly. But these programs provide something for which most PowerBook owners yearn: more storage. With System 7.0 and related utilities occupying nearly 3M of hard disk space and word processors such as Microsoft Word 5.0 requiring even more space when fully installed, a 20M or even 40M hard disk quickly can suffer from overcrowding.

Compression programs help conserve space by putting applications and documents in a less-usable form. Compression programs come in two forms: archival and "on-the-fly." Archival programs generally squeeze files more tightly but leave your data in a less-accessible format. On-the-fly programs do not squeeze as tightly but are faster because they are intended for use with files you need to access quickly. Both archival and on-the-fly programs are becoming speedier and more efficient.

Champs of the Clamps

If you spend any time accessing online services such as GEnie or America Online, you may have noticed the suffix ".sit" or ".cpt" attached to a file name. These sometimes cryptic letters signify that a popular archival utility has compressed the file.

Aladdin Systems' StuffIt Deluxe is the de facto Macintosh file compression utility. The program also is available in a watered-down shareware version called StuffIt Classic. Both programs enable you to choose from several compression methods and both have built-in virus detection. StuffIt Deluxe, however, can copy files among multiple archives and can enable you to compress files from within the Finder.

Sometime you may receive a stuffed file, commonly ending in the letters ".sit." If you don't own StuffIt Classic or Deluxe, you can obtain a free utility called UnStuffIt Deluxe. UnStuffIt Deluxe can open files created by any version of StuffIt. Other utilities claim they can open StuffIt files, but generally the claims refer to the less efficient "Classic" standard.

Like the original StuffIt, Bill Goodman's Compact Pro (originally "Compactor") made its debut as a shareware program offering faster and better compression than the established standard. Compact Pro offers only one compression method that squeezes files almost as well as StuffIt's tightest setting, and arguably performs the compression faster. At any rate, Compact Pro's attractive blend of speed and efficiency has established it as a second standard.

If you receive a compacted file, obtain a copy of the free Extractor program, which enables you to expand files squeezed with Compact Pro.

Tip: If you don't have UnStuffIt Deluxe or Extractor, be sure to tell the person compressing the files to save them as ".sea" (self-extracting archive) files. A .sea file is slightly larger than normal archives created by Compact Pro and StuffIt Deluxe because the .sea file contains code that turns files into applications. Double-clicking a .sea file enables you to expand the file without using additional software. StuffIt Deluxe and Compact Pro, as well as other utilities discussed in the next section, all can create .sea files.

6 Productivity Enhancers

Your Main Squeeze

In contrast to "archival" utilities such as StuffIt and Compact Pro (intended for tightly squeezing files to which you don't need immediate access) on-the-fly compression utilities operate very quickly, usually not squeezing files as tightly. The files created by these utilities are better-integrated with Macintosh system software than archived files. Typically, files compressed by on-the-fly utilities retain their own icons, file type, and appearance in Open dialog boxes.

Ads for on-the-fly compression utilities make some rather bizarre claims. Typically, the ads promise to double the size of your hard disk for under $100—an impossible feat. What these compression utilities actually do is shrink your files to half their original size, enabling your drive to double its capacity. This is a small trick compared to upgrading your hard drive, but it's pretty magical in itself. On-the-fly compression utilities have become very popular, and the merits of each package always make for heated arguments begging the attention of international peacekeeping forces.

Although archival utilities have entrenched themselves as a part of telecommunications, you must make the gripping decision of whether to use disk compression utilities to maximize hard disk storage. The limited hard disk space of the PowerBooks makes compression programs an alluring option, particularly on PowerBooks that ship with low-capacity hard drives.

To perform their space-conserving tricks, however, all these utilities increase the frequency of access to your hard disk. Some programs compress after you add a key code to the file name; others compress in the background. Either way, your battery depletes sooner.

Currently, four utilities promise that they now (or will soon) cram more in your PowerBook than you could alone.

Salient's DiskDoubler was the first automatic disk compression utility on the market. The program improves with each new release, incorporating advances such as creating self-extracting archives and splitting files over several disks.

SuperDisk! by Alysis was the first product to make compressed files and folders completely transparent, requiring no more the addition of an ".s" to the end of their names. Files compress after a brief delay, but changes to their names and sizes are your only clues. Files retain their special Type and Creator codes that System 7.0 uses to track which icon files should appear and which application created the icon files. Alysis is working on a product called More Disk Space that the company claims compresses applications without need to expand them again.

SuperDisk! creates self-extracting archives that can expand on either Mac- or DOS-based platforms. If you have a huge Excel worksheet you want to transfer to someone using Excel for Windows, SuperDisk! may provide the only convenient method for fitting the worksheet on a disk or saving transmission time through the modem.

Aladdin Systems' SpaceSaver is even more flexible, enabling you to use any prefix or suffix to initiate compression. In addition, the program produces self-extracting archives when you append ".sea" to a file name. SpaceSaver also creates standard StuffIt files when you append ".sit" to a file name. Like SuperDisk!, SpaceSaver does not alter file types. Therefore, utilities that scan files (such as virus-checking programs or content-searching programs like On Location), still can view the file contents. SpaceSaver also can compress in the background.

If SuperDisk! and SpaceSaver decrease the thought involved in reducing file size, Salient completely eliminates that thought with AutoDoubler. AutoDoubler may be the fastest—and perhaps the simplest to use—compression program available. Salient claims that you can compress files twice as fast as with competing products. AutoDoubler enables you to set lofty compression goals the program may never reach, but it strives toward those goals without interrupting your work.

AutoDoubler works differently from any other disk compression program. Instead of specifying which files or folders you want to squeeze, you specify a goal for the amount of disk space you want to save (see figure 6.5). AutoDoubler takes care of the rest, automatically compressing all items on the hard disk (except the System Folder) until it meets the goal or until AutoDoubler can squeeze no more.

Tip: If, in spite of your best efforts to keep only the bare essentials on your hard disk, you find yourself still cramped for space, try to do most of your compressing when your PowerBook is plugged in. If you know you're going to use certain files often and you can't recharge, exempt those files from compression. (All products mentioned in this section enable you to exclude files from compression.)

Productivity Enhancers 6

Fig. 6.5.
Salient's AutoDoubler compression program.

AutoDoubler's approach to disk compression works best with PowerBooks. AutoDoubler is fast, nearly transparent, and lighter on disk access than its competitors. The program doesn't scan at all when it detects that the PowerBook is running on battery power. This one-trick pony consumes at least 130K of RAM, plus whatever you set aside for the program's cache. Although AutoDoubler is safe, some users may find it unnerving not knowing what's squeezed or by how much.

Salient admits AutoDoubler is not the solution for everyone and recommends pairing the program with DiskDoubler. DiskDoubler, though, adds overhead to an already hefty extension, and it is not nearly as transparent as newer programs that provide features AutoDoubler lacks. If you decide to use AutoDoubler, make sure the program performs the initial crunching while your PowerBook is plugged in.

SpaceSaver is an alternative to the AutoDoubler-DiskDoubler combination. SpaceSaver is free with StuffIt Deluxe 3.0 and is available separately for a price smaller than that of SuperDisk! or DiskDoubler. SpaceSaver processes in the background like AutoDoubler with less RAM overhead, achieves comparable speeds, creates archives transparent to system software, and handily creates StuffIt archives and self-extracting archives. Although a DOS program that can unstuff files on DOS machines currently is available, most DOS owners don't have this program. As a result, SuperDisk! is your best bet if you want to save time when communicating with DOS machines.

Hitting Cruise Control

One of Apple's print ads refers to PowerBooks as computers that bring freedom. However, computers themselves do not necessarily ensure freedom from tedium. Automation utilities, though, can help increase PowerBook productivity by reducing errors associated with repetitive tasks and saving the time required to enter redundant commands. These utilities leave the tedium to the computer.

QuicKeys 2

CE Software's QuicKeys is one of the most popular Mac utilities ever written. It provided relief for users tired of taking their hands off the keyboard to initiate commands using the mouse. QuicKeys 2 still functions at this basic level for PowerBook owners, enabling you to scroll, open, close, cycle through windows, and choose menu commands without touching the trackball.

The true power of QuicKeys 2 resides in the program's sequence and extensions capabilities. Sequences enable you to string together individual QuicKeys and activate QuicKeys with a single keystroke. You can use a QuicKeys sequence to take numbers from a spreadsheet, copy them to the clipboard, open your word processor, select all the text, choose a new font, set custom margins, type your letterhead and salutation, enter today's date, insert the numbers from the clipboard, and send a fax of the final letter—all with a single keystroke.

QuicKeys 2 extensions add to its power. Note that some of the extensions require System 7.0. Through extensions, you can compress files with StuffIt and DiskDoubler, change printers, switch applications, or change sound level (see figure 6.6). You can insert the most powerful extensions, though, into QuicKeys sequences and let macros continue to run depending on which window is in front, what a menu item says, or what the cursor looks like.

Productivity Enhancers 6

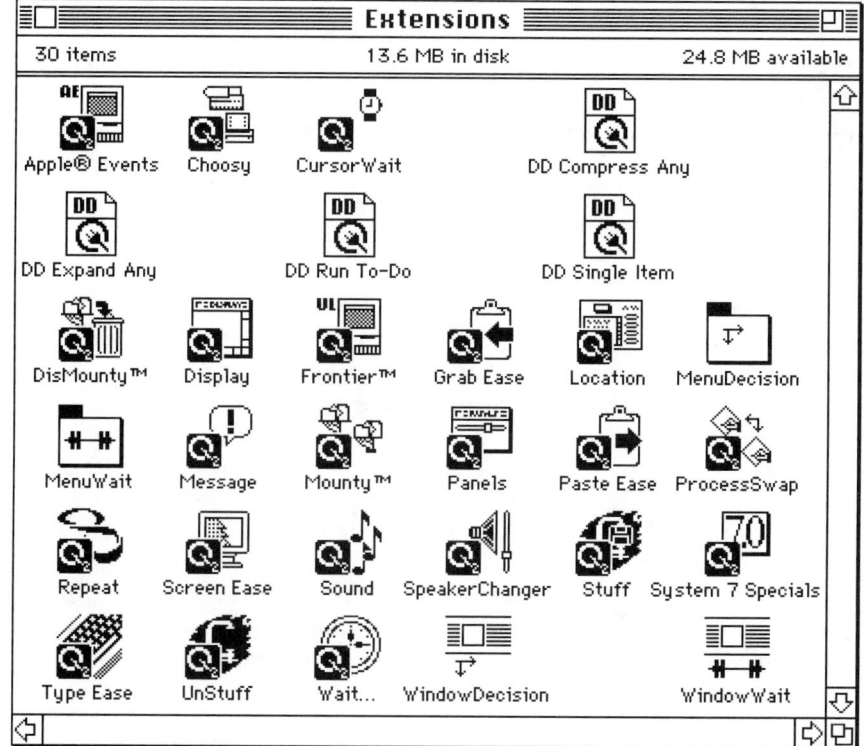

Fig. 6.6.
QuicKeys 2 extensions add to its power.

For example, using CursorWait—the QuicKeys extension that enables you to run macros based on the style of cursor on the screen—you can set up sequences that take you directly to specific folders in graphical online services such as America Online. This capability helps compensate for CursorWait's lack of automation capabilities such as those found in CompuServe Navigator.

Unfortunately, QuicKeys 2 does not include all of these extensions, particularly the powerful ones. You can obtain the extensions through online services such as CompuServe, America On-line, or GEnie.

The latest version of QuicKeys 2 takes full advantage of System 7.0 and includes extensions intended for use with the new system. One extension can turn Balloon Help on and off and switch among applications through the keyboard; another can send AppleEvents to applications. And a promising extension enables QuicKeys to serve as a familiar face on top of a powerful system-scripting language called Frontier.

Frontier

If QuicKeys is a utility you can't live without, UserLand's Frontier may soon be, too, as more applications start taking advantage of AppleEvents. Frontier is not a macro program per se. It is a scripting environment that enables you to control interaction among programs. Frontier potentially can extend the capabilities of system software and applications by automating tasks that macro programs are unable to automate.

Using Frontier, you can have the Finder search for files based on certain criteria and perform operations on the files, such as "Find all the MacDraw Pro files that are larger than 500K, stuff them, and put the files in a folder called 'Too Big to Take Along.'" You also can take advantage of scripts and macro languages already present in other programs. For example, you can, at the beginning of each week, have your communications program retrieve the next five-day forecast automatically. The program then would format the information in a program such as WordPerfect, a word processing application with a macro facility. Furthermore, when programs support the AppleEvents that enable communications between programs, Frontier will be able to provide complex automation facilities to programs that lack such features.

The disappointing news about Frontier is that to master the program and write your own scripts, you need to have some grasp of programming; scripting in Frontier's language is more daunting than in HyperTalk. Without understanding Frontier's syntax and large vocabulary of verbs and objects, you are resigned to using scripts developed by others.

KiwiPowerWindows

Kiwi Software appears to have a knack for addressing problems that people have gone crazy trying to solve. KiwiEnvelopes remains a full-featured solution for a need that few word processors satisfy. Now, KiwiPowerWindows (KPW) takes advantage of System 7.0's AppleEvents to organize windows automatically according to any layout you specify, making the most of the PowerBook's screen area.

KiwiPowerWindows provides many methods for tackling the thorny problem of desktop clutter. KPW enables you to specify whether layouts should apply to just an application (local) or to windows of any open applications (global). You also can specify whether to include the Finder's windows in layouts. You can choose from more than a dozen preset window layouts or create your own (see figure 6.7).

Productivity Enhancers 6

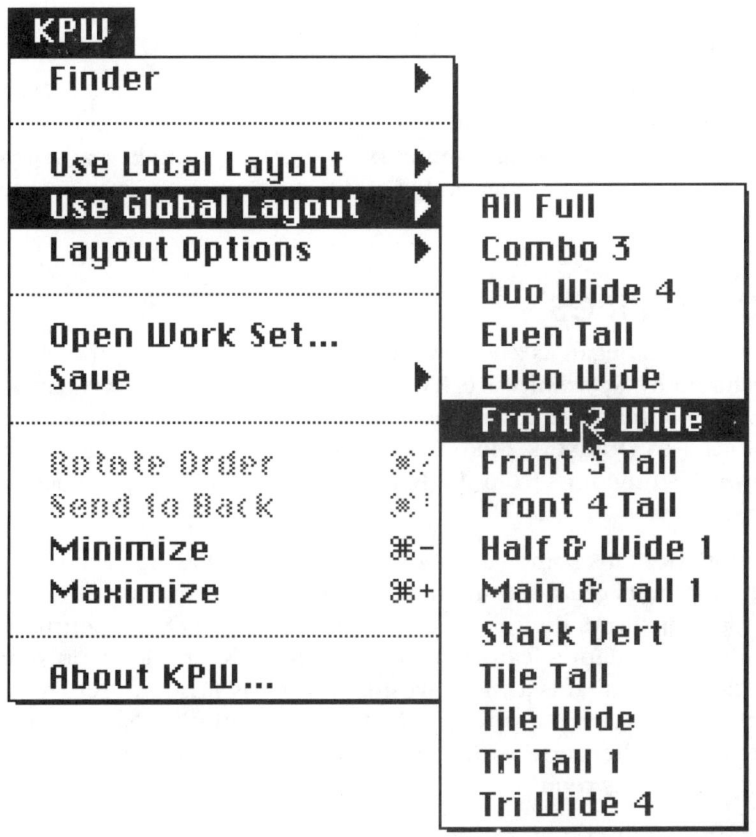

Fig. 6.7.
KiwiPowerWindows contains more than a dozen preset window layouts.

When rearranging and resizing windows, KPW is a bit sluggish, but the convenience of working in a custom environment is well worth the time invested. KPW's "work set" feature also functions as an advanced file launcher, which not only can open groups of documents and files (like On Cue II and HandOff II), but also can arrange their windows in the same size and position as when you left them.

Magic Typist

If you've ever used a glossary feature in a word processor or a "clairvoyance" feature in an address book manager, you know the value of being able to insert a long word or phrase with a few keystrokes. Tactic Software's Magic Typist extends that feature to all your applications, by automatically converting preset key sequences to long, expanded phrases. For example, you can have the PowerBook automatically enter "First National Bank" whenever you type "1NB." Magic Typist also can help with common misspellings, automatically converting "thier" to "their."

6

Hayden's PowerBook Power Book

Swiss Army Utility Knives

As one utility developer once said, "Everyone and his brother has a 'Utilities' package for the Macintosh." He may have been guilty of hyperbole, but a growing number of "integrated utilities" packages for your Mac combine a hodgepodge of different functions into a suite of programs.

Now Utilities

Now Utilities began as a somewhat-underpowered set of shareware purchased by Now Software. Two major revisions, however, have established the package as a favorite in the Mac utilities market. Now Utilities uses QuicKeys 2-like technology to enable you to to activate many of its functions from the keyboard—a boon for experienced users.

Now Utilities falls somewhat short of its claim to having each utility be at the top of its class, but many of its utilities are superior, and each component shows the results of training hard to stay competitive in the always-escalating features race. All told, Now Utilities represents an excellent value that is a wise investment for PowerBook users who can spare the RAM. Even if you can't install all ten utilities, Now's unmatched installer reports the amount of disk space and RAM each of the components requires.

SuperBoomerang is an extraordinary dialog-box enhancement utility with a clear interface. Like ShortCut, SuperBoomerang provides keyboard access to all its functions, which include renaming, deleting, and finding misplaced files. SuperBoomerang's individual features are too numerous to mention, but one of its handiest features is the capability of finding files within compressed archives.

Startup Manager is one of the best extension management programs for the Mac, and certainly one of the fastest. Startup Manager scans disks more quickly than its competitors, so the program doesn't drain your battery. Unfortunately, Startup Manager changes the types of files it creates. This has a number of drawbacks, the worst of which is that you cannot configure control panels that have been turned off. At least with System 7.0, extensions turned off upon startup appear with a big X through their icons, making it easier to recognize deactivated items.

MultiMaster is a file launching program that you can activate via a menu (with a choice of icon) or pop-up window that you can call up with an icon. MultiMaster regrettably lacks the work-set capabilities of

Productivity Enhancers 6

HandOff II or On Cue II that enable you to open multiple files with one menu selection. However, MultiMaster provides the best interface for opening files from the keyboard. MultiMaster's added value for the PowerBook is its Memory Sizer feature, which can tell you the minimum amount of RAM an application requires—a statistic not necessarily reflected in its Get Info window. Now Utilities' MultiMaster answers the question, "How low can you go?" by revealing the minimum suggested size of an application (see figure 6.8).

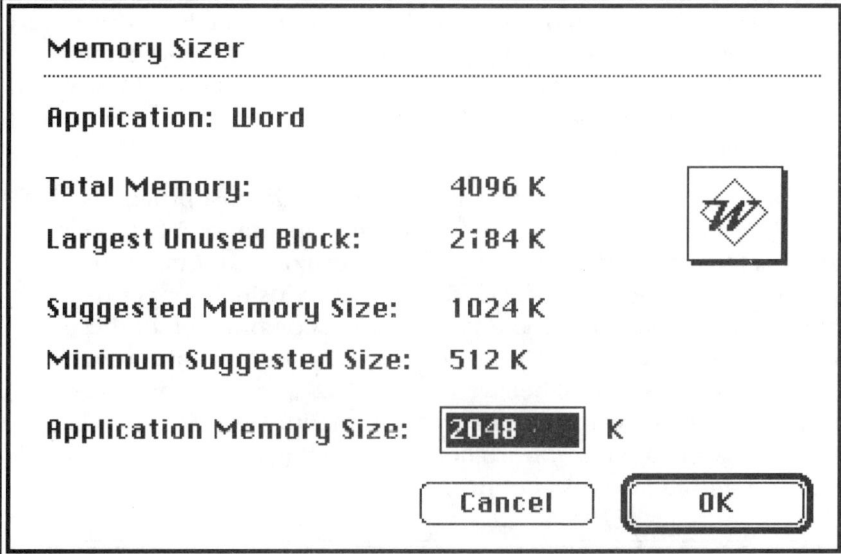

Fig. 6.8.
Now Utilities' MultiMaster answers the question, "How low can you go?"

WYSIWYG Menus is an advanced, comprehensive font menu manager that enables you to view font names in menus in their actual font, styles in their actual style, and font sizes in their actual size. WYSIWYG Menus also can group awkwardly named PostScript fonts. It is the only utility that enables you to rearrange the font menu manually. Tired of scrolling a mile and a half to reach Zapf Chancery? Drag Zapf Chancery to the top of the font menu! The program has some problems with Command-Shift key combinations in certain applications, but these problems are a minor inconvenience. Although toting many fonts causes longer startup times for many applications, if you need to work with many fonts on the road, WYSIWYG Menus is the font menu-management utility of choice.

NowMenus, like HandOff II's SuperMenu and Microseeds' HAM, enables you to access the contents of folders placed in the Apple Menu Items folder. In fact, NowMenus may be the best Apple menu brancher for PowerBook owners because the program enables you to have "drop down" menus rather than forcing you to pull them down. Instead of having to press the trackball button while perusing menus, clicking once keeps the menus dropped down. You then just click on the menu selection you want.

DeskPicture is the prodigal son of the Now family. Other programs focus on keeping you productive, but DeskPicture distracts you with your choice of background desktop picture. In consideration of computers with limited RAM, Now enables you to keep reading the picture from disk, so your PowerBook must access the hard drive every time it redraws the screen. The program, therefore, is aboard the express route on the battery-killing train. System drain would be much worse if the PowerBooks had color screens, but generally steer clear of the DeskPicture component of this otherwise fine set.

NowSave places a menu item in the File menu of most programs, providing a consistent interface for the implementation of automatic saves. Selecting NowSave enables you to designate automatic file-saving intervals. You can specify this frequency using number of minutes, keystrokes, or mouse clicks, or any combination of these options (see figure 6.9). You also can have NowSave confirm each automatic save. As a well-behaved Macintosh program, NowSave provides feedback when it initiates an automatic save. Some of the Now Utilities NowSave options demonstrate the smooth interface and high configurability typical of the Now Utilities.

Fig. 6.9. NowSave's automatic file-saving options.

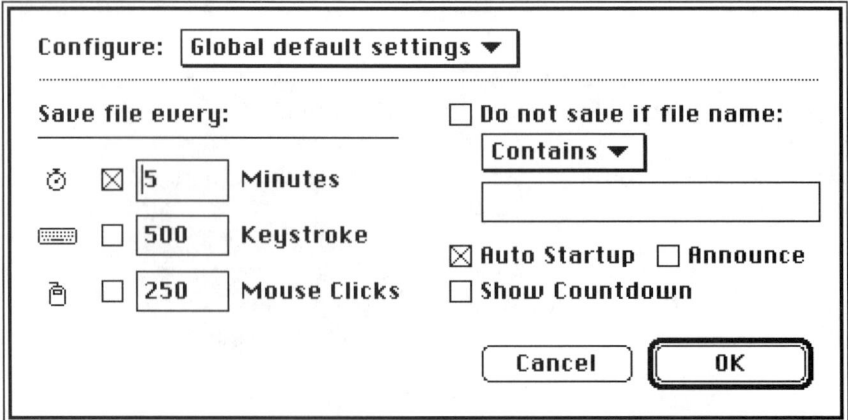

Productivity Enhancers 6

Generally, automatic saving programs are discouraged for use on portables because such programs may access the hard drive more often than necessary. Many programs, though, require only a quick write to the hard disk to update a saved document. Therefore, if you value the safety of your work more than you value battery time, NowSave is an excellent choice.

AlarmsClock is a commercial answer to the popular free program SuperClock! Both programs place a digital clock in the menu bar and enable you to count off seconds and toggle between the date and time. AlarmsClock has a bare-bones reminder feature that can flash a message in the menu bar. Although this notification method is less intrusive than the dialog boxes used by dedicated reminder programs (see Chapter 5, "Managing Time and Contacts"), it does not work well for reminders of more than a few words in length.

Because AlarmsClock is always on the screen, it is more accessible than programs configured from the Apple menu. However, because you must set reminders in a dialog box you cannot move (a modal dialog box), you can't interrupt the reminder entry process. In essence, AlarmsClock is an adequate menu bar clock, but its alarms feature satisfies only those users with the most basic requirements. A far superior variation is Visionary Software's First Things First (see Chapter 5, "Managing Time and Contacts").

Profiler is the only application in Now Utilities (aside from the Installer). Profiler creates detailed reports about your system hardware and software. These reports are useful for sending to software companies to trace incompatibilities. You can specify the level of detail you want in a report and which items you want the report to include. The reports can be quite technical. Profiler is one of the few components of Now Utilities that you won't use every day. However, Profiler may prove to be a valuable tool if you're trying to collect information about your system configuration to pass on to a technical support department, for example.

QuickTools

Advanced Software's QuickTools is a set of aggressively priced utilities that provides some overlap with Now Utilities' feature set. You could say the two sets complement each other, but QuickTools is far less appealing to PowerBook users. Although both sets are System 7.0-compatible, QuickTools does not take advantage of any System 7.0 features. Even so, the potential for these diamonds in the rough is great. Seven control panels comprise QuickTools.

6 Hayden's PowerBook Power Book

Barricade is a simple security program that anyone can defeat by starting up from a floppy. (Then again, System 7.0 startup disks are not easy to come by.)

Instant Menus, like NowMenus, is one of many utilities that enables you to pop up the menu bar anywhere on the screen. Although either program reduces the number of trips to the menu bar, the latter provides more functionality. Regardless, either program is more of a boon to users of portrait or two-page displays than it is to PowerBook owners.

Power Strip is a graphical file launcher that uses an icon-based palette rather than the Apple menu or its own menu. Power Strip enables you to launch files with a single click. As a result, the program may be the fastest method for opening applications and documents (especially on PowerBooks, on which dragging can be a bit of a drag). You can activate or hide Power Strip with a hot key, and the program looks pretty impressive on a large color monitor. Still, Power Strip eats up plenty of screen real estate.

Work Saver is a solid program that saves your work automatically at given intervals. If you have Now Utilities, NowSave has a few more options than Work Saver does.

Dialog Power enables you to select on-screen buttons from the keyboard. Unlike some shareware competitors, Dialog Power underlines the letter in each button that activates it. For example, Command-O selects "OK," and Command-R yields "Replace" when you're saving over a previous version of a file. This must-have utility—a great timesaver that should be incorporated into system software—almost justifies the price of the entire package (see figure 6.10). QuickTools' Dialog Power! can tame even a complex dialog box from the keyboard. You need only to press and hold the Command key and type the underlined letter to select the desired button.

Sunset is a nice screen saver with some imaginative modules. Although most PowerBook users leave their screen savers behind, these entertaining programs can be handy if you want to leave your system on without disrupting a network connection. Only Sunset can display modules with a white background, which makes it the dubious screen saver of choice for the PowerBooks.

QuickTools assigns the F1 to F4 function keys to the Edit menu commands Undo, Cut, Copy, and Paste. So does System 7.0. As a bonus, we will send a free PowerBook 170 to the first person to find the keys labeled F1 to F4 on the PowerBook keyboard.

Productivity Enhancers 6

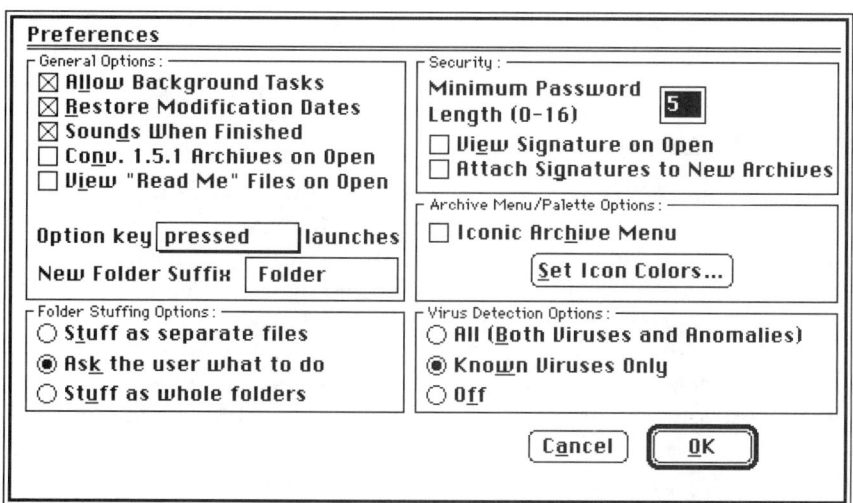

Fig. 6.10. QuickTools' Dialog Power! is a must-have utility.

Snipper is a convenient screen capture program that enables you to take pictures of windows, menus, and screen selections. The program bears a strong resemblance to Baseline Publishing's ScreenShot, which has a handy automatic-reduction feature for pictures. If the other parts of QuickTools don't excite you, ScreenShot hopefully will.

Other Aids

Certain utilities don't fall into traditional categories but are worth mentioning because they are relevant to PowerBook performance.

Intertie

The unique program Intertie, by Dantz Development, demonstrates how hardware can inspire software. Based on Dantz' powerful Retrospect backup program, Intertie can compare versions of files on two different machines and determine which files are different. Intertie then "reconciles" the files, keeping only the most recent version of the files on both Macs. The program has the potential to reduce the hassle of transferring files modified on the road back to the PowerBook.

Read My Lips

Read My Lips is a perfect companion to the microphone included with the PowerBook 140 and 170. This program takes broad strides toward a goal you may see as a feature of Macintosh system software: universal voice annotation of documents. This feature currently is limited to electronic mail packages such as CE Software's QuickMail and applications including Microsoft Word 5.0, Symmetry Software's Acta 7, and Chena Software's Fair Witness.

You access Read My Lips with a hot key in many popular applications, including most word processors. In theory, Read My Lips can work inside any application that accepts pictures (most Mac programs). The Read My Lips dialog box presents an intermediate step before you can add sound. It gives you the option to find and play existing sound notes in your document. When you press the hot key, Read My Lips presents a dialog box providing options for recording, finding, and playing sounds embedded in your document (see figure 6.11). Inserted sounds appear as "talking balloons" with a choice of several icons. To play a sound, select the desired icon and press the hot key.

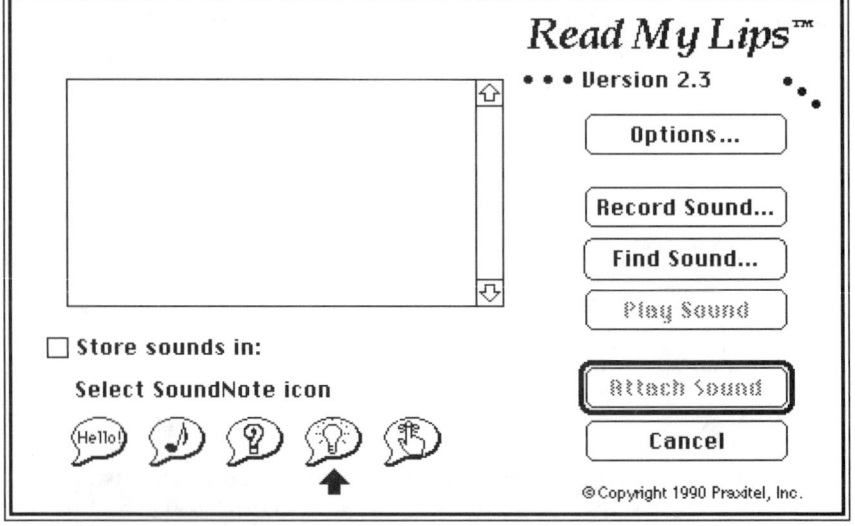

Fig. 6.11. Read My Lips finds and plays existing sounds in your document.

Read My Lips works well, especially when playing back sounds, but the process for recording sounds requires too many steps. A "quicknote" feature that would name the sound note based on the words surrounding the sound would be welcome, but such a feature may be easier to implement when more applications support AppleEvents. For now, Read My Lips is a great way to provide a consistent interface for voice annotation in your documents.

Productivity Enhancers 6

Safe at Any Speed

Productivity enhancers provide a variety of ways to push the envelope of PowerBook performance. Such programs make routine tasks easier, and streamline processes in ways that system software alone cannot.

Using too many productivity enhancers may increase your risk of problems, but you have control over that risk. The next chapter discusses how to keep your souped-up PowerBook safe from natural—and a few unnatural—predators.

Safe Computing

Life on the road is hard for any computer. PowerBooks have a rugged exterior that you may want to bolster with one of the carrying cases discussed in Chapter 1, "Portable Power." But there are other threats to your precious data from which you may want to seek protection.

Security software can protect you from just about any potential prier, from the curious child perusing the innards of the System Folder to the embittered associate trying to steal secrets. The packages act like a watchdog, making sure no one gains access to files you want to keep confidential.

Antiviral software protects you from the technological opponents of technological progress. Although present Macintosh viruses do not seek to do any harm, the problems viruses cause should encourage you to make sure epidemics do not infect your valuable software.

Security Software

Many security software packages available for the Mac offer different levels and types of protection. Some programs (such as the freeware Boris) present a simple dialog box asking for a password. You can circumvent these programs easily by holding down the Shift key at startup or starting with another disk. Other programs—predominantly the commercial ones—present thornier barriers. If you start from another disk, these programs still prevent access to your disk.

In addition, most security programs offer some sort of data encryption. Encryption scrambles a file's contents so that the data is unreadable. Most encryption programs offer a choice between their own method or DES (Data Encryption Standard). A DES-encrypted file is so tough to unscramble that an extremely powerful computer would require many years to "crack" its code. DES encryption takes more time, however, and federal law prohibits exporting products that can encrypt with DES. Again, encrypting a file doesn't prevent people from accessing that file, but—unless these people have a few supercomputers in the living room sitting idle—they can't decipher it.

> *Tip:* Remember that security software applications—particularly advanced packages such as Empower—do not take kindly to tampering. If you decided to protect your hard disk, you protect it from yourself as well. Although some packages offer override features, you save yourself a great deal of heartache if you remember your password. Pick something easy to remember but not obvious, such as your favorite pie flavor or your dentist's social security number. Also, be sure to disable security programs before using software that deals with the disk at low levels, such as formatting or file recovery software.

The Basics and Beyond

Most PowerBook users need only to prevent unauthorized access to their hard disk or the ability to encrypt a basic file occasionally. Several programs adeptly handle these modest requirements.

Fifth Generation Systems' DiskLock and Microcom's Citadel both provide hard disk locking and encryption.

DiskLock's main component is the DiskLock Installer, an incredibly simple application that installs and removes the DiskLock extension to or from your hard disk (see figure 7.1). When DiskLock is in effect, your PowerBook prompts for a password when anyone attempts to start the machine. In the great tradition of three-strikes-and-you're-out, anyone who doesn't get the password right is treated to a screen with a blinking question mark, which is "Macintoshese" for "no hard disk available." To take another crack, you must restart the PowerBook.

Safe Computing 7

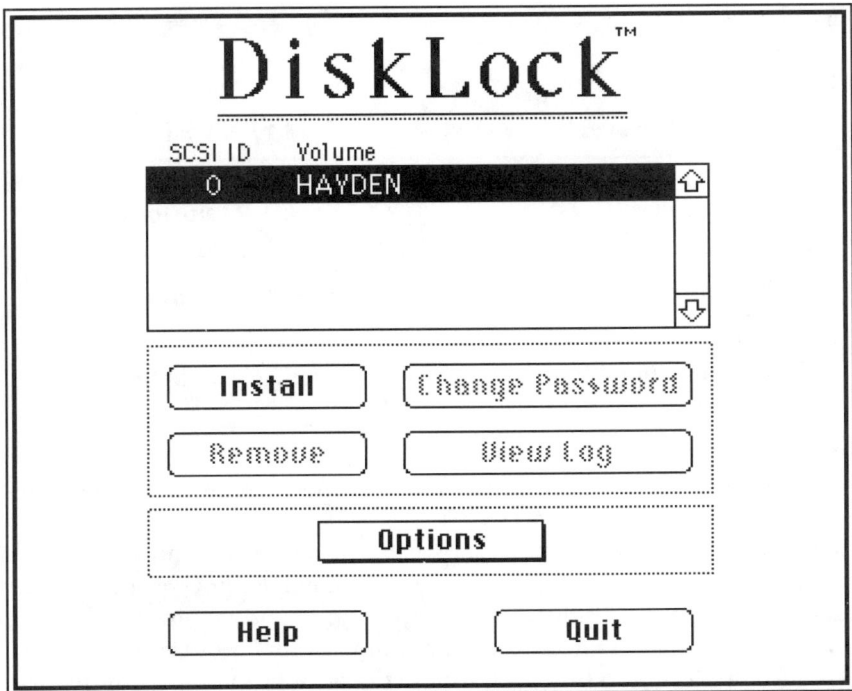

Fig. 7.1.
Fifth Generation Systems' DiskLock security software.

Although DiskLock's disk-locking interface is straightforward, it offers some flexibility in its behavior. One of DiskLock's best features is the ability to bypass the prompt upon restart, so you can avoid spending a lot of time proving that you own your hard disk. Citadel, on the other hand, notifies you of the last successful attempt after you enter the password, a practical feature for quickly determining whether anyone has been trying to access your files.

Citadel is a little more convoluted than DiskLock. An administration program must "customize" all its components before you can start using them. After the program has customized the components, the Citadel application, desk accessory, and control panel provide nearly identical functionality.

The "Customize Citadel File" option of the Citadel Administrator personalizes the package's other components so that others who own Citadel cannot override your security settings. With the administration program, you can set options for how Citadel behaves if you install its components on separate machines (see figure 7.2), although you must purchase a separate copy for each Mac. Unlike DiskLock, Citadel waits until all your extensions have loaded before prompting you for a password, which gives people a chance to twiddle with your extensions.

Fig. 7.2.
Citadel Administrator's opening screen.

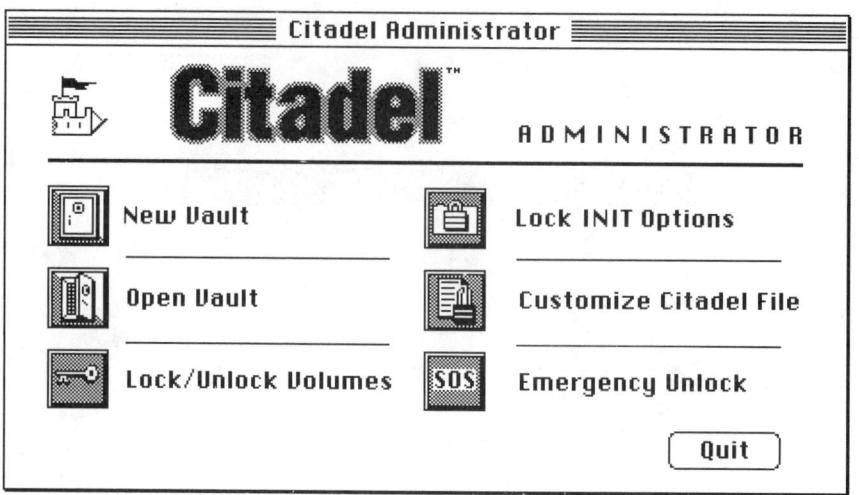

Citadel cannot encrypt folders per se, but it can create "vaults" in which you can store sensitive documents using DES encryption. These vaults appear in the Finder, but you must open and manipulate them using the Citadel desk accessory or administration application. It is a little disappointing to find such indirect manipulation in a product that shipped later than all its competitors.

Citadel comes with Shredder, a handy program for confidential documents you're sure you don't want to recover. Normally, when you empty the Trash, the disk removes the file as an entry in its directory, a sort of index that dictates where files are stored. Frequently, the file is still on the hard disk until new data overwrites where the file used to be. File recovery programs often keep an extra copy of the directory so the programs can find deleted files and recover them.

The Shredder component of Citadel rounds out the package, preventing advanced file recovery utilities from retrieving confidential files (see figure 7.3). Shredder automatically writes over deleted files. File recovery programs cannot bring shredded files back. The Trash mimics a shredder complete with slicing sound as it empties. You also can choose to have Shredder prompt you before you shred the contents of the Trash. The package even contains Disk Cleaner, which wipes free any existing deleted files still on your hard disk before you install Shredder. All that's missing is Fawn Hall.

7 Safe Computing

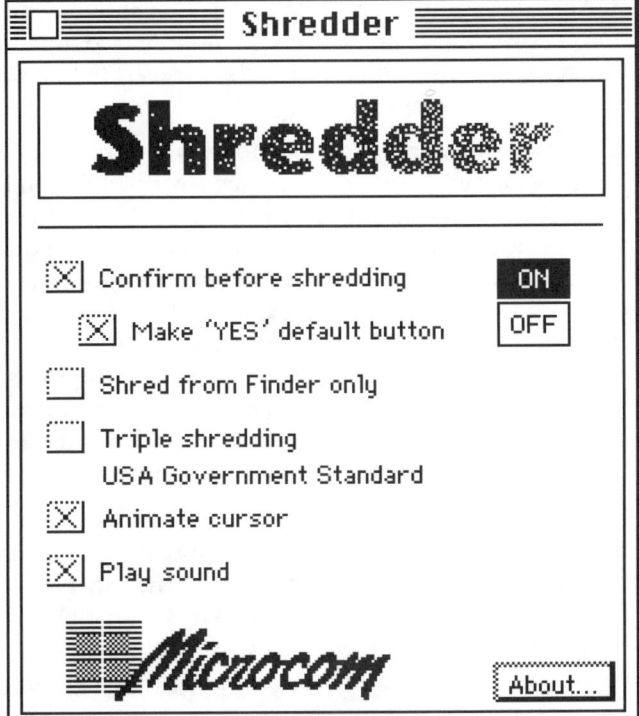

Fig. 7.3. Shredder prevents the recovery of confidential files.

Shareware Showcase

Art Shumer's MacPassword has gone through three major and countless minor upgrades in the past few years. For $40, the current version offers hard disk and folder password protection, virus detection, screen blanking, and sounds that signify successful and failed attempts to access the drive. As if that weren't enough, Shumer is gearing up to soon release MacPassword Professional, which will bridge the gap between MacPassword and commercial utilities.

FolderBolt

From a telecommunications perspective, programs that lock the entire hard disk may be inconvenient. Farallon Computing and Sophisticated Circuits offer cables that enable the Mac to be awakened by an incoming phone call (such as that from a PowerBook modem). These cables allow you to use Remote Access and Timbuktu without keeping your desktop Mac on all the time. But because disk-locking programs present their password prompts before Remote Access and Timbuktu allow you to control the machine remotely, you can't enter the password from a remote location.

Like DiskLock, FolderBolt also can lock folders, but the two programs take a different approach. FolderBolt is a control panel with just three buttons: lock folder, unlock folder, and Help. Clicking Lock or Unlock brings you to a standard Open dialog from which you can designate three levels of folder security—locked (you cannot open the folder), read only (you cannot change the contents of the folder), and drop box (you can add to the folder, but you aren't allowed to open it). You also can create FolderBolt's three folder types with programs such as FileGuard (discussed later) that use AppleShare file privileges for their folder protection, but most users will find FolderBolt's method faster and easier, especially if they're unfamiliar with System 7.0 file sharing or AppleShare.

With FolderBolt, you can avoid the simple control panel in daily use anyway because FolderBolt's shortcuts make it the most seamlessly integrated folder-locking program for the Mac. Double-clicking a locked folder causes the Mac to prompt you for the password; Shift-clicking a folder's close box lets you password-protect an unlocked folder.

With an administration program, you can set preferences for FolderBolt and open locked folders in case you forget the password. Like Citadel's Administrator, your copy of FolderBolt Administrator acts as your "signature." This signature prevents other people from using another copy of FolderBolt Administrator to override your passwords. Because FolderBolt lends itself well to neophyte use, this extra program offers some assurance that you won't lock yourself out of your folders. FolderBolt Administrator, too, can be password-protected, though, so if you want to safeguard thoroughly against password loss, keep a non-password-protected copy in a safe place.

FolderBolt also can create folder sets that allow locking and unlocking of multiple folders with a single password. Although folder sets are immensely convenient, creating them is not. You must revert to the control panel and move the folders into the set using a Font/DA Mover-like dialog box (see figure 7.4). Given FolderBolt's normal transparency, this method is disappointing. A better solution is to add a menu item to the Finder's Special menu called Folder Set. This item would automatically create a new set when you selected a group of folders. Another method could be a System 7.0 locking icon to which you could drag and drop the folders you want protected.

Safe Computing 7

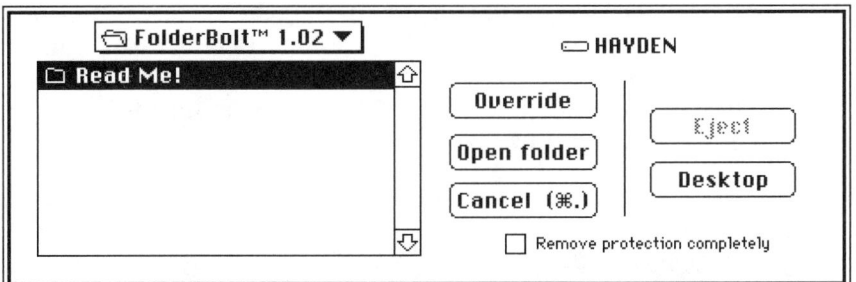

Fig. 7.4.
The FolderBolt Administrator has a Font/DA Mover-like dialog box.

A one-trick pony in the stable of Kent Marsh security products, Kent Marsh seems to have curtailed its features intentionally so that the utility doesn't cut into the sales of its other products. FolderBolt cannot lock an entire hard disk because hard disk locking is the domain of Kent Marsh's Nightwatch program. You can come close by putting all your folders in a folder set and locking that set. This procedure, however, leaves anything on the desktop vulnerable. Although FolderBolt's transparency outshines DiskLock's, FolderBolt does not encrypt files in any way because Kent Marsh's MacSafe II program handles that task.

FolderBolt lacks many of the bells and whistles of its more powerful competitors, but it remains much less complicated for the wear.

Access Management Programs

Access management packages really shine on public Macs that have multiple users, and these packages offer some features not found in simpler utilities. ASD Software's FileGuard is perhaps the most versatile security package available for the PowerBook. Its robust features suit the needs of a machine that users share (see figure 7.5). Primarily, the PowerBooks are personal machines, although, conceivably, some organizations could lend them out to teams in the field. If each member of the team needed to keep confidential information on the hard disk, FileGuard or Empower III would make an ideal traveling partner.

FileGuard and Empower III go beyond DiskLock and Citadel by offering a dizzying array of ways to keep your data safe. At the basic level, the programs can password-protect any hard disk, prompting you for the password by presenting a dialog box upon startup. Failure to provide the proper password prevents you from mounting the disk.

Both FileGuard and Empower provide folder security by using the same kinds of access controls normally provided for shared folders. In essence, these programs make your local hard disk act as a private file server to which people can "log on" by entering the correct name and password at their dialog prompts. Compared to the vault system of Citadel, this approach is familiar to most users with experience on Macintosh networks. Compared to FolderBolt's technique, this approach emphasizes versatility over simplicity.

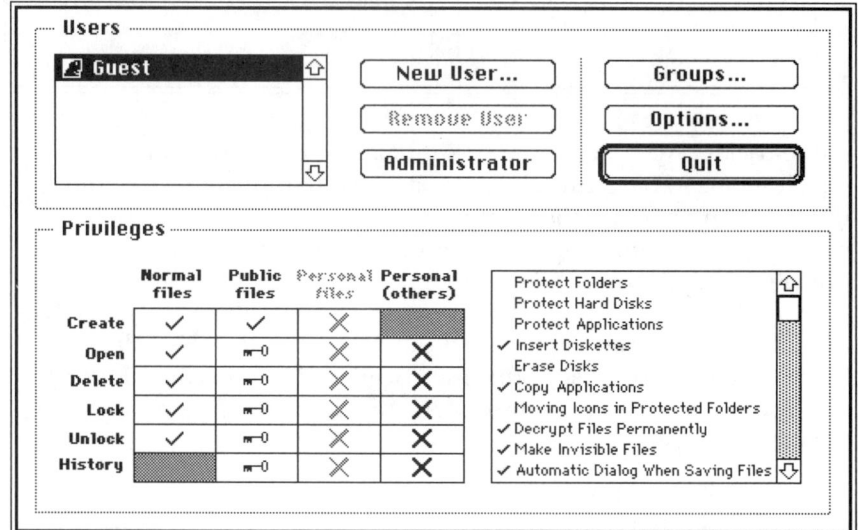

Fig. 7.5. ASD Software's FileGuard is one of the most versatile security package.

FileGuard can prompt you for a password automatically after you save a file, offering a variety of security options. FileGuard has a wonderful and natural means of encrypting documents; instead of accessing the documents through a desk accessory, you can choose to encrypt them when you are saving them or decrypt them when you are opening them (see figure 7.6). This approach is not only convenient, but it minimizes the security risks of decrypting a group of files to open only one. A foreign import, FileGuard cannot offer DES encryption, but it uses a proprietary alternative.

FileGuard also can copy-protect applications in several ways—by time, number of launches, or user. This capability is useful for ensuring that only people covered by the software's license use the software—a boon for exposed PowerBooks on the road.

FileGuard employs a "User Mover" modeled after the old Font/DA Mover that lets you sort and gather users by dragging them in and out of groups. This method is far less elegant than using System 7.0's Sharing Setup control panel. But ASD Software is working on using Sharing Setup to keep FileGuard one of the most transparent security programs available.

Safe Computing 7

Fig. 7.6. FileGuard offers a variety of security options.

Empower III's feature set strongly resembles FileGuard's. Magna also sells Empower III, which can administer other copies of Empower II over the network. This option is especially attractive if you are responsible for several Macs on a network. You can dial in using AppleTalk Remote Access and change security settings on other machines as needed. Without remote administration, you would need to resort to a screen-sharing program such as Timbuktu to change settings, and the approach still would not be as effective.

Security Summary

DiskLock and Citadel provide basic password protection without a lot of bells and whistles. If you want hard disk protection and folder protection for one machine, DiskLock is nearly foolproof, and it can encrypt whole folders automatically. If the capability of wiping confidential documents automatically is important to you, you'll find Citadel's Shredder component valuable, even if its vault metaphor can be a little confusing. DiskLock remains the most convenient tool, but the Shredder component of Citadel may be appealing to some users.

If you value flexibility in protecting and accessing certain files without having to go through the indirect manipulation of DiskLock's or Citadel's encryption, you can count on FolderBolt's slick interface to stay out of your way. Remember that when you allow access to your hard disk, though, you face administration decisions. Anything you leave unprotected is completely vulnerable to prying or malicious eyes.

Finally, if you're among the unfortunate few who are faced with sharing your PowerBook while maintaining confidentiality, you'll find smoother integration with FileGuard. Empower III, though, is a great tool for those who need to administer security privileges for others from across a network or in a remote location.

Of course, regardless of the security solution you choose, you must remain wary of the inhuman villains that could cause as much mayhem as any intruder—those that lie in the programming code of viruses.

The Terrible Trio

Essentially, three types of programs can infect your data, applications, or system files: viruses, worms, and Trojan Horses. Viruses are pieces of software that attach themselves to software. The infected software could be a commercial program, a shareware program, or even a document. Viruses have code within them that enables them to spread from program to program, and often from machine to machine. Two of the most common ways to spread viruses is to share floppy disks or to share data over an unprotected network.

The Macintosh community is fortunate that no malignant viruses have appeared to date; that is, no virus intentionally causes damage to normal software. But because viruses misappropriate resources such as disk space and RAM, and because viruses have bugs in their programming, they tend to cause errors during saving, printing, and launching applications.

Worms are similar to viruses because they replicate. Unlike viruses, worms do not require a "host" program from which to attack. There are no known worms that attack the Mac, although worms exist on other types of computers. Trojan Horses are programs that appear useful but really are insidious. An example is an obscure font-listing program that attempts to erase the Finder while the program is running.

How Serious Is the Threat?

Viruses are baffling because they rarely bring their authors fame, much less fortune. Developers clever enough to program new viruses are wasting their potential because they could be putting the effort into innumerable more socially valuable and personally profitable programs.

Safe Computing 7

Some robust viruses can spread over a network like wildfire; some have thoroughly infected Mac-intensive sites such as corporations and universities. Some Mac viruses spread merely by the insertion of a floppy disk, although System 7.0 is immune to the two known viruses that spread this way. Viruses can harm data and corrupt applications, but the most serious problems viruses pose have little to do with technical matters.

Viruses, or the threat of them, cause panic in people who use computers, especially the most important users: beginners. Shareware has a bad name because it allegedly is more susceptible to viruses, although major online services such as CompuServe and America Online meticulously screen each new file for viruses.

In reality, viruses should be one of the last culprits you suspect for system anomalies, especially if you do not regularly exchange data with other Macintosh users. Certainly, extension conflicts and corrupted System files are far more common sources of strange behavior and crashes than viruses. (Chapter 8, "Diffusing the Bomb," covers both of these problems.) Besides, only two or three Mac viruses still are widespread. Not coincidentally, those viruses were created before antiviral tools were widely available.

Many people have observed the similarity between computer viruses and human viruses. Both require a host in order to propagate, and both can be hazardous. But even the most caustic computer viruses don't cause the damage associated with certain human viruses.

Notwithstanding, several "safe" computing practices can help you avoid catching a virus. If you don't use applications or disks from other users, you are reasonably safe. If you always get software from a trusted source, such as a commercial bulletin board or one with a responsible system operator, you can take solace in the fact that most of these organizations screen all software uploaded (transferred) to their file libraries. If you are receiving software from other people, consider whether they are knowledgeable about viruses and how they obtain their software. And, of course, run the software through a virus-checking program if you have any doubts.

SAM and Virex

Symantec Antivirus for Macintosh (SAM) and Microcom's Virex are two remarkably similar de facto standards in the Mac world for combating the virus plague. Both have two components: an application that provides a place to perform batch scanning and repair of infected files, and a control panel that monitors the PowerBook for suspicious virus-like activity.

Virex INIT's options are available through a pop-up menu; SAM Intercept's options appear as a series of buttons. Virex has a slight edge in control panel interface—it's less modal—but SAM has a decided edge in the application because its menus provide a direct method of choosing files or folders to diagnose. Virex's application selects folders and files only if you press modifier keys. Unfortunately, neither utility supports drag-and-drop diagnosis as does Norton Utilities for Macintosh (see Chapter 8, "Diffusing the Bomb").

SAM and Virex have additional similarities. You can configure either program to scan entire disks or just the System Folder at startup, at shutdown, or both. Both programs can scan floppies as you insert them and with both programs you can cancel a scan by pressing Command-Period. You also can specify which word processor can open program activity logs. Both control panels support online help, although, for the record, SAM is the only antivirus tool—and was one of the first utilities—to offer Balloon Help in addition to normal online help.

One of Virex's distinguishing features enables Virex to eliminate detected viruses from the notification dialog box. Another unique feature enables you to set default buttons for dialogs so that pressing Return activates either the Repair or the Deny Access buttons (see figure 7.7).

You also can access Virex through other programs, although you will be limited to merely detecting viruses. Microcom's Carbon Copy Mac screen-sharing program uses Virex to detect a virus on an incoming file. Berkeley Systems' More After Dark package, which requires the After Dark screen saver, can perform virus scans when the screen saver is activated.

Overall, SAM is the more configurable utility. You access its wealth of options—some of which are notably obscure—from the Configure dialog. SAM can help prevent the spread of an undiscovered virus by alerting you when it detects different types of virus-like activity. SAM provides five levels of protection. The last level is Custom, in which you can choose from 14 different activities to have SAM examine (see figure 7.8). SAM also can place inoculation code in software to protect the software from viruses even without the SAM program running.

> ***Tip:*** Starting at the Basic level of protection, SAM checks for known viruses by accessing a file called SAM Virus Definitions. If you have, or are, a savvy network administrator, you can keep SAM up-to-date with the people back home.

Safe Computing 7

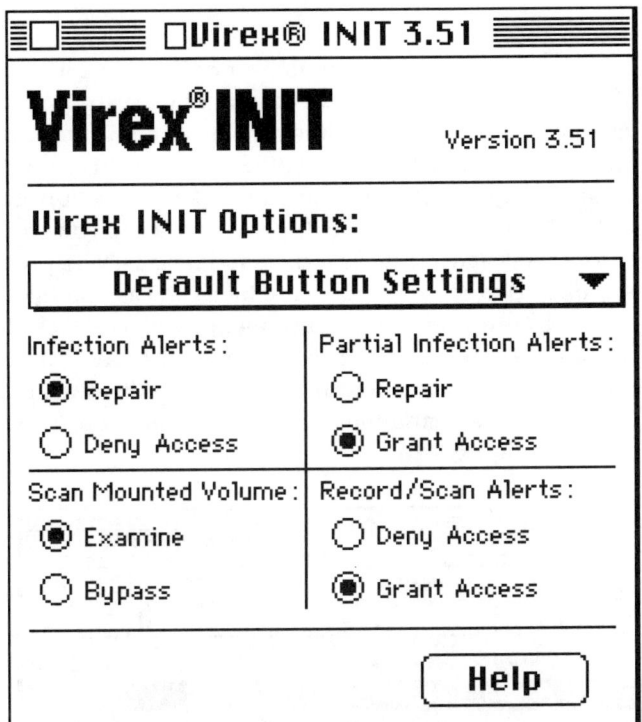

Fig. 7.7.
Virex INIT options.

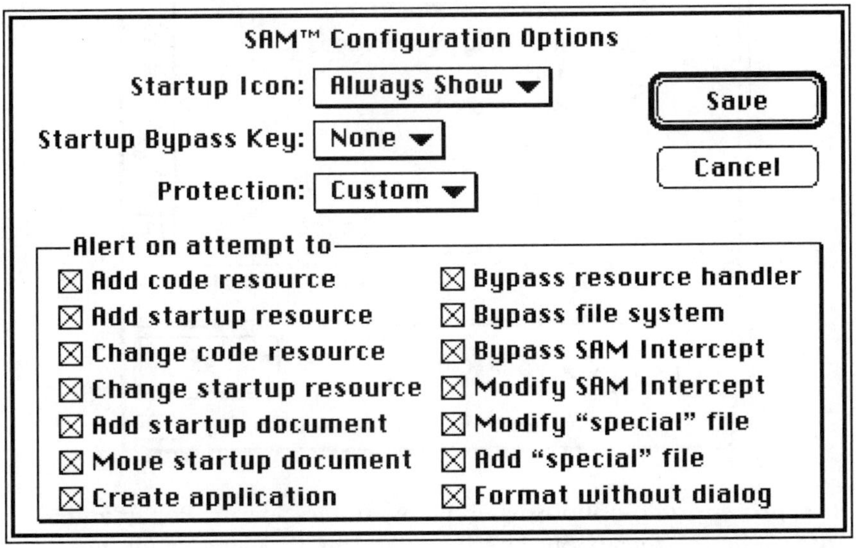

Fig. 7.8.
SAM offers 14 configuration options.

Rival

Donning an icon that could have swum out of *The Little Mermaid* and a variety of sounds depending on the results of its scans, Microseeds' Rival makes one of the least-appealing aspects of computer maintenance almost fun. Like Kent Marsh's FolderBolt, Rival is a gem of a utility because it does not get in your way. In fact, were it not for the square that Rival places around the Apple menu icon, you wouldn't even know Rival was active unless it detected a virus. The program provides seamless detection by checking files only as you open them. Rival comprises a comprehensive scanning application, including all scanning, configuration, and extensive help, within one control panel. You can configure other virus-fighting tools to act this way, but only Rival combines automatic and manual scanning and repair in a single control panel (see figure 7.9).

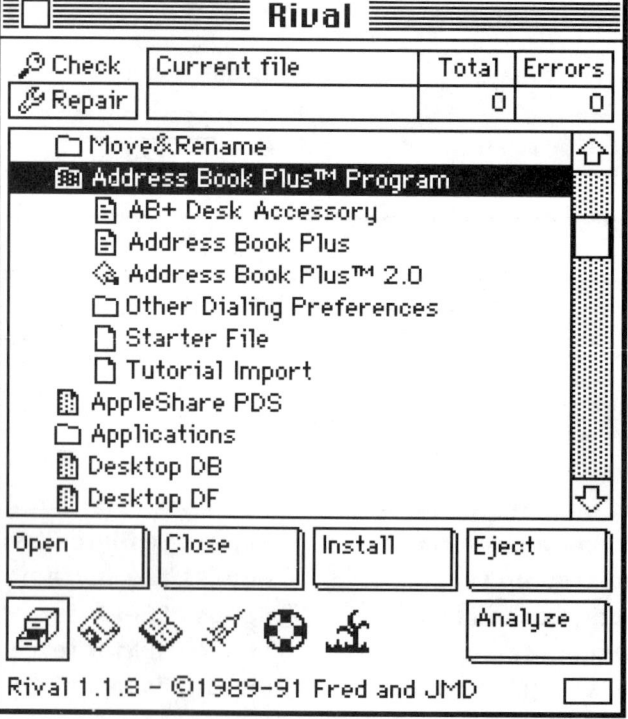

Fig. 7.9. Rival comprises a comprehensive scanning application within one control panel.

Rival presents two options when it encounters a virus: Repair and Stun. Although these options sound like Star Trek phaser settings, stunning a virus is useful if—by some major faux pas—the virus appears on a locked volume such as a CD-ROM. Antiviral utilities can't

Safe Computing 7

repair files on locked volumes because the utilities must alter the file itself to change the infected part. Stunning a virus, though, prevents the virus from spreading. Rival also can warn you if it detects an attempt to erase your hard disk, so it provides peace of mind about a particularly insidious variety of Trojan Horse.

Like Microcom and Symantec, Microseeds offers an automatic update plan and hotline support, although Microseeds has not been as quick to release vaccines to combat viruses as its larger competitors. Rival, however, can update itself by opening "vaccine" files that Microseeds makes available directly and through online services. After you have opened a vaccine, that vaccine becomes a permanent tool in Rival's arsenal of virus-fighting weapons. The ease with which you can update Rival contrasts with the cumbersome codes that you must type into certain virus fighters when a new strain of vermin is detected.

Disinfectant

Disinfectant is a free program written by the magnanimous John Norstad of Northwestern University. Disinfectant does about as good a job of detecting and repairing viruses as anything on the market. However, it lacks some of the bells and whistles of other packages, such as automatic updates when a new virus is discovered and phone support. Nonetheless, Norstad has responded promptly to each new viral discovery with a new version of Disinfectant.

Disinfectant does have some minor anomalies under System 7.0 (for example, you must place its protection extension in the System Folder proper rather than in the Extensions folder), but, all told, the program works well. Because Disinfectant is designed to contain a complete solution in one file, it uniquely can install its protection extension from within the application.

> *Tip:* If you're really bored at the airport, try setting a new application size for Disinfectant. Normally, you set the size by selecting the application, double-clicking in the "Current Size" field, typing in a new value, and closing the Get Info window. This technique does not work with Disinfectant, because—as a tool combatting deviant software—Disinfectant does not allow attempts to change its internals in any way. So, try as you might, you can't change its memory partition, although you can knock yourself out trying. It's almost as exciting as looking for new snowglobes at the souvenir shop, but not quite.

Sometime soon, a System 7.0-savvy Disinfectant 3.0 will arrive, providing a way for modular updates so that you don't have to get a whole new copy of Disinfectant if some loser decides to program a new virus. Although Disinfectant technically "competes" with the commercial utilities mentioned previously, many of the commercial utility authors work with Norstad to ensure that reliable virus detection is not a luxury. Those on a tight budget may find Disinfectant to be their free ticket.

Keep in mind that although many old antiviral programs—mostly freeware—still might be available, most of them check for only selected viruses and are unsupported. Notable exceptions include Disinfectant, Jeff Shulman's shareware VirusDetective, and Chris Johnson's GateKeeper. VirusDetective is a configurable desk accessory that can search for virtually any pattern inside a file; GateKeeper is an excellent tool for controlling the behavior of specific applications, ensuring that they don't do anything suspicious. Either arguably is more configurable than its commercial cousins.

DOS Viruses

If you need to work with DOS or Windows-based data in your Mac, you need not worry about the innumerable and vicious DOS-based viruses unless the virus already has damaged the data. Otherwise, your PowerBook is immune to DOS viruses—unless, of course, it's running DOS under SoftPC. If this is the case, you need a separate DOS virus-checking program. If you're comfortable with SAM, Norton Anti-Virus for the PC generally is considered to be among the best. Norton Anti-Virus uses similar terminology because Symantec owns both programs. Ah, the perils of owning such a versatile computer....

The Bottom Line

Although Rival's integration and interface is appealing, you can approach its convenience using other programs. Disinfectant certainly provides a great bargain by providing 75 percent of the functionality of commercial programs in a free package.

Neither Rival nor Disinfectant, however, can detect suspicious behavior; the programs check only for known viruses. The chance of discovering an unknown virus is very small, but it's nice to know you have some protection available in SAM and Virex. Using SAM's advanced features produces many false alarms, but if you have the patience, you eventually can make SAM unobstructive. SAM also ships with SAM Intercept, Jr., a lean godsend for people in RAM-tight environments.

Safe Computing 7

The Bomb Squad

In reality, of course, malicious intruders and viruses cause a small fraction of all problems. Most difficulties are caused by the types of problems that just seem to occur naturally over time—corrupted applications, extension conflicts, damaged System files, and directory damage. The final chapter should help you track down the causes of system errors and provide a quick fix—enough to last until you can get more in-depth when you have more time and better resources at hand.

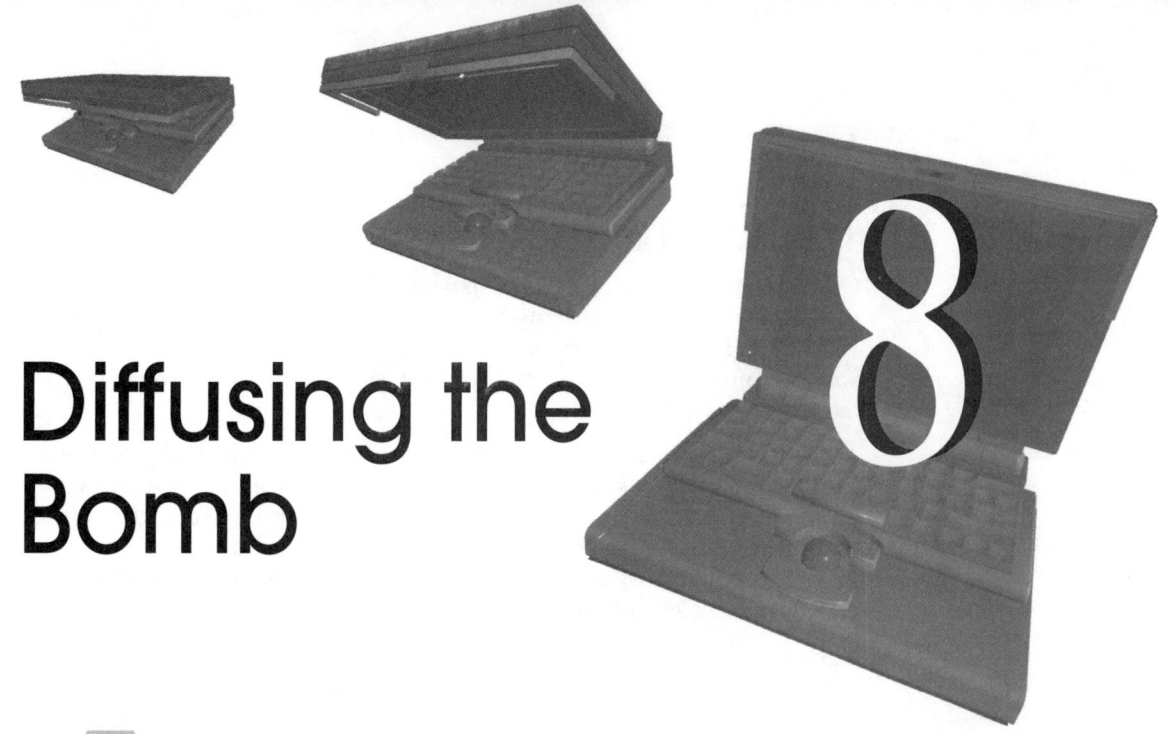

Diffusing the Bomb

8

Anyone who has seen the classic Dr. Seuss cartoon "The Cat in the Hat" may remember when the forward feline marks everything in the house under the rationale of "calculatus eliminatus"—the process of elimination. Successful Macintosh troubleshooting requires a bit of experience, luck, and black magic, along with the process of elimination. If you keep digging methodically, you'll eventually be able to eliminate the cause of woes on your own.

As opposed to question-and-answer troubleshooting chapters that answer random questions and teach you nothing, this chapter lends some insight into what causes things to go wrong and presents the information in a nontechnical fashion. On the road, you probably will be less concerned with minor problems that can wait until you have better support resources available, and more concerned with eliminating problems that interfere with your time-critical tasks.

Essentially, problems can occur at six levels: the document, application, application extension, system extension, system software, and hardware. After you determine the layer at which a problem occurs, fixing the problem usually is straightforward.

The Hard Facts

One of the most useful determinations to make early on is whether the problem you're experiencing is software- or hardware-related. Hardware problems actually consume less troubleshooting time than software problems. Unfortunately, you can't do much yourself if your hard disk really has died.

Apple has instituted a plan in which you can send PowerBooks directly to the company for service. If you call 1-800-SOS-APPL, you can make arrangements to have your PowerBook picked up by overnight courier and returned to you in a matter of days. If you opt to take advantage of this service, you may get your PowerBook back faster than through traditional dealer channels.

Hardware problems often display symptoms that cannot be caused by software, such as a PowerBook that won't turn on or a floppy drive that won't read a variety of disks. Sometimes, though, you can't tell at first glance whether hardware or software is causing the problem. For example, if you see a blinking question mark upon startup, you don't know whether a damaged System file or a dead hard disk is responsible without further investigation.

Sometimes, a sneaky hardware defect can cause a problem that software traditionally causes, such as a system error. Often, such a problem is caused by a hard disk that unexpectedly stops or by failing RAM or some other faulty chip on the PowerBook's logic board. Because of difficulties with SCSI termination, you also should remove any devices attached to the PowerBook's SCSI chain prior to troubleshooting system errors.

Hardware problems often are less predictable than software problems. Crashes caused by software problems often occur while you're saving, printing, or switching among applications. Hardware-based problems caused by failing components tend to occur more randomly and with no help from you.

If your RAM is failing, for example, your machine may crash at a random time after startup. One good way to test for failing RAM is to start up with the System 7.0 Disk Tools disk and just leave your PowerBook turned on for a while. If a RAM chip is going bad, the Mac is likely to crash after just a few minutes.

Disk-o-Tech

Testing a hard disk is trickier, especially for intermittent problems. Because Macintosh system software reads and writes extensively to the

Diffusing the Bomb 8

hard disk, intermittent hard disk problems are nearly indistinguishable from system software problems. In fact, if you have problems reading to or writing from your hard disk, the culprit more likely is damaged system software than a damaged hard drive—especially on a new PowerBook. This situation illustrates Murphy's Law of Hardware Inertia, which states that functioning hardware usually continues functioning, and broken hardware is not likely to spring back to life.

If the hard disk icon appears on the desktop but cannot start the Mac, you can assume that system software is responsible for this failure. For a hard disk that just refuses to start up or appear on the desktop, a quick way to tell whether it's a hard disk problem is to start up from a floppy containing a hard disk formatting utility, such as Apple's HD Setup application.

Launch the hard disk formatting utility (located on the System 7.0 Disk Tools floppy disk). If the hard disk doesn't appear in the list of valid hard drives, the problem probably is hardware-related. The problem might be as simple as a loose cable connecting the hard drive to the logic board. If that's not the problem, you should check to see whether your hard disk is under warranty.

> *Tip:* Apple's HD Setup application often fails to recognize completely functional hard disks because such disks do not contain the Apple label. If you use a third-party hard disk (such as those from CMS and Microtech), be sure to test it with the utility supplied by the hard disk vendor.

If the formatting utility indicates that it can see the hard disk, you can breathe a sigh of relief. At least you have determined that the hard disk is receiving power and sending a signal through the SCSI chain. While you are using the formatting utility, you might as well take advantage of the testing features many of these utilities offer. A test usually scans your hard disk looking for damaged sectors that could cause data loss. Smart formatting software automatically takes these bad sectors out of commission so that your data doesn't get written onto those sectors.

A less reliable method for testing intermittent hard disk problems is to start up from a System 7.0 floppy disk and just open and close some folders on the hard disk. You also can test writing operations by copying some files to and from the hard disk. Do not open any files, however, because doing so causes the hard disk's System to take over, leaving you susceptible to any problems the System may have.

Beating the System

The Macintosh System file is an extraordinarily complex piece of software that is responsible for many tasks. In addition to managing nearly every conceivable task—from memory handling to printing—the System file acts as a liaison between the PowerBook hardware and application software. This relationship makes the System file susceptible to damage. It's difficult to determine the exact cause of a corrupted System file; but this condition commonly causes system errors and oddities.

If your System file is seriously damaged, you'll have a rude awakening when you try to restart your PowerBook and you see the notorious blinking question mark. If you can start up from a floppy disk containing system software, you can be sure that the system file is the problem. Partially damaged system files can cause frequent crashes in many programs, cause just one program to bomb, or even prevent one feature in one program from working properly.

You often can solve the problem of a faulty System file by reinstalling System 7.0—a simple but tedious procedure if you have all the disks available. Five disks may seem like a cumbersome insurance policy—until you need them. Even PowerBook 100 owners should reconsider leaving their external floppy drives behind. Is the extra pound or so worth the possibility of not being able to fix—or even start—your machine?

Sometimes, though, even the Installer program cannot repair a damaged System file. This may occur because the Installer only updates selected parts of the System file and leaves other parts alone. The damage sometimes lies in locations that the Installer cannot repair. If the Installer cannot repair the damage, salvage any important fonts or sounds (important sounds?) by dragging the files out of the System file. Then, delete the System file and reinstall System 7.0. If the problem was a corrupted System file, your PowerBook should work just fine. If the System file was not the problem, your hard disk may have directory damage. An application such as Norton Utilities for Macintosh (discussed later) may be able to help.

Sometimes, hard disks do not appear on the desktop because of damaged or incompatible drivers. A hard disk driver is software that manages communications between the hard disk and the system software. Apple's HD SC Setup Utility has an Update button that may be able to repair a damaged hard disk driver. Other formatting utilities

Diffusing the Bomb 8

have functional equivalents. Many hard disk formatting utilities enable you to update the hard disk driver without forcing you to erase the hard disk (see figure 8.1). You always should make sure you have the most recent version of formatting software. Luckily, most vendors—including Apple—offer free updates of their formatting software.

Fig. 8.1. Apple's HD SC Setup Utility enables you to update the hard disk driver without erasing the hard disk.

If the vendor did not supply a formatting utility (tsk, tsk) or if you want an application that provides more options than generic formatting utilities, you should consider Silverlining from La Cie, Ltd. This trustworthy utility recognizes Apple and third-party drives and provides a host of methods for customizing your hard disk. Such options include a choice of icons and a software-based "access light" that flashes in the top-left corner of the Mac screen. A less expensive but arguably more elegant formatting program is the System 7.0-savvy Drive7 from Casa Blanca Works, a company that appears to be finding a niche for inexpensive, useful utilities.

Assuming you have backups of your important work, you can try reformatting your hard disk as a last resort. Although you will lose all the data on your hard disk, reformatting sometimes can clear up problems or repair severe directory damage that data recovery programs cannot fix. If your formatting utility is unable to reformat the drive, you might try another formatting utility. Beyond that, your hard disk probably has serious physical problems, and you must either have the drive repaired or replace it.

The Soft Touch

Because PowerBooks have a finite number of hardware components, an Apple dealer can diagnose what is wrong with the machine relatively easily. Authorized Apple dealers have diagnostic tools that further facilitate the process. Certainly, fewer variables exist than in the thousands of Macintosh programs that contain millions of lines of potentially conflicting programming code.

What causes system errors and other problems? The answer often is more complex than an error code number with an explanation such as "unimplemented trap." Macintosh software responds to an almost infinite number of actions that users perform in various regions of the screen. Consequently, Macintosh software is, by necessity, more complex than character-based software such as Lotus 1-2-3 for DOS.

This complexity should not reflect negatively on the collective competence of Mac programmers. On the contrary, the entire PowerBook environment provides a smoother road than the parade of Unrecoverable Application Errors Microsoft Windows users endure.

Troubleshooting software—although far from fun—enhances your expertise and enables you to resolve problems more quickly the next time they appear. Improving your troubleshooting skills also makes you more productive in the long run. Although some problems can take even experienced Macintosh consultants hours to resolve, you'll fix more problems in less time if you use a diagnostic approach.

To reiterate, Mac software problems can occur at five levels: document, application, application extension, system extension, and system software. The preceding section discussed system software problems. Problems that can occur at the other four levels are discussed in the following sections. You won't always have a clear indication of the level at which the problem occurs. Often, however, you can quickly narrow down the possible offenders.

8 Diffusing the Bomb

What's Wrong, Doc?

Document corruption problems are among the easiest to detect but can be the most frustrating to fix. Essentially, if you are only having trouble with one document, and the others are of a similar file size and complexity, it's easy to detect the corrupted document. If the problem occurs in more than one file, you should suspect something other than the document. The document may contain garbled or overlaid text, or it may refuse to open, save, or print (those pesky PostScript errors). Perhaps scrolling to a part of the document causes a system error.

As long as you can open a document, you have a chance of recovering most of its content. Select small pieces of the document and cut and paste them into another document. If scrolling to part of the document causes you to crash, try scrolling past that section. Sometimes, you can select what comes after the corrupted part of your document. As a result, you'll need to re-create only the section that somehow became corrupted.

If you can't open the file, your chances for recovering the bulk of the file are much greater if the file is text-oriented, such as a word processing document. You also may have luck opening the file from within another application; for example, Microsoft Word can read MacWrite files. Several free and shareware programs can read the data parts of word processing files, enabling you to salvage much of a seemingly corrupted file.

Interrupting This Program

Application errors also are easy to spot but are even easier to fix. Application errors often occur after the occurence of a system error that is so severe that the application becomes corrupted. An application that ran well yesterday refuses to open today although you haven't changed anything. As a rule, you should try to increase the RAM allocation from the application's "Get Info" window, because a lack of available RAM often causes problems for applications.

Sometimes, a corrupted System file can cause this condition. To eliminate any doubt, replace the application on your hard disk with a fresh copy from the master disk or a backup disk. If the program is well-designed, any previously set preferences should remain intact.

Tip: Although carrying a complete set of backup floppies with you may seem unreasonable, you may want to consider taking backup copies of your most important applications along with a set of System 7.0.1 floppies. If an application is too large to fit on a floppy, you can compress the program into a self-extracting archive using StuffIt Deluxe or Compact Pro. In this format, the archive can self-expand onto your hard disk.

Weighing Your Options

Application extensions have a variety of names depending on the application the programs extend. Quark calls its extensions QuarkXTensions, Aldus calls them Aldus Additions, Claris calls them Add-Its, and Adobe calls them plug-ins. Regardless of the name, application extensions provide an easy way to customize an application's features. The Find File command in Microsoft Word 5.0 enables you to search for files based on a variety of criteria (see figure 8.2). Such a feature is an example of an application extension that adds new capabilities to a program in a modular way.

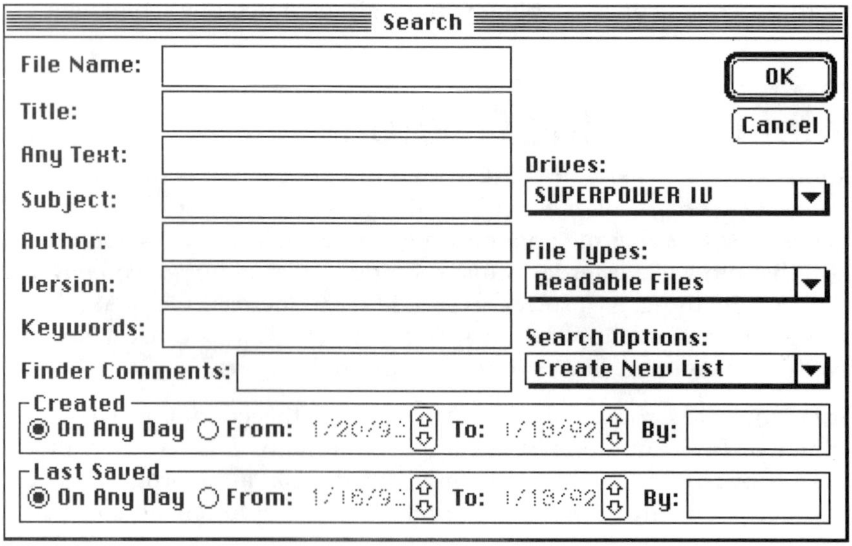

Fig. 8.2. Microsoft Word 5.0's Find File command.

Diffusing the Bomb 8

Extensible, modular applications are exciting because they provide a way for developers to add dream features to programs without a time-consuming upgrade to the application itself. Such applications also enable you to continue working with applications with which you are comfortable.

For example, let's say you do a lot of scientific reports and you need an equation editor integrated into your word processor. Because this is not a feature that the majority of people need, a developer may be reluctant to make an equation editor a feature of the program. If someone else could develop an equation editor extension to your word processor, the extension would fill your need. You would not have to wait for an upgrade or choose another word processor that may contain an equation editor.

On the other hand, application extensions add yet another layer of complexity to the Macintosh environment. From a technical-support perspective, they introduce the concept of "fourth-party developers" who create extensions for applications written by third parties (such as Aldus or Claris) that second parties (you) use on machines by first parties (such as Apple). At this rate, you soon may need an attorney present to turn on your PowerBook!

If you use application extensions and have a problem (although the problem may not necessarily surface when using the extension's features), try disabling the extension or extensions and restarting. With most applications that support extensions (such as QuarkXPress or SuperPaint), you can disable the extension by dragging modules out of a special folder that the application searches when it launches. For example, SuperPaint keeps these files in a folder called "SP Pouch." At least one application, Canvas by Deneba Software, enables you to select which extensions you want to use via an innovative tool picker that appears when you launch the application.

When you discover an extension that's causing a problem, you may need to contact the developer of the extension rather than the application developer for technical assistance.

Application extensions currently cause a relatively small percentage of problems. This situation, however, is likely to change as more applications adopt a modular approach to adding features. Soon, presentation programs such as Aldus Persuasion and word processors such as MacWrite Pro will enable you to add features through their developers' extension schemes.

INIT-Wits

Unlike application extensions—which slowly continue to gain popularity among developers and users—system extensions also have been popular with Mac users for several years. System extensions have been known by many arcane names, among them control panels, INITs, cdevs, RDEVs, and startup documents. System extensions, however, comprise some of the most well-known Mac programs (such as After Dark, DiskDoubler, QuicKeys 2, and Virex).

System extensions are programs that run when your Mac starts up. Extensions usually display their icons in a row at the bottom of the startup screen. Typically, extensions add functionality to the standard operating environment, providing magic such as automatic virus scans, screen savers (not as valuable on a PowerBook), automatic file compression, and hierarchical Apple menus.

The System automatically places extensions in either the Control Panels folder or the Extensions folder when you drag extension icons to the System Folder. However, extensions also can work if they are "loose" in the System Folder (some older extensions operate better there). The Control Panel folder contains extensions called control panels (formerly cdevs); you can double-click and configure these control panels. This is a big switch for old Mac hands who remember when they could not open control panels from the Finder. (Actually, extremely old Mac hands may remember when control panels didn't exist!)

You cannot open extensions (formerly INITs) in the Extensions folder by double-clicking. You can access some extensions, though, such as the LaserWriter and StyleWriter extensions, through the Chooser. Other extensions just provide functionality; you cannot configure them. The DiskDoubler extension, for example, places a DD menu in the Finder and does not need a control panel interface. You change options from the DD menu itself.

Extensions use hard disk space and RAM. Although many extensions consume minimal amounts of RAM, owners of 2M PowerBooks will be hard-pressed to run any extensions. Provided you have enough RAM, there is no limit to the number of extensions you can use. Some power users run more than 30 extensions; this provides many added functions but uses a great deal of RAM.

A problem with extensions is that they sometimes conflict with system software, applications, and even each other. Extensions cause conflicts

Diffusing the Bomb 8

so often that they should be among the first items you check when troubleshooting problems. You can turn off all extensions by holding down the Shift key as the PowerBook starts up. The standard welcome message changes to "Welcome to Macintosh. Extensions off."

Extension Headaches

For more sophisticated extension management, a good extension manager makes all the difference. An extension manager enables you to turn off different extensions selectively upon startup. This eliminates much of the tedium associated with troubleshooting extensions. An extension manager also enables you to change the order in which extensions load.

By default, extensions load alphabetically within three folders. All extensions in the Extensions folder load first, followed by control panels in the Control Panels folder. Any extensions loose in the System Folder load last.

For example, KiwiPowerWindows loads before On Location Extension, because both extensions belong in the Extensions Folder. AlarmsClock, however, loads after both of these files, because it is a control panel. You sometimes can resolve extension conflicts by having one extension load before another. This strategy is especially good if you see crashes upon startup even before you arrive at the Finder.

If you are lucky, you discover which extension caused the system error. You then can experiment using an extension manager to move an offending extension earlier (or later) in the startup sequence. Most extension managers offer the option of automatically disabling the extension that was loading when the system error occurred.

> ***Tip:*** You also can use the rearrange feature of an extension manager to have an important extension—such as a virus checker—load early in the sequence. As a result, the extension can check for viruses in other extensions. If you have security software that uses an extension to prompt for the password (such as MacPassword), you may want to rename the software so that it loads before the extension manager itself. Doing so prevents knowledgeable intruders from using the extension manager to turn off the security software.

Most extension managers let you save groups of extensions in sets. You can create a minimal set that contains just your essential extensions, or exclude an extension when you know you'll be using an application that is incompatible with your extension.

> ***Tip:*** Although most extension managers technically are control panels, you must place them in the Extensions folder, because the PowerBook examines the Extensions folder first when it starts loading extensions. To access your extension manager in the Control Panels folder, place an alias of your extension manager program in that folder.

Ricardo Batista (an Apple employee) wrote a capable, free extension manager aptly named Extensions Manager. Like most extension managers in its genre, you can configure Extensions Manager's control panel by opening the panel or holding down the spacebar upon startup. Extensions Manager uniquely enables you to designate the types of files you regard as extensions (see figure 8.3). This feature may become more important as programmers write new utilities as applications that you can place in the System Folder's Startup Items folder.

Fig. 8.3. Extensions Manager enables you to select the file types you want to manage upon startup.

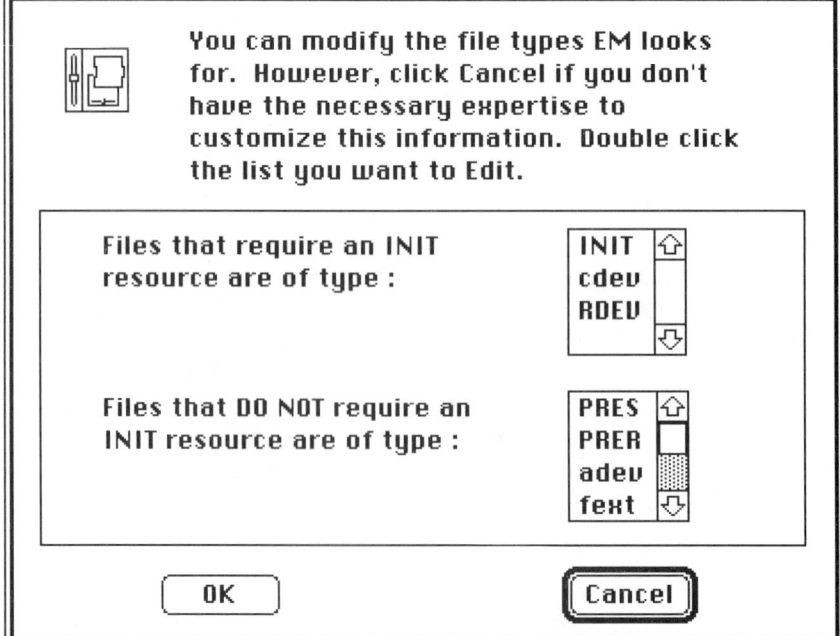

Diffusing the Bomb 8

Other extension managers include Startup Manager (part of Now Software's Now Utilities), On Startup (part of Icom Simulations' On Cue II), and Microseeds' INITPicker.

Startup Manager enables users with many extensions to display all the startup icons in two or three rows. Startup Manager also changes the file type of the extension. You cannot configure disabled control panels for the next restart. Startup Manager provides a unique Links feature that enables you to specify, for example, two extensions that should never run together or to specify that one extension depends on another (see figure 8.4).

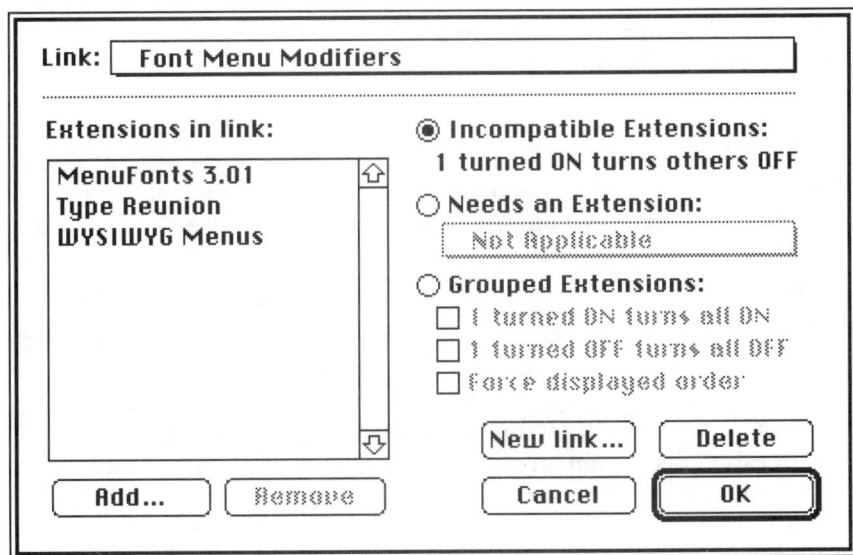

Fig. 8.4.
Now Utilities' Startup Manager enables you to create relationships among extensions.

For example, CE Software's QuicKeys 2 is not fully functional unless CEToolbox loads before QuicKeys 2. Using Startup Manager, you can specify that CEToolbox must load if you select QuicKeys 2. Startup Manager also provides thorough reports on extensions and the order in which the extensions load. This feature can be useful for sending to a technical support department if you cannot resolve an extension conflict by reordering extensions.

Icom Simulation's On Startup may be even faster than Startup Manager, but On Startup lacks Startup Manager's icon-wrapping and linking features. Billed as a "safe" extension manager, On Startup does not change the file types of extensions and control panels, taking the novel approach of moving disabled extensions into folders where they won't load.

Although On Startup's method probably is superior to Startup Manager's, it's more a question of convenience than safety. On Startup's interface is partly inspired by Extensions Manager, but On Startup has most of the bells and whistles of a commercial contender. If nothing else, its startup icon of a match igniting wins hands-down for the best animation in an extension manager icon.

Microseeds' INITPicker, once the CEO of extension managers, has not undergone a major revision in some time. The main gripe with INITPicker is—despite updates that promised better speed—the program scans the System Folder for new extensions more slowly than its competitors.

INITPicker provides a convenient method for determining the file type and size of the extensions it manages, and the program does not change or move the extensions. This approach is more seamless than those of other utilities, but it gives you no indication that an extension has been disabled. This lack of feedback can be confusing if you don't remember which extensions you turned off. When opened, most control panels are smart enough to realize that they were not loaded upon startup, but some may give you confusing error messages.

> *Tip:* When using an extension manager to troubleshoot extensions, keep halving the number of your extensions as you restart until you determine the source of the trouble. For example, when an application crashes with all your extensions loaded, but it doesn't crash when an extension manager disables them all, use the halving procedure to help you narrow the cause of the crash.

To determine the exasperating extension, try loading all extensions that start with the letters A through M and see whether the application crashes. If it does, you know the problem is among those extensions. You can keep restarting, using half of that set (that is, trying A through G and then A through D, and so on) until you determine which extension is causing the problem. Of course, if the application does not crash with extensions that begin with the letters A through M, you should start narrowing down the culprit from the N through Z set.

As this example illustrates, even a good extension manager cannot eliminate the tedious and battery-consuming troubleshooting process. You may have to restart several times to determine the cause of the problem. You could avoid much of this trouble if another user already knew which extensions conflicted and what he or she should do to resolve the conflicts.

Someone does know: Baseline Publishing sells INITInfo Pro, a HyperCard stack that contains a plethora of information on extensions and how they go bump in the Mac. The information in INITInfo Pro has been collected largely from members of CompuServe's on-line community, which boasts some of the most knowledgeable names in the Mac community. A demonstration version of INITInfo is available on-line from CompuServe.

The Norton Anthology

Symantec's Norton Utilities for Macintosh is the premiere data recovery package for the Mac. You won't find many unqualified recommendations in this book, but in spite of Norton Utilities' somewhat high price for a utilities package and partial incompatibility with System 7.0, you should buy this collection. The Norton Utilities Disk Doctor component can quickly scan and repair directory damage on hard disks, and its Unerase feature often resurrects files you emptied in the Trash. Unerase achieves much of its magic through a control panel called FileSaver (see figure 8.5), which makes a copy of your directory in case your original directory becomes corrupted. Although the program attempts to track the last 500 deleted files, you probably won't be able to recover many older ones.

Symantec also sells a similar product called SUM (Symantec Utilities for Macintosh) II, but Symantec plans to incorporate the more popular features of SUM in the next major release of Norton Utilities.

> ***Tip:*** Unless you buy your software at a Mac-specific store such as California's Computerware or one of the Mac mail-order houses, specify that you want Norton Utilities *for Macintosh*. Norton Utilities also is a highly regarded package in the DOS world, and you may receive the PC version if you're not vocal.

Norton Utilities also contains Speed Disk, a program that takes parts of files that have been spread out over the hard disk and puts them in one contiguous block (see figure 8.6). This process, called fragmentation, happens to all disks that have been used for a while. Programs such as Speed Disk are called defragmenters or optimizers.

8 Hayden's PowerBook Power Book

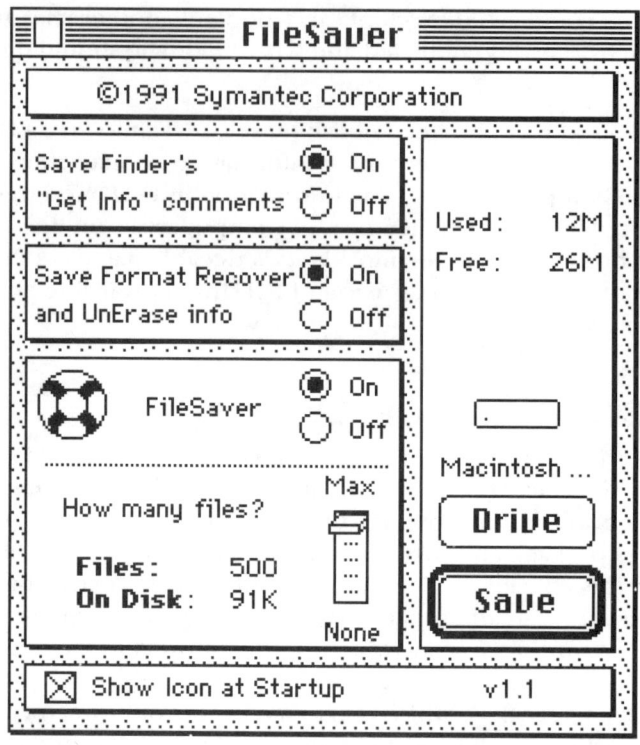

Fig. 8.5. The Norton Utilities FileSaver control panel.

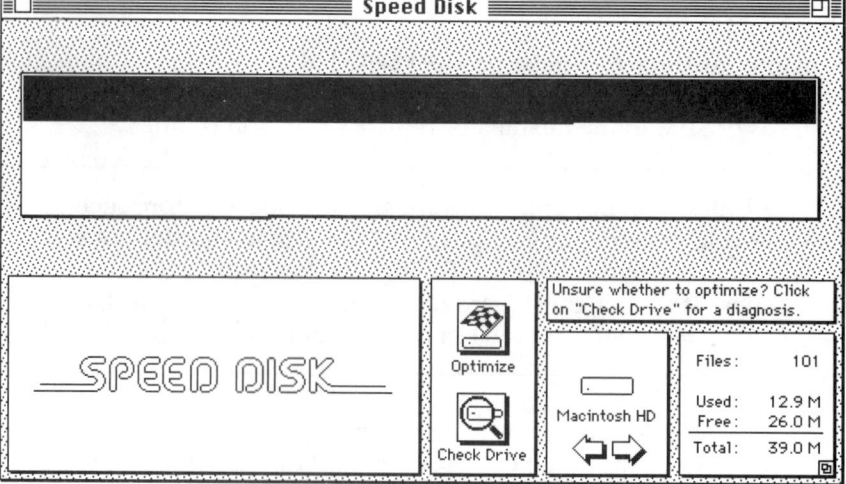

Fig. 8.6. The Norton Utilities Speed Disk.

Diffusing the Bomb 8

Disk Express II—a competitor to Speed Disk—keeps your hard disk constantly optimized by shuffling parts of files when you're not busy at your Mac. The usefulness of this constant disk-chugging has been debated, and it is of even more dubious value in the disk access-sensitive world of the PowerBooks. Generally, your PowerBook should not suffer from the slowdown associated with severe fragmentation if you use a program such as Speed Disk once per month.

The MacTools Deluxe collection offers some features Norton Utilities lacks, including a capable backup application and file security software. You can run the optimizer from the startup disk, whereas you must boot Speed Disk from a floppy disk to defragment your internal hard disk. The Rescue program (the counterpart to Disk Doctor) provides advice for specific problems that can circumvent running MacTools Deluxe; the Rescue Program's Mirror program (similar to Norton's FileSaver program) can update its copy of the directory via a hot key.

Both Symantec and Central Point Software reportedly are readying new versions of their programs for release in 1992, so keep your eyes on the software shelves.

In contrast to data recovery programs, which take a mostly reactive approach to saving the day, four packages can help you foresee and prevent problems.

Last Resort

Last Resort by Working Software performs like a modest safety net. This small control panel remembers each keystroke you type and stores it in a file. Unlike file recovery programs that update only at shutdown, Last Resort works constantly. As a result, you have some sort of automatic backup for text-based documents even if a problem prevents you from saving your work. Using Last Resort's control panel interface, you can specify how often you want the program to write keystrokes to its backup file (see figure 8.7).

If you need to recover text from a Last Resort file, don't expect a beautiful layout to be preserved. Last Resort's clearly stated purpose is to record everything you type, including text you've deleted and replaced. You may have to spend some time re-creating the document from fragments contained in the Last Resort file.

Fig. 8.7.
Last Resort records every keystroke.

Last Resort also poses a security risk because it records passwords you may have typed to access network services or password-protected documents from programs such as Excel, WordPerfect, and MicroPhone II. Anyone who can access the backup file may be able to determine your passwords. If you don't work with confidential documents, or if your entire hard disk is password protected, Last Resort pays for itself in saved frustration.

What Knowledge Lurks

Teknosys' Help may be the next best thing to traveling with a Macintosh expert—and you don't even have to feed it. Although most file recovery programs can detect basic problems such as multiple System Folders, Help! goes an order of magnitude deeper to provide a detailed, beautifully formatted report on your hardware and software (see figure 8.8). Teknosys' Help! screen doubles as a printed report. You can navigate the wealth of information the program provides by using the pop-up menu in its lower left corner.

Diffusing the Bomb 8

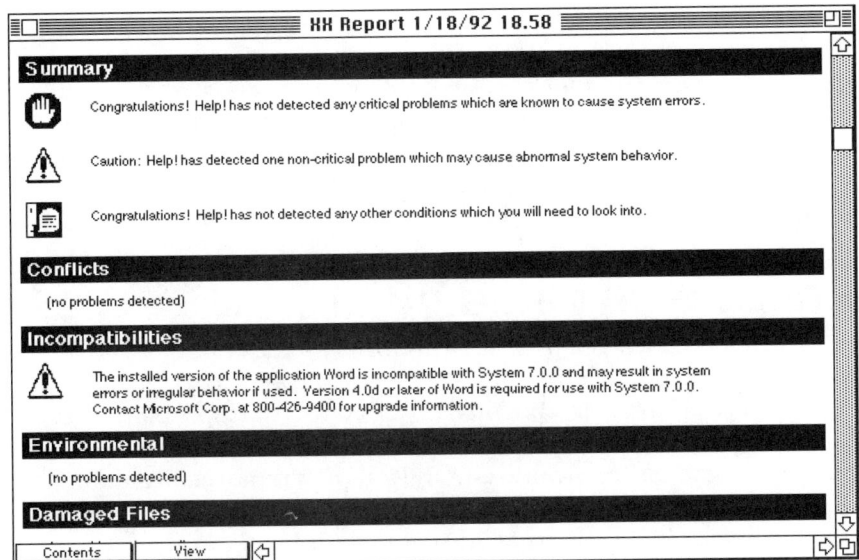

Fig. 8.8. Teknosys' Help! produces a detailed report.

Help! is easy to use, which is fortunate because the last thing you need when your PowerBook isn't working properly is a stress-inducing application. To create a report, double-click on the Help! application icon and click the New Report button. Help! asks you to select a system version number. You then choose which disk to analyze. This step is provided for users with multiple drives attached to their desktop Mac. Chances are however, you only need to select the startup disk. After you select the disk, Help! treats you to an entertaining display in which you see small icons fly out of a Mac and onto a report.

The brain of Help! is a file called Knowledgebase, which Help! uses to determine incompatibilities and store information about whom to contact. If you are using an old version of Thunder 7 with your PowerBook, Help! may tell you "Thunder 7 1.0 is incompatible with System 7.0. You should use Thunder 7 1.04. Please contact Baseline Publishing at 901-682-9676." The previous example sounds like something you might see in Apple's Compatibility Checker, but Knowledgebase can diagnose INIT conflicts and hardware conflicts.

Help! is superbly implemented, but its usefulness depends on how thorough and current the Knowledgebase remains. Teknosys intends to update the information file every six months. However, the pace at which Mac software is developed and updated unfortunately ensures that Help! is always playing catch-up with the products it diagnoses.

Help!'s nontechnical explanations of complex incompatibilities are useful to beginners. The program, however, is most useful when an experienced user can interpret the program's results. Remember that Help! may not always provide the proper advice because the program lacks completely up-to-date information. If Teknosys can enlist the cooperation of other vendors to maintain the accuracy of Help!, the program can remain a powerful weapon in a troubleshooting arsenal.

Hanging on a Heartbeat

Micromat's MacEKG is a product with the right idea but the wrong focus for a broad audience. This startling control panel performs a series of eye- and ear-dazzling diagnostics upon startup, compiling and recording statistics for hard disk and CPU speed (see figure 8.9). MacEKG's diagnostics include an "MPR" (mean performance rating). The Export Log button makes comparing figures in a spreadsheet easy. You can control how often MacEKG compares the figures.

Fig. 8.9. MacEKG performs a series of dazzling diagnostics.

Diffusing the Bomb 8

MacEKG is at home in a service department that needs to trace hardware problems. PowerBook owners who want insight into what goes wrong may feel cheated unless their hardware has legitimate problems. MacEKG routinely performs hard disk checks that may result in wasted battery time.

The product's appeal (besides the quasi-robotic voices that announce "All systems nominal") is that it scans at startup, much like a virus protection program. This type of scan should be applied in more mainstream applications—such as a scan for directory damage upon startup with Norton Utilities for Macintosh.

Crashing the Party

There's not much that's frustrating about using a Mac, but only Mac users know the frustration resulting from the appearance of the message "Sorry, a system error occurred." Since the dawn of the Macintosh era, Mac users have tried to make their machines more reliable. Several good techniques have been discovered, such as giving applications plenty of RAM and keeping extensions down to a minimum, but the bombings haven't stopped.

Through the years, several "anti-crashing" programs have appeared in freeware and shareware forms under various names. No conclusive testing ever proved such programs worked, however.

That may change, though, with Crash Barrier, by Casady & Greene, which takes a three-tiered approach to diffusing the bomb. In presenting an alternative system error dialog box, Crash Barrier goes into more depth about why a program locked up. These explanations may satisfy your curiosity more than your deadline, but they induce less head-scratching than wondering about the nature of an "F-Line error."

Second, Crash Barrier offers you a variety of choices when a system error occurs, including several choices that may keep you going long enough to save your work. Crash Barrier's "Fix It" button often fails to highlight, but undoing system errors does not seem like a trivial task. Crash Barrier contains a few options that have always been available by typing codes after pressing the programmer's switch. However, Crash Barrier makes the options more accessible, complete with on-screen explanations. Crash Barrier also can warn you when memory is so low that a crash is likely, but this feature itself seems to crash the system in its initial release.

8 Hayden's PowerBook Power Book

Finally, in a concession that even its anti-crashing mechanisms are not foolproof, Crash Barrier includes an auto-saving function comparable to Now's NowSave or Advanced Sofware's QuickTools (see figure 8.10). In addition to providing more options when a system occurs, Crash Barrier provides a multitude of methods to configure its automatic saving rules. You can set Crash Barrier to save at regular intervals or after a given number of mouse clicks or keystrokes.

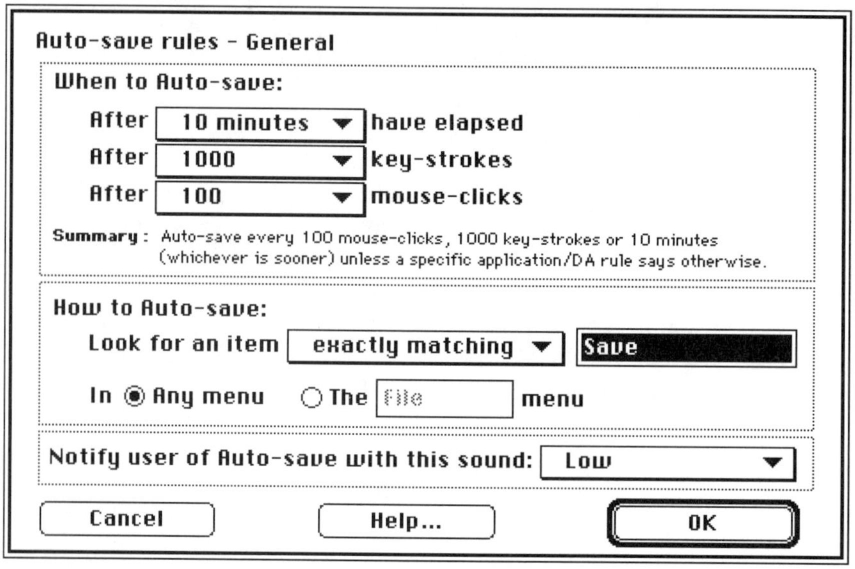

Fig. 8.10. Crash Barrier provides an automatic saving feature.

All system software malfunctions once in a while. Crash Barrier is no substitute for memory protection, which protects other programs when one program crashes. This feature may appear in a future version of system software. Until then, Crash Barrier represents the best protection from system errors you can get.

Product Directory

Notes: The following list is alphabetical by product name. All prices are suggested retail. Some products have different pricing structures for multiple or LAN purchases. Please contact the vendor if you have any questions.

1-Shot Worksheet
Baseline Publishing
1770 Moriah Woods Blvd., Suite 14
Memphis, TN 38117
(800) 926-9676
(901) 682-9676
$99.95

AccessPC
Insignia Solutions
526 Clyde Ave.
Mountain View, CA 94043
(415) 694-7600
$99.95

ACT! for Macintosh
Contact Software International, Inc.
1840 Hutton Dr., #200
Carrollton, TX 75006
(800) 365-0606
(214) 919-9500
$395

Acta 7
Symmetry Software
8603 E. Royal Palm Rd., Suite 110
Scottsdale, AZ 85258
(800) 624-2485
(602) 998-9106
$149

Active Memory
ASD Software, Inc.
4650 Arrow Highway, E-6
Montclair, CA 91763
(714) 624-2594
$199 for two users

ADB 10-Key
Sophisticated Circuits
19017 120th Ave. N.E., Suite 106
Bothell, WA 98011
(206) 485-7979
Price unavailable at press time.

Hayden's PowerBook Power Book

Address Book
Jim Leitch
$30
Available from online services and user groups.

Address Book Plus
Power Up Software Corp.
2929 Campus Drive
San Mateo, CA 94403
(800) 851-2917
(415) 345-5900
$99.95

Adobe Type Manager (ATM)
Adobe Systems
1585 Charleston Road
P.O. Box 7900
Mountain View, CA 94039
(800) 344-8335
(415) 961-4400
$99

After Dark
Berkeley Systems
2095 Rose St.
Berkeley, CA 94709
(510) 540-5535
$49.95

AgentDA
TeamBuilding Technologies
836 Bloomfield
Otremont, Quebe
H2V 3S6 Canada
(514) 278-3010
$99

AlSoft Power Utilities
AlSoft, Inc.
P.O. Box 927
Spring, TX 77383
(713) 353-4090
$129

Amazing Paint
CE Software
1801 Industrial Circle
P.O. Box 65580
West Des Moines, IA 50265
(515) 224-1995
$79.95

America Online
America Online, Inc.
8619 Westwood Center Dr.
Vienna, VA 22182
(800) 227-6364
(703) 448-8700
Access software is free. Online rates vary.

AppleTalk Remote Access
Apple Computer, Inc.
Cupertino, CA 95014
(800) 776-2333
(908) 996-1010
$199

AutoDoubler
Salient Software
124 University Ave., Suite 300
Palo Alto, CA 94301
(415) 321-5375
$79.95

Automobile Power Adapter
Lind Electronic Design Co., Inc.
6416 Cambridge St.
St. Louis Park, MN 55426
(612) 927-6303
$189.95

Auxiliary Power Pack
Lind Electronic Design Co., Inc.
6416 Cambridge St.
St. Louis Park, MN 55426
(612) 927-6303
$99.95

BeagleWorks
Beagle Bros.
6215 Ferris Sq., Suite 100
San Diego, CA 92121
(619) 452-5500
$299

BeHierarchic
Fabien Octave
$10
Available from online services and user groups.

Bernoulli 90 Transportable removable drive
Iomega Corp.
1821 W. 4000 S.
Roy, UT 84067
(800) 456-5522
(801) 778-1000
$1,198

Product Directory

BookView video card
Computer Care
Ford Centre
420 N. Fifth St., Suite 1180
Minneapolis, MN 55401
(612) 371-0061
$395

Carbon Copy Mac
Microcom, Inc.
500 River Ridge Dr.
Norwood, MA 02062
(800) 822-8224
(617) 551-1000
$99

Chinon CDA-431 CD-ROM drive
Chinon, Inc.
660 Maple Ave.
Torrance, CA 90503
(213) 533-0274
$795

Citadel
Microcom, Inc.
500 River Ridge Dr.
Norwood, MA 02062
(800) 822-8224
(617) 551-1000
$149.95

ClarisWorks
Claris Corp.
5201 Patrick Henry Drive
Santa Clara, CA 95052
(800) 544-8554
(408) 987-7000
$299

ClearVue/SD21 monitor
RasterOps
2500 Walsh Ave.
Santa Clara, CA 95051
(800) 729-2656
(408) 562-4200
$2,199

ClickChange
Dubl-Click Software
9316 Deering Ave.
Chatsworth, CA 91311
(818) 700-9525
$79.95

Compact Pro
Bill Goodman
$25
Available from online services
and user groups.

CompuServe Information Manager (CIM)
CompuServe Information Service
5000 Arlington Centre Blvd.
Columbus, OH 43220
(800) 848-8199
(614) 457-8600
$39.95

CompuServe Information Service (CIS)
CompuServe Information Service
5000 Arlington Centre Blvd.
Columbus, OH 43220
(800) 848-8199
(614) 457-8600
Online rates vary.

CompuServe Navigator
CompuServe Information Service
5000 Arlington Centre Blvd.
Columbus, OH 43220
(800) 848-8199
(614) 457-8600
$99.95

Connect, Inc.
10101 Bubb Rd.
Cupertino, CA 95014
(800) 262-2638
Online rates vary.

Connections
Concentrix Technology
1875 South Grant St., Suite 760
San Mateo, CA 94402
(415) 726-1700
$199

Contact Ease
Westware
10148 Diamond Head Ct.
Spring Valley, CA 92077
(800) 869-0871
(619) 660-0356
$395

Crash Barrier
Casady & Greene, Inc.
22734 Portola Dr.
Salinas, CA 93908
(800) 359-4920
(408) 484-9228
$79.95

DAtabase
Baseline Publishing
1770 Moriah Woods Blvd., Suite 14
Memphis, TN 38117
(800) 926-9676
(901) 682-9676
$129.95

DateBook
After Hours Software
5636 Van Nuys Blvd., Suite B
Van Nuys, CA 91401
(818) 780-2220
$125

DayMaker
Pastel Development Corp.
81 Franklin St., Suite 3B
New York, NY 10013
(212) 431-3421
$99

Delphi Information Systems
31416 Agoura Rd.
Westlake Village, CA 91361
(800) 251-7385
(800) 325-9450
Online rates vary.

DeskPaint and DeskDraw
Zedcor
4500 E. Speedway, #22
Tucson, AZ 85712
(602) 881-8101
$199.95

Diconix M150 Plus printer
Diconix (Eastman Kodak Co.)
PPP Customer Information Center
901 Elm Grove Rd.
Rochester, NY 14653-6224
(800) 344-0006
$699

Disinfectant
John Norstad
Free
Available from online services
and user groups.

DiskDoubler
Salient Software
124 University Ave., Suite 300
Palo Alto, CA 94301
(415) 321-5375
$79.95

DiskExpress II
ALSoft, Inc.
P.O. Box 927
Spring, TX 77383
(713) 353-4090
$89.95

DiskLock
Fifth Generation Systems
10049 N. Reiger Road
Baton Rouge, LA 70809
(800) 873-4384
(504) 291-7221
$189

DiskTop
CE Software
1801 Industrial Circle
P.O. Box 65580
West Des Moines, IA 50265
(515) 224-1995
$99.95

DOS Mounter
Dayna Communications, Inc.
50 S. Main St.
Salt Lake City, UT 84144
(801) 531-0600
$89.95

DoubleTalk
Baseline Publishing
1770 Moriah Woods Blvd., Suite 14
Memphis, TN 38117
(800) 926-9676
(901) 682-9676
$149.95

Drive7
Casa Blanca Works, Inc.
148 Bon Air Center
Greenbrae, CA 94904
(415) 461-2249
Price unavailable at press time.

Dynodex
Portfolio Systems, Inc.
10062 Miller Ave., Suite 201
Cupertino, CA 95014
(800) 729-3966
$125

DynoPage
Portfolio Systems, Inc.
10062 Miller Ave., Suite 201
Cupertino, CA 95014
(800) 729-3966
$125

Product Directory

Easy Alarms
Essential Software
Address information unavailable at press time.
$59.95

Empower III
Magna
2540 N. First St., Suite 302
San Jose, CA 95131
(408) 433-5467
$396

Fair Witness
Chena Software
905 Harrison St.
Allentown, PA 18103
(215) 770-1210
$495

The Far Side Computer Calendar for Macintosh
Amaze!, Inc.
11810 115th Ave., NE
Kirkland, WA 98034
(800) 367-4802
(206) 820-7007
$69.95

File Director
Fifth Generation Systems
10049 N. Reiger Road
Baton Rouge, LA 70809
(800) 873-4384
(504) 291-7221
$129

FileGuard
ASD Software, Inc.
4650 Arrow Highway, E-6
Montclair, CA 91763
(714) 624-2594
$249

First Things First
Visionary Software
P.O. Box 69447
Portland, OR 97201
(503) 246-6200
$69.95

FolderBolt
Kent Marsh Ltd.
P.O. Box 460289
1200 Post Oak Blvd., Suite 210
Houston, TX 77056
(800) 325-3587
(713) 623-8618
$129.95

Frontier
UserLand Software
490 California Ave., Suite 202
Palo Alto, CA 94306
(415) 325-5700
$179

GateKeeper
Chris Johnson
Free
Available from online services and user groups.

GEnie
GE Information Services
401 N. Washington St.
Rockville, MD 20850
(301) 340-4000
Online rates vary.

Get-a-Grip
Premier Technology, Inc.
1072 Folsom St.
San Francisco, CA 94103
(415) 255-9300
$29.95

GreatWorks
Symantec Corp.
10201 Torre Ave.
Cupertino, CA 95014
(800) 441-7234
(408) 253-9600
$299

HAM (Hierarchical Apple Menu)
Microseeds Publishing, Inc.
5801 Benjamin Ctr. Dr., Suite 103
Tampa, FL 33634
(813) 882-8635
$99

HandiWorks
MacVonk USA
313 Iona Ave.
Narbeth, PA 19072
(215) 660-0606
$175

HandOff II
Connectix
125 Constitution Drive
Menlo Park, CA 94025
(800) 950-5880
(415) 324-0727
$79.95

A Hayden's PowerBook Power Book

HDI-20 External 1.4 MB Floppy Disk Drive
(for use with PowerBook 100 only)
Apple Computer, Inc.
20525 Mariani Ave.
Cupertino, CA 95014
(800) 776-2333
(908) 996-1010
$279

HDI-30 SCSI Disk Adapter
Apple Computer, Inc.
20525 Mariani Ave.
Cupertino, CA 95014
(800) 776-2333
(908) 996-1010
$49

HDI-30 SCSI System Cable
Apple Computer, Inc.
20525 Mariani Ave.
Cupertino, CA 95014
(800) 776-2333
(908) 996-1010
$49

Helium
Robert L. Matthews
$7
Available from online services and user groups.

Help!
Teknosys, Inc.
3923 Coconut Palm Dr., Suite 111
Tampa, FL 33619
(800) 873-3494
(813) 620-3494
$149

In Control
Attain Corporation
5 Irving Terrace
Cambridge, MA 02138
$129.95

INITInfo Pro
Baseline Publishing
1770 Moriah Woods Blvd., Suite 14
Memphis, TN 38117
(800) 926-9676
(901) 682-9676
$69.95

INITPicker
Microseeds Publishing, Inc.
5801 Benjamin Ctr. Dr., Suite 103
Tampa, FL 33634
(813) 882-8635
$69

Instant Update
ON Technology, Inc.
One Cambridge Center
Cambridge, MA 02142
(617) 225-2545
$495 for two users

Intertie
Dantz Development
1400 Shattuck Ave., Suite 1
Berkeley, CA 94709
(510) 849-0293
$149

INTouch
Advanced Software
1095 E. Duane Ave., Suite 103
Sunnyvale, CA 94086
(800) 346-5392
(408) 733-0745
$79.95

KiwiPowerWindows
Kiwi Software, Inc.
6546 Pardall Road
Santa Barbara, CA 93117
(800) 321-5494
(805) 685-4031
$80

LapLink Mac III
Traveling Software, Inc.
18702 N. Creek Pkwy.
Bothell, WA 98011
(800) 662-2652
(206) 483-8088
$189.95

Last Resort
Working Software Inc.
P.O. Box 1844
Santa Cruz, CA 95061
(408) 423-5696
$50

Product Directory

Liberty portable hard disks
Liberty Systems
122 Saratoga Ave., #16
Santa Clara, CA 95051
(408) 983-1127
Price varies with configuration.

LightningScan 400
Thunderware, Inc.
21 Orinda Way
Orinda, CA 94563
(800) 445-1166
(415) 254-6581
$495

MacCalc
Bravo Technologies
P.O. Box 10078
Berkeley, CA 94709
(510) 841-8552
$139

MacEKG
MicroMAT Computer Systems
7075 Redwood Blvd.
Novato, CA 94947
(800) 829-6227
(415) 898-6227
$99

Macintosh PowerBook 100
Apple Computer, Inc.
20525 Mariani Ave.
Cupertino, CA 95014
(800) 776-2333
(908) 996-1010
Price varies with configuration.

Macintosh PowerBook 100 Battery Recharger
Apple Computer, Inc.
20525 Mariani Ave.
Cupertino, CA 95014
(800) 776-2333
(908) 996-1010
$159

Macintosh PowerBook 100 Rechargeable Battery
Apple Computer, Inc.
20525 Mariani Ave.
Cupertino, CA 95014
(800) 776-2333
(908) 996-1010
$99

Macintosh PowerBook 140
Apple Computer, Inc.
20525 Mariani Ave.
Cupertino, CA 95014
(800) 776-2333
(908) 996-1010
Price varies with configuration.

Macintosh PowerBook 140/170 Battery Recharger
Apple Computer, Inc.
20525 Mariani Ave.
Cupertino, CA 95014
(800) 776-2333
(908) 996-1010
$159

Macintosh PowerBook 140/170 Rechargeable Battery
Apple Computer, Inc.
20525 Mariani Ave.
Cupertino, CA 95014
(800) 776-2333
(908) 996-1010
$99

Macintosh PowerBook 170
Apple Computer, Inc.
20525 Mariani Ave.
Cupertino, CA 95014
(800) 776-2333
(908) 996-1010
Price varies with configuration.

Macintosh PowerBook Fax/Data Modem
Apple Computer, Inc.
20525 Mariani Ave.
Cupertino, CA 95014
(800) 776-2333
(908) 996-1010
$349

MacLink Plus/Translators
DataViz
55 Corporate Drive
Trumbull, CT 06611
(203) 268-0030
$199

MacMike
Premier Technology, Inc.
1072 Folsom St.
San Francisco, CA 94103
(415) 255-9300
$59.95

Hayden's PowerBook Power Book

MacPassword
Art Shumer
$40
Available from online services and user groups.

MacRecorder Driver
Macromind-Paracomp, Inc.
Free
Available from online services and user groups.

MacRecorder Voice Digitizer
Macromind-Paracomp, Inc.
600 Townsend St.
San Francisco, CA 94103
(415) 442-0200

MacSafe II
Kent Marsh Ltd.
P.O. Box 460289
1200 Post Oak Blvd., Suite 210
Houston, TX 77056
(800) 325-3587
(713) 623-8618
$189.95

MacTools Deluxe
Central Point Software
15220 N.W. Greenbrier Pkwy, #200
Beaverton, OR 97006
(800) 888-8199
(503) 690-8090
$129

Magic Typist 1.1
Tactic Software Corp.
11925 S.W. 128th St.
Miami, FL 33186
(800) 344-4818
(305) 378-4110
$99

MenuChoice
Kerry Clendenning
$15
Available from online services and user groups.

MicroPhone II
Software Ventures, Inc.
2907 Claremont Ave.
Berkeley, CA 94705
(415) 644-3232f
$215

Microsoft Works
Microsoft Corp.
One Microsoft Way
Redmond, WA 98052
(800) 426-9400
(206) 882-8080
$249

More Disk Space
Alysis Software
1231 31st Ave.
San Francisco, CA 94122
(415) 566-2263
$99.95

NetModem networkable modems
Shiva Corp.
One Cambridge Center
Cambridge, MA 02142
(800) 458-3550
(617) 864-8500
Price varies with configuration.

NightWatch
Kent Marsh Ltd.
P.O. Box 460289
1200 Post Oak Blvd., Suite 210
Houston, TX 77056
(800) 325-3587
(713) 623-8618
$149.95

Nisus Compact
Paragon Concepts, Inc.
990 Highland Dr., #312
Solana Beach, CA 92075
(800) 922-2993
(619) 481-1477
$150

Norton Utilities for the Macintosh
Symantec Corp.
10201 Torre Ave.
Cupertino, CA 95014
(800) 441-7234
(408) 253-9600
$199

Notebook Display Adapters
Envisio, Inc.
5365 W. Bald Eagle Blvd.
White Bear Lake, MN
(612) 653-7694
Price varies with configuration.

Product Directory A

Notebook Keypad
2855 Campus Drive
San Mateo, CA 94403
(415) 572-2700
$139.95

Notebook Traveler carrying cases
Kensington Microware Ltd.
2855 Campus Drive
San Mateo, CA 94403
(415) 572-2700
$79.95 for Compact model
$129.95 for Deluxe model

Now Utilities
Now Software
520 S.W. Harrison, Inc., Suite 435
Portland, OR 97201
(800) 237-3611
(503) 274-2800
$129

Num Lock
Masaaki Takahashi
Free
Available from online services
and user groups.

On Cue II
Icom Simulations
648 S. Wheeling Rd.
Wheeling, IL 60090
(708) 520-4440
$99

On Location
ON Technology, Inc.
One Cambridge Center
Cambridge, MA 02142
(617) 225-2545
$129.95

Outbound Notebook System
Outbound Systems
4840 Pearl E. Circle
Boulder, CO 80301
(303) 786-9200
Price varies with configuration.

Panorama II
ProVUE Development, Inc.
15180 Transistor Lane
Huntington Beach, CA 92649
(714) 892-8199
$395

PhoneNET Liaison
Farallon Computing, Inc.
2000 Powell St., Suite 600
Emeryville, CA 94608
(510) 596-9000
$395

PICTure This
FGM
131 Elden St., Suite 108
Herndon, VA 22070
(703) 478-9881
$99

MagentaCase
Magenta Seven, Inc.
5109 Holly Ridge Dr., Suite 209
Raleigh, NC 27612
(919) 787-2787
$85

PowerBundle carrying case
T/Maker Co.
1390 Villa St.
Mountain View, CA 94041
(415) 962-0195
Price unavailable at press time.

PowerModem internal modem
PSI Integration
2205 Hamilton Ave., Suite 220
San Jose, CA 95125
(800) 622-1722
(408) 559-8544
$299

PowerPort/V.32 internal modem
Global Village Communications
1204 O'Brien Dr.
Menlo Park, CA 94025
(800) 736-4821
(415) 329-0700
$799

PowerSleep
Urs Calibran
Free
Available from online services and
user groups.

PowerView
Radius, Inc.
1710 Fortune Dr.
San Jose, CA 95131
(800) 227-2795
(408) 434-1010
$599

Hayden's PowerBook Power Book

Prodigy
Prodigy Services
445 Hamilton Ave.
White Plains, NY 10601
(800) 822-6922, ext. 556
$49.95. Online rates vary.

QBlazer
Telebit Corporation
1315 Chesapeake Terrace
Sunnyvale, CA 94089
(408) 734-4333
$745

QuickDEX II
Casady & Greene, Inc.
22734 Portola Dr.
Salinas, CA 93908
(800) 359-4920
(408) 484-9228
$60

QuicKeys 2
CE Software
1801 Industrial Circle
P.O. Box 65580
West Des Moines, IA 50265
(515) 224-1995
$149

QuickTools
Advanced Software
1095 E. Duane Ave., Suite 103
Sunnyvale, CA 94086
(800) 346-5392
(408) 733-0745
$79.95

Read My Lips
Praxitel
1631 Sheffield Dr.
Ypsilanti, MI 48198
(313) 485-6278
(313) 487-5349
$119

Remember?
David Warker
$20
Available from online services and user groups.

Retriever II
Exodus Software
8620 Winton Road, Suite 304
Cincinnati, OH 45231
(513) 522-0011
$150

Rival
Microseeds Publishing, Inc.
5801 Benjamin Ctr. Dr., Suite 103
Tampa, FL 33634
(813) 882-8635
$99

RoadRunner 80 MB internal hard disk
Microtech International, Inc.
158 Commerce St.
East Haven, CT 06512
(800) 626-4276
(203) 468-6223
$773

RunPC/Remote
Argosy Software, Inc.
113 Spring S., 5th Fl.
New York, NY 10012
(212) 274-1199
$219

ScreenShot
Baseline Publishing
1770 Moriah Woods Blvd., Suite 14
Memphis, TN 38117
(800) 926-9676
(901) 682-9676
$59.95

SCSI/Link external EtherNet adapter
Dayna Communications, Inc.
50 S. Main St.
Salt Lake City, UT 84144
(801) 531-0600
$399

ShadowWriter
Gizmo Technologies
P.O. Box 14177
Fremont, CA 94539
(510) 623-7899
$129

Product Directory A

ShortCut
Aladdin Systems, Inc.
Deer Park Center, Suite 23A-171
Aptos, CA 95003
(408) 685-9175
Price unavailable at press time.

Siesta
Andrew Welch
$5
Available from online services
and user groups.

Smart Alarms and Appointment Diary
JAM Software
P.O. Box 1345
Point Reyes Station, CA 94956
(415) 663-1041
$125

SmartCom II
Hayes Microcomputer Products, Inc.
P.O. Box 105203
Atlanta, GA 30348
(404) 441-1617
$149

SoftAT
Insignia Solutions
526 Clyde Ave.
Mountain View, CA 94043
(415) 694-7600
Price unavailable at press time.

Software Bridge/Mac
Argosy Software, Inc.
113 Spring S., 5th Fl.
New York, NY 10012
(212) 274-1199
$159

SpaceSaver
Aladdin Systems, Inc.
Deer Park Center, Suite 23A-171
Aptos, CA 95003
(408) 685-9175
$59.95

StuffIt Deluxe
Aladdin Systems, Inc.
Deer Park Center, Suite 23A-171
Aptos, CA 95003
(408) 685-9175
$99.95

StyleWriter inkjet printer
Apple Computer, Inc.
20525 Mariani Ave.
Cupertino, CA 95014
(800) 776-2333
(908) 996-1010
$599

Suitcase II
Fifth Generation Systems
10049 N. Reiger Road
Baton Rouge, LA 70809
(800) 873-4384
(504) 291-7221
$79

SuperClock! 3.9
Steve Christensen
Free
Available from online services
and user groups.

SuperDisk!
Alysis Software
1231 31st Ave.
San Francisco, CA 94122
(415) 566-2263
$89

SuperOffice
110 Great Rd.
Bedford, MA 01730
(617) 275-2140
$395

Symantec Antivirus for Macintosh (SAM)
Symantec Corp.
10201 Torre Ave.
Cupertino, CA 95014
(800) 441-7234
(408) 253-9600
$99.95

System 7.0
Apple Computer, Inc.
20525 Mariani Ave.
Cupertino, CA 95014
(800) 776-2333
(908) 996-1010
$99

System 7 Tune-Up
Apple Computer, Inc.
Free
Available from online services
and user groups.

Hayden's PowerBook Power Book

Telebridge
Shiva Corp.
One Cambridge Center
Cambridge, MA 02142
(800) 458-3550
(617) 864-8500
$599

Thunder 7
Baseline Publishing
1770 Moriah Woods Blvd., Suite 14
Memphis, TN 38117
(800) 926-9676
(901) 682-9676
$99.95

Timbuktu 4.0
Farallon Computing, Inc.
2000 Powell St., Suite 600
Emeryville, CA 94608
(510) 596-9000
$149

Timbuktu/Remote 2.0
Farallon Computing, Inc.
2000 Powell St., Suite 600
Emeryville, CA 94608
(510) 596-9000
$195

TimeBook
ProAct Software
555 Bryant St., Suite 231
Palo Alto, CA 94301
(415) 853-8463
$109

ToDo!
Andrew Welch
$15
Available from online services
and user groups

TouchBASE
After Hours Software
5636 Van Nuys Blvd., Suite B
Van Nuys, CA 91401
(818) 780-2220
$125

TrashMaster
The HandOff Corporation
P.O. Box 811
Allen, TX 75002
(214) 727-2329
$69.95

Up-to-Date
Now Software
520 S.W. Harrison, Inc., Suite 435
Portland, OR 97201
(800) 237-3611
(503) 274-2800
$99

Virex
Microcom, Inc.
500 River Ridge Dr.
Norwood, MA 02062
(800) 822-8224
(617) 551-1000
$99.95

VirusDetective
Jeff Shulman
$45
Available from online services
and user groups.

Wallpaper
Thought I Could Software
107 University Place, Suite 4D
New York, NY 10003
(212) 673-9724
$59.99

White Knight
FreeSoft Co.
150 Hickory Drive
Beaver Falls, PA 15010
(412) 846-2700
$139

Word for Word/Macintosh
Mastersoft
6991 E. Camelback Rd., Ste. A-320
Scottsdale, AZ 95251
(602) 277-0900
$149

Product Directory

WriteMove inkjet printer
GCC Technologies
580 Winter St.
Waltham, MA 02154
(800) 422-7777
(617) 890-0880
$549

WriteNow
T/Maker Co.
1390 Villa St.
Mountain View, CA 94041
(415) 962-0195
$199

ZTerm
Dave Alverson
$30
Available from online services and user groups.

Index

1-Shot Worksheet program, 61
32-bit addressing, 39

A

AccessPC program, 79-80
Acta 7 outlining program, 65
adapters, third-party internal
 display, 20
Address Book Plus address
 manager, 114-116
address managers, 109
 free-form
  INTouch, 111-113
  QuickDEX II, 110-111
 structured
  Address Book Plus, 114-116
  Connections, 118-120
  Dynodex, 114-116
  TouchBASE, 116-118
addressing, 32-bit, 39
Adobe Type Manager (ATM)
 control panel, 34-35
Advanced Software's INTouch,
 111-113
Advanced Software's QuickTools,
 141-143

After Hours Software's
 TouchBASE, 116-118
AgentDA scheduling program,
 104-106
Alarming Events reminder program, 97-98
AlarmsClock program, 141
aliases, 32-33
Alverson, Dave, 64
Alysis SuperDisk!, 131-132
Amaze! Inc.'s Far Side Calendar,
 108
Amazing Paint graphics program,
 64
America Online online service,
 88-89
Antivirus for Macintosh (SAM),
 157-158, 162
Apple
 HDI-20 External 1.4 Megabyte
  Floppy-Disk Drive, 15
 HDI-30 SCSI System Cable, 11
 StyleWriter printer, 23
Apple File Exchange (AFE), 78
Apple LocalTalk networks, 68
Apple menu, 126

Hayden's PowerBook Power Book

Apple Menu Items folder
  accessing, 139-142
  DAs, 33-34
  moving files to, 127
AppleShare networks, 71
AppleTalk Filing Protocol (AFP), 71
AppleTalk Remote Access (ARA), 71-74
applications
  errors, 171-172
  extensions, 172-173
  hiding, 28-29
  modular, 173
  opening, 28-29
Argosy Software MountPC, 79-80
Argosy Software RunPC/Remote, 83-84
Art Shumer's MacPassword, 151
ASCII format, DOS files, 82
ASD Software's FileGuard, 153-156
Attain Software's In Control, 103-104
automatic saves, 140-142
automation programs, 134
  KiwiPowerWindows (KPW), 136-137
  QuickKeys 2, 134-137
  Tactic Software's Magic Typist, 137
  UserLand's Frontier, 136

B

background
  AppleTalk Remote Access (ARA), 71-74
  desktop pictures, 140
  indexing, 129
  Liaison, 74
backups, 172
Balloon Help, 29
Banyan VINES, 71
Barricade security program, 142
Baseline Publishing 1-Shot Worksheet program, 61
Baseline Publishing DAtabase program, 62
Baseline Publishing DoubleTalk, 76-77
batteries
  external packs, 21
  PowerBook 100, 16
Battery desk accessory, 46
BeagleWorks, 57, 66
BeHierarchic file launcher, 126
BookView video card, 20
Bravo Technologies MacCalc spreadsheet program, 61

C

cables, HDI-30 SCSI System, 11
Caps Lock extension, 44
Caps Lock key, 44
Carbon Copy Mac, 76
carrying cases, third-party, 25
Casady & Greene's QuickDEX II, 110-111
cdevs, *see* control panels
CE Software Amazing Paint graphics program, 64
CE Software's Alarming Events, 97-98
CE Software's DiskTop, 127
chips, comparing, 5, 7
Chris Johnson's GateKeeper, 162
Citadel security program, 148-150, 155
Claris XTND, 80-82
ClarisWorks, 55-56, 66
Clean Up (Special menu) command, 36
ClearVue/SD21 two-page grayscale monitor, 20

Index

ClickChange control panel, 36-37
clocks, 141
commands
    Clean Up (Special menu), 36
    Find (File menu), 30-31
    Make Alias (File menu), 32
    Publish (Edit menu), 40-41
    Sharing (File menu), 39
    Sleep (Special menu), 45
    Subscribe (Edit menu), 40-41
communications programs, 64-65
Compact Pro file compressor, 130
CompuServe Information Service (CIS), 89-91
Computer Care BookView video card, 20
Concentrix Software's Connections, 118-120
CONNECT online service, 91
Connections address manager, 118-120
Connectix' HandOff II, 124-126
Contact Ease lead manager, 120
control panels, 33
    ClickChange, 36-37
    file launchers, 126-127
    Memory, 37-39
    Portable, 47-48
    Sharing Setup, 39
    Siesta shareware, 45
.cpt file extension, 130
CPUs (central processing units), comparing, 5-7
crashes, software related, 166

D

Dantz Development's Intertie, 143
data encryption, 148-150
DAtabase program, 62
databases, 62-63
DataViz MacLink/Plus, 83
dates, 141
DayMaker scheduling program, 101-103
Dayna DOS Mounter, 79-80
DaynaPORT SCSI/Link external SCSI device, 21
Delphi online service, 91
DES (Data Encryption Standard), 148
desk accessories (DAs)
    Apple Menu Items folder, 33-34
    Battery, 46
    Timbuktu, 75
    Timbuktu/Remote, 75
DeskDraw graphics program, 63
DeskPaint graphics program, 63
DeskPicture desktop program, 140
Desktop, 36-37
desktops, background pictures, 140
dialog boxes
    enhancements, 138, 142
    Open and Save, 128
Dialog Power dialog-enhancement program, 142
Disinfectant anti-virus program, 161-162
disk caches, 37
DiskDoubler file compressor, 131-133
DiskLock security program, 148-150, 155
disks
    hard, 166-167
    unreadable, 166
DiskTools file finder, 127
DiskTop file finder, 127
documents
    opening automatically at startup, 34

placing in menus, 124
universal voice annotation, 144
DOS, viruses, 162
DOS Mounter program, 79-80
DOS PCs
   and Macintosh, 77-78
      accessing via serial cables or modems, 83
      controlling remotely, 83-84
      emulating, 84-86
      file-format translation systems, 80-82
      graphics formats, 82-83
      network transfers, 87
      reading disks, 78
      saving in ASCII format, 82
      terminal emulation, 86
      using files, 79-80
DoubleTalk terminal emulation program, 76-77
drivers, 168
Dubl-Click Software's ClickChange control panel, 36-37
Dynodex address manager, 114-116

E

Easy Alarms reminder program, 98-99
encryption, 148-150
Envisio Notebook Display Adapters, 20
errors, application, 171-172
Essential Software's Easy Alarms, 98-99
Ethernet networks, 68
Exodus Software Retriever II database, 62
extension manager, 175-179
extension mapping, 79-80
extensions, 33
   applications, 172-173
   Caps Lock, 44
   disadvantages, 123-124
   managing, 138
   QuicKeys, 134-135
   system, 174-175
   System 7 TuneUp package, 42
Extractor file decompressor, 130

F

Fabien Octave's BeHierarchic, 126
Far Side Calendar scheduling program, 108
Farallon Liaison, 74
Farallon PhoneNET networks, 68
Farallon Timbuktu, 75
Farallon Timbuktu/Remote, 75
faxes, 92-94
FDHDs (Floppy disks, high-density), 78
Fifth Generation Systems' DiskLock, 148-150, 155
Fifth Generations' DiskTools, 127
file compressors, 129
   archival, 130
   on-the-fly, 131-134
file decompressors, 130
file finders, 127-129
file launchers, 124-127, 142
file reminders
   Now Utilities' AlarmsClock, 141
FileGuard security program, 153-156
files
   .sea (self-extracting archive), 130
   comparing on different machines, 143
   copying and moving with keyboard, 127

Index

DOS
   translating to Macintosh, 80-82
   using on Macintosh, 79-83
extensions, 130
launching multiple, 125
list views, 127
managing with keyboard, 32
moving to Apple Menu Items folder, 127
Num Lock keyboard definition, 22
sharing
   networks, 70-71
   modems, 71-77
   SCSI-docking, 69-70
   swapping floppy disks, 69
shredding deleted, 150
System
   damaged, 166
   repairing, 168
   viewing lists, 29-30
Find (File menu) command, 30-31
Finder, 28
   managing with keyboard, 31-32
   searching with, 30-31
First Things First reminder program, 99-101
floppy disks
   DOS, reading on Macintosh, 78
   HDI-20 External 1.4 Megabyte drive, 15
   swapping, 69
FolderBolt security program, 151-153
folders
   Extensions, 176
   locking, 152-153
   hierarchical menu items, 126
   shared, 39-40

fonts
   rearranging menus, 139
   TrueType format, 34-35
   viewing WYSIWYG, 139
formats
   ASCII, saving DOS files, 82
   graphics, transferring DOS files, 82-83
Freesoft White Knight, 87
Frontier automation program, 136

G

GateKeeper anti-virus program, 162
GCC Technologies' WriteMove printer, 23
GEnie online service, 91
Gizmo Technologies ShadowWriter, 73
Global Village Communications PowerPort/v.32 modem, 23
Global Village Comunications PowerPort/v.32, 74
graphics, 63-64
graphics formats, transferring DOS files, 82-83
GreatWorks, 53-54, 66

H

HAM (Hierarchical Apple Menu) file launcher, 126
HandiWorks, 57
handles, add-on, 25
HandOff Corporation TrashMaster, 36
HandOff II file launcher, 124-126
hard disks
   drivers, 168
   icon, 167
   locking, 148-150
   space, conserving, 12-13

testing, 166
hardware
　reports, 141
　troubleshooting, 166
Hayes SmartCom II, 87
HD SC Setup Utility, 168
HDI-20 External 1.4 Megabyte Floppy-Disk Drive, 15
HDI-30 SCSI System Cable, 11
Helium shareware program, 29
help, Balloon, 29

I

Icom Simulations' On Cue II, 124-127
Icom Simulations' On Disk, 127-128
icons
　applying labels to, 31
　hard disk, 167
　managing with keyboard, 31-32
In Control scheduling program, 103-104
indexing, background, 129
INITs, *see* extensions
Insignia SoftPC, 84-86
Insignia Solutions AccessPC, 79-80
installation, System 7, 168
integrated software, 52
　BeagleWorks, 57-66
　ClarisWorks, 55-56, 66
　GreatWorks, 53-54, 66
　HandiWorks, 57
　Microsoft Works, 52-53
　versus lean, 50-51
integrated utilities packages
　Advanced Software's QuickTools, 141-143
　Now Software's Now Utilities, 138-141

Inter-Application Communication (IAC), 41
internal expansion slots, 14
Intertie program, 143
INTouch address manager, 111-113

J–K

JAM Software's Smart Alarms, 96
Jeff Shulman's VirusDetective, 162
John Norstad's Disinfectant, 161-162
Kensington Microware carrying cases, 25
Kensington's Notebook Keypad, 22
Kent Marsh's FolderBolt, 151-153
keyboard, 8-9
　accessing from, 127
　copying and moving files with, 127
　initiating mouse commands, 134
KiwiPowerWindows (KPW) automation program, 136-137

L

Label menu, 31
labels, applying to icons, 31
LAN Manager networks, 71
LapLink Mac III program, 83
lead management programs, 120
lean software, 57, 66
　communications, 64-65
　databases, 62-63
　graphics, 63-64
　spreadsheets, 61
　versus integrated, 50-51
　word processing, 58-61
Liaison program, 74
Lind Electronic Design external

Index

batter y pack, 22
list view, 29-30
LocalTalk networks, 68, 70
locking
    folders, 152-153
    hard disks, 148-150
logic board chips, faulty, 166

M

Macintosh
    and DOS PCs, 77-78
        accessing via serial cables
            or modems, 83
        controlling remotely, 83-84
        emulating, 84-86
        file-format translation
            systems, 80-82
        graphics formats, 82-83
        network transfers, 87
        reading disks, 78
        saving in ASCII format, 82
        terminal emulation, 86
        using files, 79-80
    applications compatibility with
        System 7.0, 43
    System 7.0, 27-48
Macintosh PowerBook Fax/Data
    Modem, 14
Macintosh System 7.0, 71
MacLink/Plus program, 83
MacMike microphone, 16
MacNet, *see* CONNECT online
    service
MacPassword security program,
    151
MacRecorder Voice Digitizer, 16
Macromind-Paracomp's
    MacRecorder Voice Digitizer, 16
MacTOPS networks, 71
MacVonk HandiWorks, 57
MagentaCase carrying cases, 25
Magic Apple utility, 127
Magic Typist automation pro-
    gram, 137
Magna's Empower III, 155-156
Make Alias (File menu) command,
    32
mapping extension, 79-80
Masaaki Takahashi Num Lock, 22
math coprocessors, 17
memory
    RAM, 42-45
    virtual, 38-39
Memory control panel, 37-39
menu bar, accessing, 142
menus
    Label, 31
    placing programs and docu-
        ments, 124
Microcom Carbon Copy Mac, 76
Microcom's Citadel, 148-150, 155
Microcom's Virex, 157-162
MicroPhone II terminal emulation
    program, 87
microphones, 16
Microseeds' HAM (Hierarchical
    Apple Menu), 126
Microseeds' Rival, 160-162
Microsoft LAN Manager, 71
Microsoft Works, 52-53
Microtech RoadRunner 80M
    internal hard disk, 12
modem ports, 68
modems
    accessing DOS PCs, 83
    adding through internal
        expansion slots, 14
    file sharing
        AppleTalk Remote Access
            (ARA), 71-74
        Baseline Publishing
            DoubleTalk, 76-77
        Farallon Liaison, 74
    screen sharing
        Farallon Timbuktu, 74-75

Microcom Carbon Copy
    Mac, 76
  third-party, 23
modes
  Power-Saver, 46
  Sleep, 14, 45
modular applications, 173
MountPC program, 79-80
MultiMaster file launcher,
  124-127, 138-139

N

NetModem, 74
NetWare networks, 71
networks
  comparing, 68
    SCSI devices for connecting to
      third-party add-ons, 21
  DOS files, transferring, 87
  files, transferring, 70-71
Newer Technologies RAM expan-
  sion cards, 24
Nisus Compact word processor,
  59-61
Norton Utilities, 179-181
Notebook Display Adapters, 20
Novell NetWare, 71
Now Software's Now Utilities,
  138-141
Now Software's Up-to-Date,
  106-107
Now Utilities' MultiMaster,
  124-127
Now Utilities utilities package,
  138-141
NowMenus Apple menu brancher,
  139-142
NowSave auto-saving program,
  140-141
Num Lock keyboard definition
  file, 22

numeric keypads, third-party, 22

O

On Cue II file launcher, 124-127
On Disk file finder, 127-128
On Location file finder, 128-129
online services
  America Online, 88-89
  CompuServe Information
    Service (CIS), 89-91
  CONNECT, 91
  Delphi, 91
  GEnie, 91
  Prodigy, 91-92
Outbound Notebook System, 7-8

P

Panorama II database program,
  63
Paragon Concepts Nisus Compact
  word processor, 59-61
password protection, 151-154
Pastel Development's DayMaker,
  101-103
Personal Information Managers
  (PIMs), 95, 120
PhoneNET networks, 68, 70
pointing devices, 9-10
Portable control panel, 47-48
Portfolio Systems' Dynodex,
  114-116
ports
  modem, 68
  printer, 68
  SCSI, 11, 69
  serial, 10-11
  video out, 18-20
PostScript fonts, 34-35
Power Strip graphical file
  launcher, 142
Power Up's Address Book Plus,
  114-116

Index

Power-Saver mode, 46
PowerBook 100
  comparing to Macintosh, 6-7
  comparing with other
    PowerBooks, 15-17
  SCSI-docking, 69-70
PowerBook 140
  comparing to Macintosh, 6-7
  comparing with other
    PowerBooks, 17
PowerBook 170
  comparing to Macintosh, 6-7
  comparing with other
    PowerBooks, 17-18
PowerBooks
  hard disks, 12-13
  internal expansion slots, 14
  keyboard, 8-9
  pointing devices, 10
  power saving features, 14
  sleeping, 45, 47
  resting, 47
  screens, 10
  SCSI ports, 11
  serial ports, 10-11
  sounds, 12
  third-party add-ons
    battery packs, 21
    carrying cases, 25
    connecting to networks, 21
    modems, 23
    numeric keypads, 22
    printers, 23
    RAM, 24
  trackballs, 9
  video-out ports, 18-20
PowerBundle carrying case, 25
PowerModem, 23
PowerPort/v.32, 74
PowerPort/v.32 modem, 23
PowerSleep program, 45
PowerView SCSI device, 18-20
Premier Technology add-on

handles, 25
Premier Technology's MacMike, 16
printer ports, 68
printers, third-party, 23
Prodigy online service, 91, 92
Profiler report generator, 141
programs
  1-Shot Worksheet, 61
  accessing from Open and Save
    dialog boxes, 128
  AccessPC, 79-80
  Acta 7 outlining, 65
  address, *see* address managers
  Amazing Paint graphics, 64
  anti-virus, 157-162
  assigning default options, 125
  automation, 134-135
  Bravo Technologies MacCalc
    spreadsheet, 61
  Carbon Copy Mac, 76
  ClickChange control panel, 36-37
  copy-protecting, 154
  Dantz Development's Intertie, 143
  DAtabase, 62
  DeskDraw graphics, 63
  DeskPaint graphics, 63
  DOS Mounter, 79-80
  DoubleTalk terminal emulation, 76-77
  fax, 92-94
  file compression, 129-134
  file finders, 127-129
  file launchers, 124-127
  Helium shareware, 29
  integrated, 52
    BeagleWorks, 57, 66
    ClarisWorks, 55-56, 66
    GreatWorks, 53-54, 66
    HandiWorks, 57
    Microsoft Works, 52-53

versus lean, 50-51
integrated utilities packages, 138-143
LapLink Mac III, 83
lead management, 120
lean, 57-66
Liaison, 74
MacLink/Plus, 83
MicroPhone II terminal emulation, 87
MountPC, 79-80
Nisus Compact word processor, 59-61
opening automatically at startup, 34
Panorama II database, 63
placing in menus, 124
PowerSleep, 45
QuicKeys 2, 29
Read My Lips, 143-144
reminder, see reminder programs, 95
Retriever II database, 62
RunPC/Remote, 83-84
scheduling, see scheduling programs, 101
security, 147-148
ShadowWriter, 73
SmartCom II terminal emulation, 87
SoftPC, 84-86
terminal emulation, 86
TrashMaster utility, 36
Wallpaper, 36
White Knight terminal emulation, 87
WriteNow word processor, 58-59
XTND, 80-82
Zedcor graphics, 63
ZTerm communications, 64-65
protocols, Zmodem, 64-65
PSI PowerModem, 23

Publish (Edit menu) command, 40-41

Q

QBlazer, 74
QBlazer modem, 23
question mark, blinking, 166
QuickDEX II address manager, 110-111
QuicKeys 2 automation program, 134-135
QuicKeys 2 program, 29
QuickTools utility package, 141-143

R

Radius PowerView SCSI device, 18-20
RAM
 adding, internal expansion slots, 13-14
 available amounts, 42-43
 failing, 166
 third-party expansion cards, 24
RAM disks, 44-45
RasterOps ClearVue/SD21 two-page grayscale monitor, 20
Read My Lips program, 143-144
reminder programs
 CE Software's Alarming Events, 97-98
 Essential Software's Easy Alarms, 98-99
 JAM Software's Smart Alarms, 96
 Visionary Software's First Things First, 99-101
rest system, 14
Retriever II database, 62
Rival anti-virus program, 160-162
RoadRunner 80M internal hard

Index

disk, 12
RunPC/Remote program, 83-84

S

Salient AutoDoubler file compressor, 132-133
Salient's DiskDoubler, 131-133
saving, automatic intervals, 140-142
scheduling programs
    Amaze! Inc.'s Far Side Calendar, 108
    Attain Software's In Control, 103-104
    Now Software's Up-to-Date, 106-107
    Pastel Development's DayMaker, 101-103
    Team Building Technologies' AgentDA, 104-106
screen savers, 142
screens, 10
    blanking, 151
    capturing, 143
    sharing with modems, 74-76
scripts, creating, 136
SCSI (Small Computer System Interface)
    chain, 167
    devices, third-party, 18-21
    docking, 69-70
    ports, 11
    termination, 166
SCSI/Link external SCSI device, 21
.sea (self-extracting archive) files, 130
searching, 30-31
security, 142, 147-148
security programs
    AppleTalk Remote Access (ARA), 72-73

Art Shumer's MacPassword, 151
ASD Software's FileGuard, 153-156
Fifth Generation Systems' DiskLock, 148-150, 155
Kent Marsh's FolderBolt, 151-153
Magna's Empower III, 155-156
Microcom's Citadel, 148-150, 155
sequencing QuicKeys, 134
serial cables, accessing DOS PCs, 83
serial ports, 10-11, 68
ShadowWriter program, 73
shared folders, 39-40
Sharing (File menu) command, 39
Sharing Setup control panel, 39
Shiva NetModem, 74
Shiva Telebridge, 74
Siesta shareware control panel, 45
.sit file extension, 130
Sleep (Special menu) command, 45
Sleep mode, 45
sleep mode, 14
slots, internal expansion, 14
Smart Alarms reminder program, 96
SmartCom II terminal emulation program, 87
Snipper screen capture program, 143
SoftPC program, 84-86
software
    crashes, 166
    reports, 141
    troubleshooting, 170
Software Ventures MicroPhone II, 87

Sophisticated Circuits numeric keypad, 22
sound, creating, 143-144
sounds, 12
SpaceSaver file compressor, 132-134
spreadsheets, 61
Startup Items folder, 34
Startup Manager, 177
Startup Manager extension management program, 138
StuffIt Classic file compressor, 130
StuffIt Deluxe file compressor, 130
StyleWriter printer, 23
Subscribe (Edit menu) command, 40-41
Sunset screen saver, 142
SuperBoomerang dialog-box enhancement program, 138
SuperDisk! file compressor, 131-132
SuperDrives, 78
SuperOffice lead manager, 120
Symantec Antivirus for Macintosh (SAM), 157-162
Symmetry Software Acta 7 outlining program, 65
System 7 TuneUp extension package, 42
System 7.0, 27-28
   aliases, 32-33
   Balloon Help, 29
   compatibility of Macintosh applications, 43
   Desktop, 36-37
   Finder, 28
   free RAM available, 42-43
   Finder, managing with keyboard, 31-32
   memory, expanding, 37-39
   opening/hiding applications, 28-29

publishing and subscribing, 40-41
reinstalling, 168
searching with, 30-31
shared folders, 39-40
System Folder, 33-34
Trash, 36
TrueType font format, 34-35
Version 7.0.1, 43-44
   Battery DA, 46
   Caps Lock extension, 44
   Portable control panel, 47-48
   putting PowerBook to sleep, 45
   RAM disks, 44-45
viewing file lists, 29-30
System 7.0 Disk Tools, 166
System 7.0 networks, transferring files, 71
system extensions, 174-175
System files, 168
System Folder, 33-34
system rest, 14

T

T/Maker PowerBundle carrying case, 25
T/Maker WriteNow word processor, 58-59
Tactic Software's Magic Typist, 137
Team Building Technologies' AgentDA, 104-106
Telebit Corporation QBlazer modem, 23
Telebit QBlazer, 74
Telebridge, 74
terminal emulation programs, 86
Thought I Could Software Wallpaper, 36
Timbuktu desk accessory, 75
Timbuktu/Remote desk accessory, 75

Index

times, 141
TOPS networks, *see* MacTOPS networks
TouchBASE address manager, 116-118
trackballs, 9
Trash, 36
TrashMaster utility, 36
Traveling Software LapLink Mac III, 83
Trojan Horses, 156
troubleshooting, 165-186
    applications
        extensions, 172-173
        errors, 171-172
    extension manager, 175-179
    hardware, 166
    Norton Utilities, 179-181
    returning PowerBook, 166
    software, 170
    system extensions, 174-175
TrueType font format, 34-35
Type 1 PostScript fonts, 34-35
Type Manager (ATM) control panel, 34-35

U

Unerase, 179
UnStuffIt Deluxe file decompressor, 130
Up-to-Date scheduling program, 106-107
UserLand's Frontier, 136
utilities
    HD SC Setup Utility, 168
    Magic Apple, 127

V

video out ports, third-party add-ons, 18-20
views, list, 29-30
VINES networks, transferring files, 71
Virex anti-virus program, 157-158, 162
virtual memory, 38-39
virus detection, 130, 151
VirusDetective anti-virus program, 162
viruses, 156, 175
    DOS-based, 162
    threat of, 156-157
Visionary Software's First Things First, 99-101

W

Wallpaper, 36
Wallpaper program, 36
Welch, Andrew, 45
Westware's Contact Ease, 120
Westware's SuperOffice, 120
White Knight terminal emulation program, 87
windows
    customizing, 136-137
    hiding, 28-29
    hiding automatically, 125
    organizing, 136-137
word processing programs, 58-61
Work Saver auto-saving program, 142
Works (Microsoft), 52-53
worms, 156
WriteMove printer, 23
WriteNow word processor, 58-59
WYSIWYG Menus font menu manager, 139

X–Y–Z

XTND program, 80-82

Zedcor graphics program, 63
Zmodem protocol, 64-65
ZTerm communications program, 64-65

How This Book Was Created

This book is especially cool because it (along with all Hayden titles) was created entirely on a computer. The text was written on a Macintosh IIci and PowerBook 170 using MacWrite II 1.1 and Microsoft Word 5.0. Screenshots were taken using Baseline Publishing's ScreenShot. Considerable distraction and sanity checks were caused by Stick Software's Solarian II. The product directory was assembled from a FileMaker Pro database. Files were sent to the publisher using AppleTalk Remote Access.

The text was edited on a Macintosh IIsi and a PowerBook 140 using Microsoft Word 5.0. Pages were assembled and the index was generated on a Macintosh IIfx and Macintosh IIci using Aldus PageMaker 4.2. Final output was printed on a Optrotech imagesetter.

The cover was designed using Adobe PhotoShop and QuarkXpress, and icons and other images were created using Adobe Illustrator and Aldus FreeHand. Even all correspondence—from the initial book contract to "the manuscript looks great" and "where is my check?" letters—were created in Microsoft Word. Pretty neat, huh?

Sams—Covering The Latest In Computer And Technical Topics!

Audio

Advanced Digital Audio	$39.95
Audio Systems Design and Installation	$59.95
Compact Disc Troubleshooting and Repair	$24.95
Handbook for Sound Engineers: The New Audio Cyclopedia, 2nd Ed.	$99.95
How to Design & Build Loudspeaker & Listening Enclosures	$39.95
Introduction to Professional Recording Techniques	$29.95
The MIDI Manual	$24.95
Modern Recording Techniques, 3rd Ed.	$29.95
OP-AMP Circuits and Principles	$19.95
Principles of Digital Audio, 2nd Ed.	$29.95
Sound Recording Handbook	$49.95
Sound System Engineering, 2nd Ed.	$49.95

Electricity/Electronics

Active-Filter Cookbook	$24.95
Basic Electricity and DC Circuits	$29.95
CMOS Cookbook, 2nd Ed.	$24.95
Electrical Wiring	$19.95
Electricity 1-7, Revised 2nd Ed.	$49.95
Electronics 1-7, Revised 2nd Ed.	$49.95
How to Read Schematics, 4th Ed.	$19.95
IC Op-Amp Cookbook, 3rd Ed.	$24.95
IC Timer Cookbook, 2nd Ed.	$24.95
RF Circuit Design	$24.95
Transformers and Motors	$29.95
TTL Cookbook	$24.95
Understanding Digital Troubleshooting, 3rd Ed.	$24.95
Understanding Solid State Electronics, 5th Ed.	$24.95

Games

Master SimCity/SimEarth	$19.95
Master Ultima	$16.95

Hardware/Technical

First Book of Modem Communications	$16.95
First Book of PS/1	$16.95
Hard Disk Power with the Jamsa Disk Utilities	$39.95
IBM PC Advanced Troubleshooting & Repair	$24.95
IBM Personal Computer Troubleshooting & Repair	$24.95
Microcomputer Troubleshooting & Repair	$24.95
Understanding Fiber Optics	$24.95

IBM: Business

10 Minute Guide to PC Tools 7	$9.95
10 Minute Guide to Q&A 4	$9.95
First Book of Microsoft Works for the PC	$16.95
First Book of Norton Utilities 6	$16.95
First Book of PC Tools 7	$16.95
First Book of Personal Computing, 2nd Ed.	$16.95

IBM: Database

10 Minute Guide to Harvard Graphics 2.3	$9.95
Best Book of AutoCAD	$34.95
dBASE III Plus Programmer's Reference Guide	$24.95
dBASE IV Version 1.1 for the First-Time User	$24.95
Everyman's Database Primer Featuring dBASE IV Version 1.1	$24.95
First Book of Paradox 3.5	$16.95
First Book of PowerPoint for Windows	$16.95
Harvard Graphics 2.3 In Business	$29.95

IBM: Graphics/Desktop Publishing

10 Minute Guide to Lotus 1-2-3	$9.95
Best Book of Harvard Graphics	$24.95
First Book of Harvard Graphics 2.3	$16.95
First Book of PC Paintbrush	$16.95
First Book of PFS: First Publisher	$16.95

IBM: Spreadsheets/Financial

Best Book of Lotus 1-2-3 Release 3.1	$27.95
First Book of Excel 3 for Windows	$16.95
First Book of Lotus 1-2-3 Release 2.3	$16.95
First Book of Quattro Pro 3	$16.95
First Book of Quicken In Business	$16.95
Lotus 1-2-3 Release 2.3 In Business	$29.95
Lotus 1-2-3: Step-by-Step	$24.95
Quattro Pro In Business	$29.95

IBM: Word Processing

Best Book of Microsoft Word 5	$24.95
Best Book of Microsoft Word for Windows	$24.95
Best Book of WordPerfect 5.1	$26.95
First Book of Microsoft Word 5.5	$16.95
First Book of WordPerfect 5.1	$16.95
WordPerfect 5.1: Step-by-Step	$24.95

Macintosh/Apple

First Book of Excel 3 for the Mac	$16.95
First Book of the Mac	$16.95

Operating Systems/Networking

10 Minute Guide to Windows 3	$9.95
Best Book of DESQview	$24.95
Best Book of Microsoft Windows 3	$24.95
Best Book of MS-DOS 5	$24.95
Business Guide to Local Area Networks	$24.95
DOS Batch File Power with the Jamsa Disk Utilities	$39.95
Exploring the UNIX System, 2nd Ed.	$29.95
First Book of DeskMate	$16.95
First Book of Microsoft Windows 3	$16.95
First Book of MS-DOS 5	$16.95
First Book of UNIX	$16.95
Interfacing to the IBM Personal Computer, 2nd Ed.	$24.95
The Waite Group's Discovering MS-DOS, 2nd Edition	$19.95
The Waite Group's MS-DOS Bible, 4th Ed.	$29.95
The Waite Group's MS-DOS Developer's Guide, 2nd Ed.	$29.95
The Waite Group's Tricks of the UNIX Masters	$29.95
The Waite Group's Understanding MS-DOS, 2nd Ed.	$19.95
The Waite Group's UNIX Primer Plus, 2nd Ed.	$29.95
The Waite Group's UNIX System V Bible	$29.95
Understanding Local Area Networks, 2nd Ed.	$24.95
UNIX Applications Programming: Mastering the Shell	$29.95
UNIX Networking	$29.95
UNIX Shell Programming, Revised Ed.	$29.95
UNIX: Step-by-Step	$29.95
UNIX System Administration	$29.95
UNIX System Security	$34.95
UNIX Text Processing	$29.95

Professional/Reference

Data Communications, Networks, and Systems	$39.95
Handbook of Electronics Tables and Formulas, 6th Ed.	$24.95
ISDN, DECnet, and SNA Communications	$49.95
Modern Dictionary of Electronics, 6th Ed.	$39.95
Reference Data for Engineers: Radio, Electronics, Computer, and Communications, 7th Ed.	$99.95

Programming

Advanced C: Tips and Techniques	$29.95
C Programmer's Guide to NetBIOS	$29.95
C Programmer's Guide to Serial Communications	$29.95
Commodore 64 Programmer's Reference Guide	$24.95
Developing Windows Applications with Microsoft SDK	$29.95
DOS Batch File Power	$39.95
Graphical User Interfaces with Turbo C++	$29.95
Learning C++	$39.95
Mastering Turbo Assembler	$29.95
Mastering Turbo Pascal, 4th Ed.	$29.95
Microsoft Macro Assembly Language Programming	$29.95
Microsoft QuickBASIC Programmer's Reference	$29.95
Programming in ANSI C	$29.95
Programming in C, Revised Ed.	$29.95
The Waite Group's BASIC Programming Primer, 2nd Ed.	$24.95
The Waite Group's C Programming Using Turbo C++	$29.95
The Waite Group's C: Step-by-Step	$29.95
The Waite Group's GW-BASIC Primer Plus	$24.95
The Waite Group's Microsoft C Bible, 2nd Ed.	$29.95
The Waite Group's Microsoft C Programming for the PC, 2nd Ed.	$29.95
The Waite Group's New C Primer Plus	$29.95
The Waite Group's Turbo Assembler Bible	$29.95
The Waite Group's Turbo C Bible	$29.95
The Waite Group's Turbo C Programming for the PC, Revised Ed.	$29.95
The Waite Group's Turbo C++ Bible	$29.95
X Window System Programming	$29.95

Radio/Video

Camcorder Survival Guide	$14.95
Radio Handbook, 23rd Ed.	$39.95
Radio Operator's License Q&A Manual, 11th Ed.	$24.95
Understanding Fiber Optics	$24.95
Understanding Telephone Electronics, 3rd Ed.	$24.95
VCR Troubleshooting & Repair Guide	$19.95
Video Scrambling & Descrambling for Satellite & Cable TV	$24.95

For More Information, See Your Local Retailer Or Call Toll Free
1-800-428-5331

All prices are subject to change without notice. Non-U.S. prices may be higher. Printed in the U.S.A.

Find The Latest Technology And Most Up-To-Date Information In Hayden Books

Mastering Turbo Debugger
Tom Swan
This book is for accomplished IBM PC MS-DOS programmers who have mastered Pascal, C, or assembly language and who need useful guidelines for quickly finding and fixing the bugs in their code.

700 pages, 7 3/8 x 9 1/4, $29.95 USA
0-672-48454-4

UNIX Networking
Stephen G. Kochan and Patrick H. Wood, Editors
This book provides a comprehensive look at the major aspects of networking in the UNIX system. It's a must for both computer professionals and students with a basic understanding of programming and networking.

600 pages, 7 3/8 x 9 1/4, $29.95 USA
0-672-48440-4

Advanced C: Tips and Techniques
Paul Anderson and Gail Anderson
456 pages, 7 3/8 x 9 1/4, $29.95 USA
0-672-48417-X

Exploring the UNIX System, Second Edition
Stephen G. Kochan and Patrick H. Wood
450 pages, 7 3/8 x 9 1/4, $29.95 USA
0-672-48447-1

Mastering Turbo Assembler
Tom Swan
600 pages, 7 3/8 x 9 1/4, $29.95 USA
0-672-48435-8

Mastering Turbo Pascal 5.5, Third Edition
Tom Swan
912 pages, 7 3/8 x 9 1/4, $29.95 USA
0-672-48450-1

Programming in ANSI C
Stephen G. Kochan
450 pages, 7 3/8 x 9 1/4, $29.95 USA
0-672-48408-0

Programming in C, Revised Edition
Stephen G. Kochan
476 pages, 7 3/8 x 9 1/4, $29.95 USA
0-672-48420-X

UNIX Shell Programming, Revised Edition
Stephen G. Kochan and Patrick H. Wood
460 pages, 7 3/8 x 9 1/4, $29.95 USA
0-672-48448-X

UNIX System Administration
David Fiedler and Bruce H. Hunter
336 pages, 7 3/8 x 9 1/4, $29.95 USA
0-810-46289-3

UNIX System Security
Steven G. Kochan and Patrick H. Wood
330 pages, 7 3/8 x 9 1/4, $34.95 USA
0-672-48494-3

UNIX Text Processing
Timothy O'Reilly and Dale Dougherty
680 pages, 7 3/8 x 9 1/4, $29.95 USA
0-810-46291-5

See your local retailer or call:
1-800-428-5331.